THE TIME OF THE

TROLLEY

BY WILLIAM D. MIDDLETON

A KALMBACH PUBLICATION

Library of Congress Catalog Card Number:
67-20155

First printing, August 1967. Second printing, February 1968.

To Frank Julian Sprague,
Naval officer, engineer, and inventor, whose
ingenuity and tireless effort, more than those
of any other man, made possible the age
of electric traction, this book is dedicated.

PROBABLY no industry played a more central role in the development of the American city than did the street railway. When the first horsecar line made its inaugural run down New York's Bowery in 1831, the United States was still a rural nation; scarcely one American in 12 lived in the city, and the nation's largest municipality (New York) had little more than 200,000 inhabitants. By the time the streetcar had for the most part vanished from the American scene more than a century later, close to two-thirds of the nation's populace lived in cities, over a hundred of which by then had passed 100,000 in population.

Unlike such no less necessary but largely unseen urban public utilities as the power and telephone companies, or the water and sewage works, the street railway impressed itself on the public consciousness to a remarkable degree. The trolley car was a visible and noisy part of the urban scene, and during the age of electric traction no place of consequence seemed complete without it. Until the family automobile became a commonplace, the streetcar performed a remembered role in the urban existence. Whether for travel to and from work, or for an outing to the theater, a park, or a ball game, riding on the cars was a part of the fabric of daily life.

For the many who knew it, the trolley car is generally remembered with a good deal of nostalgia and affection. In retrospect at least, the time of the trolley seems less hurried and less urgent than the present urban world of high-speed freeways and automobile commuting. Some of my own recollections may perhaps be typical. Still sharp in my mind's eye, for example, are such pleasant memories of the traction era as the delightful escape from the steamy heat of a Midwestern summer afforded by the exhilarating ride through the woods on the big trolleys of St. Louis' line to Creve Coeur Lake; the incomparable bargain of a single seven-cent fare that bought an afternoon's riding around the loop of New Orleans' St. Charles-Tulane belt; or the unforgettable sound — heard from a Loop hotel room on a summer evening — of Chicago's "big red Pullmans" as they pounded rhythmically through the intricate specialwork of a downtown intersection.

It has been my endeavor here to present the entire story of urban rail transportation. Consequently, I have included material devoted to animal railways, cable cars, and other varieties of mechanical traction, and to rapid transit lines, without which — even though they may seem outside the scope suggested by the title of this volume — the story would be incomplete.

The author extends most sincere thanks and appreciation to the many individuals who have contributed in some measure to the preparation of this volume. The superb quality and range of the pictorial material has been made possible only through the willing assistance and interest of dozens of collectors, photographers, institutions, and corporations, whose contributions are individually credited. Particular thanks are due the late Howard E. Johnston, LeRoy O. King, and Stephen D. Maguire, who made available their extensive personal collections; to Suzanne T. Cooper and George H. Menge of the Library of Congress, who helped in locating rare items in the Library's collections; to John H. White Jr., Curator of Land Transportation at the Smithsonian Institution, who assisted with material from the files of the Institution; to Freeman H. Hubbard, Editor of *Railroad* Magazine, who made available valuable material in the magazine's files; and to the *Headlights* editorial staff and the librarian of the Electric Railroaders' Association, who lent a number of choice pictorial items. For assistance with a wide variety of background and regional information, the contributions of Allan H. Berner, Roger Borrup, O. R. Cummings, Frank P. Donovan Jr., Robert W. Gibson, Gene D. Gordon, Wayne C. Olsen, and Felix E. Reifschneider are gratefully acknowledged. Special thanks are due J. H. Price, who furnished a large part of the information for the overseas chapter. And finally, the author's sincere thanks to Mrs. Grace Hankinson, who typed the final manuscript, and to Stephen D. Maguire, E. Harper Charlton, and James W. Walker Jr., who aided in checking proofs for accuracy.

Much of the historical information that forms the basis for this volume has been drawn from the scores of publications devoted to the history of the street railway era painstakingly prepared by both individuals and the members of the several railway enthusiast groups, usually without profit to their authors. Of particular value have been the journals of the Central Electric Railfans' Association, Electric Railroaders' Association, Electric Railway Historical Society, *Interurbans*, Light Railway Transport League, various chapters of the National Railway Historical Society, Pacific Railroad Publications, and a series of historical monographs published by Felix E. Reifschneider, as well as a number of individual efforts.

William D. Middleton.

Ewa, Hawaii
April 1967

An open "smoking car" rolled down Broadway on underground-conduit trackage in 1897. — *Library of Congress.*

A two-horse open car clip-clops briskly down New York's Grand Street, which is brilliant-ly illuminated by newfangled electric street lights, in this woodcut by W. A. Rogers for an 1889 issue of *Harper's Weekly*. — *Collection of William D. Middleton.*

Before the Trolley

Horse-drawn omnibuses remained a part of the New York scene long after the development of the street railway. This double-deck stage was placed in service on the run up Fifth Avenue to Central Park in 1889. Street railways were never permitted on Fifth Avenue. — *Library of Congress.*

The New York & Harlem Railroad, the first street railway, began operating along the Bowery in 1832 with two of these handsome cars manufactured by John Stephenson. The historic event is depicted in this Clyde O. DeLand painting now owned by the Continental Insurance Companies. — *Library of Congress.*

THERE was a time, not really so many years ago, when the trolley car seemed an indispensable part of urban America. More utilitarian than graceful in appearance, the big electric cars dominated the downtown scene as they moved awkwardly, one after another, through crowded streets at rush hour. By night the trolley car was a cheerful sight as it rumbled noisily through suburban streets, casting a warm yellow glow on the darkened pavement from a brightly lighted interior. Until the noiseless streamliners came along in the declining years of the street railway, the trolley car was an undeniably noisy vehicle; and such characteristic sounds as the dissonant clang of its bell, the *lung-a-lung-a-lung* hammering of its air compressor, the whispering sound of the trolley gliding along the overhead wire, and the rhythmic clash of steel wheels on intricate trackwork echoing in canyonlike streets as a car moved through a downtown intersection were indelibly impressed in the memories of generations of Americans.

In contemplating the few remnants of the street railway era that have survived into the present day or the relatively marginal role played by the trolley car's colorless bus successors in an automobile-oriented midcentury America, it is difficult to imagine the great size and strength enjoyed by the street railway industry less than a half century ago when the trolley car represented an almost universal means of urban transportation — or, indeed, to realize the central and vital role played by the trolley car and its rail-borne predecessors in the development of urban America.

America in the post-Revolutionary War period was a fundamentally different society from the one it is today. In 1790, when the census-takers made the first of their decennial rounds, the United States was an overwhelmingly rural nation. Of the fewer than 4 million Americans then living in the republic, barely 1 in 20, or a little over 200,000 people, lived in the city; Philadelphia, then the nation's largest city, had a population of less than 55,000. But already, as the commerce and industry of the new nation developed, the cities were growing rapidly, and a trend was in motion toward the urbanization of America which has continued without interruption to the present time.

By 1830 more than a million people lived in American cities. The Erie Canal had been completed in 1825, and New York, with an unsurpassed natural harbor, had become the center of American commerce. The population of the thriving city had passed 200,000, a sufficient number to displace Philadelphia as the largest American metropolis.

As long as the cities remained relatively small and compact, urban transportation had presented little difficulty. Those who weren't wealthy enough to own or hire a horse and carriage, or who didn't have access to a horse, simply walked. But as the cities grew, getting around in them became increasingly difficult. Some form of urban public transportation not only became desirable but seemed imperative if the cities were to continue their growth.

What was probably the first regular urban transportation service was opened in Paris in 1819 when a line of horse-drawn stagecoaches began operating in the city. A similar line of what by then had become known as omnibuses began running in London 10 years later. New York City got its first public transportation in 1827 when a man named Abraham Brower inaugurated a regular stagecoach service up and down Broadway at a fixed fare. Four years later a large omnibus built for Brower by John Stephenson, a coachmaker who was destined to become one of the leading street railway carbuilders of the 19th century, began running on Broadway between Bond Street and the Battery at a fare of 12½ cents. Omnibus services quickly became popular; within only a few years hundreds of them were operating in New York and similar services were being operated in Philadelphia and Boston.

At almost the same time, however, the greater efficiency of the then new railway suggested itself as a means of providing a superior urban transportation service; and on April 25, 1831, America's first street railway, the New York & Harlem Railroad Company, was incorporated with John Mason, president of the Chemical Bank of New York City, at its head. Rails were laid along the Bowery from Prince Street to 14th Street, and coachbuilder John Stephenson turned out a pair of handsomely decorated cars, each bearing the name *John Mason* in honor of the railway's president. The cars were fitted with cast-iron wheels and incorporated a number of fea-

JOHN STEPHENSON

John Stephenson (1809-1893), Irish-born New York carriage builder, constructed both the first omnibus and the first streetcar to run on the streets of the city. His firm became the leading street railway carbuilder for most of the 19th century. — *Smithsonian Institution.*

Before horsecar architecture evolved into a style of its own, early streetcars closely resembled their omnibus predecessors. This car operated on Broadway in New York during the 1850's. — *Collection of LeRoy O. King.*

13

New England's first horsecar line (below) opened between Boston and Cambridge in 1856. Travel aboard the Cambridge cars was a congenial outing if the sketch above is representative. — *Library of Congress (below); New York Public Library (above).*

14

Because of its operating economy the one-horse, one-man "bobtail" car was one of the most popular car types with street railway operators. Passengers, who had to board the cars by the small step at the rear and then push their way to the front of the car to deposit their fare, weren't nearly as fond of it. This bobtail operated on a Washington (D. C.) line. — *Smithsonian Institution.*

Small's automatic fare collector, developed in 1884, permitted passengers on one-man horsecars to deposit their fares without having to reach the fare box beside the driver at the front of the car. — *Street Railway Journal.*

Many regarded the horse-drawn streetcars as a menace to life and limb. This imaginative woodcut, which appeared in an 1865 issue of *Frank Leslie's Illustrated Newspaper,* was part of a more or less continuous editorial campaign carried on by *Leslie's* against reckless horsecar operation. — *Library of Congress.*

tures later patented by Stephenson, chief among them an arrangement whereby the center of gravity was lowered by dropping the entrance to each of the three compartments below the tops of the wheels and placing the seats above the wheels. "They resemble an omnibus, or rather several omnibuses attached to each other, padded with fine cloth and with handsome glass windows, each capable of containing outside and inside, fully 40 passengers," stated a contemporary description.

By the afternoon of November 14, 1832, all was in readiness, and a crowd of 60 distinguished guests rode the cars in a gala opening celebration. The *Morning Courier & New York Enquirer* reported:

> Officials of the New York & Harlem Railroad, with Mayor Walter Bowne and others of distinction, left the city hall in carriages to the depot near Union Square where two splendid cars, each with two horses, were in waiting. The company was soon seated and the horses trotted off in handsome style, with great ease, at the rate of about 12 miles, followed by a number of private barouches and horsemen. Groups of spectators greeted the passengers of the cars with shouts and every window in the Bowery was filled.

That evening the event was celebrated with a festive dinner at City Hall, including speeches heralding the dawn of a new era of speed in city transportation. "This event will go down in the history of our country as the greatest achievement of man," declared Mayor Bowne in what might be termed a masterful piece of overstatement.

The new service proved popular, and soon Stephenson constructed three additional cars for the railway — the *Mentor,* the *For-Get-Me-Not,* and the *President.* Two years later New Orleans became the second American city to have a street railway. Horsecars went into service on the Magazine Street branch of the New Orleans & Carrollton Railroad early in January 1835, and a few weeks later a second branch opened on Jackson Street.

After these beginnings, more than 20 years went by before further interest was shown in street railways. But by 1850, when the population of urban America had grown to more than 3½ million and there were no less than a half-dozen cities exceeding 100,000 in population, the need for more adequate urban transportation had become greater than ever. Early in the 1850's further street railway lines were constructed in New York City, and the Brooklyn City Railroad began horsecar operation in 1853.

Boston became the next city to enjoy street railroad service. The first section of the 3-mile Cambridge Railroad was opened between Boston and Cambridge on March 26, 1856, beating a rival line into operation by the purchase of secondhand cars from the Brooklyn City Railroad. In order to popu-

Just the thing for warm weather travel was this two-mule, four-bench Hawaiian Tramways open car shown in front of the Royal Government buildings on Honolulu's King Street in 1888. — *Public Archives, State of Hawaii.*

The upper deck of this 1859-model horsecar was clearly a delightful place for a summer outing. Double-deckers, however, never became popular in North America. — *Smithsonian Institution.*

The 19th century horsecar was often a joy to behold. This elaborately decorated specimen operated on the Mount Auburn & Boston line. — *Collection of LeRoy O. King.*

larize its service, the Cambridge line tried the novel idea of letting everyone ride free, and within a week it was transporting more than 2000 passengers a day. After some two months of free transportation, the line's conductors began to ask for fares. The

public was outraged at this imposition. Many demanded that the company's franchises and privileges be revoked, and a few extremists even suggested that the line's officials should be hanged on Boston Common.

Philadelphia's first street railway began operating 2 years later, and by 1859 lines were running in Baltimore, Pittsburgh, Cincinnati, and Chicago as well.

These early street railways were not always received with universal acclaim. Carriage owners asserted that the rails in the streets constituted a serious hazard to the safety of their horses and vehicles, and it was widely believed that the speeding horsecars would take a terrible toll of pedestrian traffic. Said the Philadelphia *Sunday Dispatch* in 1857, when the city's first horsecar line was under construction: "It is perhaps scarcely worthwhile to allude to the fact that in New York City they kill one person each week on city railroads and mangle

three or four on an average in the same space of time. Human life is really of little value nowadays."

Often the early street railways suffered the ill will of cabmen and carters. Soon after the Montreal City Passenger Railway opened in 1861 it experienced trouble on this score. Cab drivers and carters hooted and yelled at the street railwaymen, stoned the cars, and placed obstacles on the tracks. Stern measures were taken to repress such ruffianism. Reported the Montreal *Gazette* after one such inci-

Interior appointments of this 1886 Boston car, constructed by the Metropolitan Railroad Company in its own shops, were considerably more luxurious than in most horsecars in order to satisfy the wealthy Beacon Street and Commonwealth Avenue trade on the company's Back Bay line. The ceiling was covered with a "tastefully decorated" painted cotton lining, windows were of a large "parlor-car style," and the seats were stuffed with curled hair and covered with moquette. Oil lanterns provided interior illumination. The cards above the windows marked one of the earliest uses of this type of advertising. — *Street Railway Journal.*

Discriminating travelers on New York's Third Avenue Railroad rode aboard this richly furnished drawing-room car constructed for the horsecar line in 1871 by the Pullman Palace Car Company. The car made four round trips daily except Sunday. — *Courtesy of Pullman Company and Railroad Magazine.*

16

17

Rather than struggle with snow removal, several Canadian cities simply converted their horsecar lines to sleigh operation when heavy snows came. This runner-equipped horsecar was constructed for the Winnipeg Street Railway by the John Stephenson Company of New York City. — *Smithsonian Institution*.

dent, "As a warning to those who have by placing [sic] obstructions in the track and otherwise interfered with the running of the cars, we have to state that Hermidas Racette was yesterday committed to gaol by Mr. Coursol on a charge of felony, the prisoner having placed a stone upon the track upon the approach of the cars."

The question of Sunday operation was another hot issue for the early street railways. When the Ridge Avenue & Manayunk Railway Company in

This dramatic drawing by I. P. Pranishnikoff for an 1877 issue of *Harper's Weekly* shows the tracks being cleared by big horse-drawn snow sweepers in New York City. — *New-York Historical Society*.

Philadelphia decided to begin Sunday service during the 1860's, the management attempted to mollify the more puritanical element with the diplomatic announcement that "this service will enable persons residing temporarily in the country to attend their usual places of worship in the city." Despite this ploy there was a storm of protest and the mayor finally had to work out a compromise agreement whereby the cars would not begin operating until 1 p.m. and their bells would be removed and the horses walked rather than trotted past the churches. Even at that, some drivers were arrested, and writs of *habeas corpus* obtained. The issue wasn't settled until the Supreme Court of Pennsylvania finally ruled in favor of Sunday operation in 1867.

Winter posed still another problem for early horsecar operators. Before the advent of street railways, cities had made no effort to remove snow from their streets. During the winter months a few streetcar systems in such northern cities as Toronto and Montreal simply converted to the operation of sleighs similar in construction to their regular horsecars, but most lines found it more expedient to remove snow from their tracks to enable continued operation. This usually brought loud protests, since it ruined the sleighing. Some lines favored the use of salt for snow removal, a practice that had to be discontinued in Boston after the chairman of the Board of Health ruled that it was injurious to the public health because it worked as salt does in an

Two conflicting views of street railway travel are reflected in these drawings from the horsecar era. The idyllic scene above of life on the tramway is from a German publication of 1882. A less favorable view was presented in a drawing (below) which appeared in a New York weekly shortly after a crime aboard one of the cars. — *Both photos, New York Public Library.*

ice cream freezer, lowering temperatures 10 degrees and giving pedestrians violent colds.

Whatever their problems, the horsecar systems developed rapidly to meet the increasing demand for urban transportation. As early as 1855 New York City's horsecar lines were transporting well over 18 million passengers a year, and within the next 30 years their traffic approached 188 million. In 1881 there were in the United States some 415 street railway companies operating 18,000 cars pulled by more than 100,000 horses and mules over 3000 miles of track and doing an annual business in the vicinity of 1¼ billion dollars.

If Americans were quick to make use of street railway service, they were equally quick to find fault with it. Editorializing on the inadequacies of the city's streetcar and omnibus service in 1886, the New York *World* declared: "For filth, dilapidation, and a general appearance of squalor and slovenliness some of the streetcar lines of this city cannot be surpassed in the civilized world. Ladies and gentlemen are compelled to sit down on seats sticky with nastiness, breathe loathsome air, and look out of cracked windows that are splashed with dirt from one end of the year to the other. Some of these cars are washed only by the rain." And so on.

The earliest horsecars were little more than omnibus bodies mounted on flanged cast-iron wheels, but this arrangement gradually evolved into a style of car more suitable for street railway service. The usual arrangement consisted of a closed car with a single passenger compartment provided along each side with longitudinal seats which accommodated anywhere from 20 to 30 people. Perhaps the most widely used type was a small single-end car that could be drawn by one horse. A platform was provided for the driver at the front end and passengers entered from the rear. Sometimes a full platform was installed at the rear, but more often — in what was usually known as a "bobtail" car — only a step, leading to a rear entrance door, was supplied. These smaller cars were usually operated by one man, and passengers had to struggle all the way to the front of the car to deposit fares in a money box next to the driver. In 1884 an inventor named Small came up with an "automatic fare collector" that obviated this difficulty. This was simply an inclined brass channel running forward from the rear of the car into which a passenger deposited his fare; it then rolled forward into the fare box.

Almost as numerous as the one-horse cars, and generally employed on the more heavily trafficked routes, were larger cars drawn by two horses and usually provided with both a driver and a conductor to collect the fares. These larger cars often had full platforms at front and rear and could be quickly reversed at the terminus of the line simply by walk-

For the men who drove the cars from their unprotected front platform, winter could be cruel. This drawing of a driver's misery appeared in a 19th century periodical. — *New York Public Library*.

A New York newsboy's narrow escape from death or disfigurement under grinding car wheels was depicted in a drawing accompanying an article in an 1893 issue of *Once a Week* decrying the street accidents that were a daily occurrence. — *Courtesy of Railroad Magazine*.

21

Crowded rush-hour conditions on the Broadway line in 1889 were slightly exaggerated by an artist of the period.

ing the team around to the opposite end of the car.

The closed car was by far the most common type, but many systems also maintained fleets of open cars, fitted with transverse benches running the full width of the car and full-length running boards for boarding. These were operated in summer service. Less widely used was the double-decker, which was tried by a few systems but never attained any degree of popularity.

Horsecars were constructed of wood, the lightest and most easily fabricated material then available. The carbody normally was built upon a heavily framed floor platform, which had to have sufficient strength to support the running gear. In order to avoid excessive weight, sides and roofs were built of lightweight three-ply veneers. Horsecars were almost invariably four-wheel vehicles, with the axle bearings spring-supported in pedestals attached directly to the floor platform.

Interior appointments were generally of a rudimentary sort. Seats were usually of solid wood construction or were made of molded three-ply birch or mahogany veneers. In the more luxurious cars, seats were covered with rattan or carpet — some were even upholstered. At least one line, New York's Third Avenue Railroad, operated a plush extra-fare drawing-room car constructed by the Pullman Palace Car Company.

One of the most vexing problems faced by horsecar operators was that of car ventilation and heating, there being almost as many opinions on this subject as there were passengers. Most lines provided no heat at all, only straw on the floor to help keep their passengers' feet from freezing. Some lines that did supply heat placed a coal-burning heater on the front platform and carried hot air into the car with registers. New York's Second Avenue line used a box furnace mounted under the car and fired from outside. Pipes carried hot air under the seats, an arrangement that occasionally resulted in a car's being set afire.

When the public demanded heat in cars, most horsecar operators regarded it as an unnecessary frill or even downright unhealthy. Complained one official, "If you heat the cars, the next thing they will want is Axminster carpets and satin cushions." Commented President W. H. Hazard of the Brooklyn City Railroad, "The people want it, so we must give it to them whether it is detrimental to health or not." He evidently thought better of it, though, and removed the heaters from his cars in the spring of 1871. To one sarcastic letter writer, who offered to take up a collection to put them back if the company was too poor to do it, Hazard replied, "Keep the money and buy yourself an overcoat!"

If horsecar accommodations frequently left something to be desired, the cars themselves often were a joy to behold. Most lines painted their cars in bright colors and decorated them handsomely with elaborate lettering and striping. Among the most ornate cars were those of Boston's Highland Street Railway, which painted them in the plaid of the Scottish

ARE YOU GOING FAR? — NOT FAR.

ONLY TO THIS CAR! TA! TA!

Boy meets girl — humor in the horsecar age as depicted by a colorful pair of 1882 lithographs. — *Library of Congress*.

Highlanders. In the center of each carside was a panel painted with a historical scene or a portrait of the Massachusetts governor for whom the car was named.

Despite the success of horsecars in accommodat-ing the demand for transportation, animal traction as a means of street railway motive power had some serious shortcomings. To begin with, horsecars were not very fast. Most lines managed an average speed of only 5 or 6 mph, and this set a limit to the size of

Overcrowding of the horsecars, as shown in this drawing by Sol Eytinge Jr., was an entirely too frequent happen-ing. Horses were usually good for no more than 3 to 5 years of such service. — *New York Public Library*.

23

urban areas which could effectively be served by street railways. More important, horses were an extremely expensive form of motive power.

Street railway systems had a tremendous investment tied up in their horses and stables. Most companies had to have 5 to 10 horses for each car they operated, and the street railway systems in major cities owned thousands of the animals. As late as 1890, for example, 15,000 horses were engaged in street railway service in New York City alone. A good street railway horse cost around $125, and its keep usually amounted to anywhere from 40 to 60 cents a day.

Street railway work was hard on horses, and most were good for no more than 3 to 5 years of service before they had to be sold for less arduous work. A rather remarkable exception to this rule was "Old Crooked Tail," a five-year-old purchased by the Chicago City Railway in 1863. More than 21 years later Old Crooked Tail was still going strong in daily service, having worked seven days a week without missing a day for 21 years 5 months. During this time the gelding had covered 120,540 miles in 17,090 round trips over the railway. Citing this performance, a letter writer to the *Street Railway Journal* claimed a record length of service for Old Crooked Tail.

Once a car was in motion, it could be moved along by the horses without too much difficulty, and hand brakes on the car saved them much of the strain in stopping the heavy load. Getting the cars started, though, was extremely hard on street railway horses. In the heavy New York City traffic, for example, horses in street railway service were

Caring for the large number of horses required for street railway service was a costly item for horsecar operators. Mechanical devices helped to keep the costs down. An 1884 issue of the *Street Railway Journal* showed the newly invented Pennington's Grooming Machine which had a cylindrical brush driven by a flexible shaft. — *Street Railway Journal.*

often required to start a full car from a dead stop as many as a dozen times in the space of two city blocks. Inventors developed all manner of devices designed to ease the starting of the cars, but no one was able to come up with anything that was really workable in solving the problem. Typical of these was the "car starter" devised by A. R. Witmer of Safe Harbor, Pa., in 1886. It consisted of springs coiled about the car axles and a clutch arrangement whereby the springs were wound up by the momentum of the car in stopping. The spring tension was used to help start the car.

Still another problem for the animal railways was the down-to-earth one of manure. A Dr. Kemp of New York City, after a careful study of the subject, estimated that each street railway horse deposited 10½ pounds of solid matter in the streets daily, creating an obvious sanitation problem along a heavily traveled horsecar line. Disposal of manure from the stables was another problem. Most companies solved this problem by selling it; and earnings from the sale of manure often represented a sizable part of a company's income. One system that reported annual revenues of a little over $400,000 from passengers, earned almost $14,000 from the sale of manure during the same period.

During the Great Epizootic in 1872, horsecar service was maintained in Boston only because drivers and conductors offered to pull the cars by hand. — *Library of Congress.*

An earlier attempt to apply human power to the street railway was this unique contraption which operated briefly at New Orleans in 1866. The former horsecar was powered by a man who turned the large handwheel on the front platform. Reduction gears and the rooftop "walking beam" arrangement transmitted the power to the paddle-wheel-like device at the rear, which was fitted with eight iron "shoes." Speed was obviously limited. — *Duke-Middleton Collection.*

A typical horsecar of the 1860's is shown here on the Lynn & Boston Railroad. During the 1860's carbuilders began to adopt the "monitor roof," which had a raised deck running the length of the carbody with windows in the sides of the deck for better illumination and ventilation. — *Smithsonian Institution.*

Labor disputes were not uncommon on the street railways of the late 19th century, when labor unions were beginning their rise to power. These woodcuts from the February 9, 1889, issue of *Harper's Weekly* illustrate some of the violence in the streets of New York and Brooklyn after the street railway companies attempted to restore service with "scab" labor during a strike of nearly 7000 streetcar men that tied up 26 car lines in the two cities. The principal disagreement stemmed from the companies' refusal to recognize the Knights of Labor, or any other labor organization, as the bargaining agent for the car men. A demand for a wage increase to $2.25 for a 12-hour day was also an issue. — *All drawings, collection of William D. Middleton.*

The fragrant odor of the manure pits brought continuous complaints from residents in the vicinity of horsecar barns, and despite the use of all kinds of favorite disinfectants no one ever came up with a real solution to the problem.

Street railway horses were subject to an almost endless variety of ailments, and the pages of early *Street Railway Journals* were filled with discussions of veterinary problems. Numerous remedies were published for such common horse afflictions as colic, corns, collar gall, shoulder strains, severe coughs, runny noses, and pink eye. Proper shoeing of horses for the rough service on cobblestoned pavements was the subject of continuous debate. Many felt that the horses shouldn't be shod at all, but for those who preferred shoes, a tremendous variety of patented ones were available.

The vulnerability of street railway systems to animal ailments became evident late in 1872 when an epidemic of a horse disease known as Epizootic Apthnae, or the "Great Epizootic," swept through stables in the cities of eastern North America. The disease, previously known in Europe, reached America in 1870, grew to epidemic proportions in Montreal and Toronto 2 years later, then spread swiftly through the principal cities of the eastern United States. Thousands of horses died from it, and many others were disabled. In a large number of cities, street railway service had to be severely curtailed or discontinued altogether; in some, service was maintained only by hiring gangs of the unemployed to draw the cars through the streets.

The devastating effect of the Great Epizootic served only to intensify a search that had already been going on for years to find a suitable means of mechanical traction for street railways. The earliest efforts in this direction had been to apply the steam locomotive to street railway service, but this form of motive power had obvious drawbacks. The smoke, cinders, and noise of steam locomotives

27

In the aftermath of the great Blizzard of 1888, twice the usual motive power was required to keep this Philadelphia Traction Company car moving on the 12th and 16th streets line. — *Smithsonian Institution*.

Although cable railway tracks were already laid, an almost endless procession of horsecars along New York's Broadway dominated this 1893 scene at Madison Square. — *Library of Congress*.

A two-mule bobtail car laid over at the end of the Louisville Street Railway's line to the Exposition grounds in 1883. A handy water barrel supplied refreshment for the animals. — *Smithsonian Institution*.

This self-contained steam-powered streetcar, built by the Baldwin Locomotive Works, operated for about four months on the Market Street Railroad at Philadelphia during the 1876 Centennial Exhibition. — *Collection of H. L. Broadbelt.*

hauling several passenger cars were used, an arrangement that proved more adaptable to suburban-type services than it did to the purely urban street railway systems with their frequent-service requirements. Steam dummy lines were constructed in a number of cities, and sometimes they developed into important systems. San Francisco, for one, had an extensive system. The city's first steam dummy line, the Market Street Railroad, began operating down the principal thoroughfare in 1860, but was replaced by horse operation only 7 years later. In subsequent years a number of steam-operated systems of a more or less suburban character were developed in connection with the city's cable railways to carry passengers to such destinations as the Seal

To help promote the sale of lots in his Coronado development, San Diego financier Elisha S. Babcock Jr. constructed the Coronado Beach Railroad. Horses provided the motive power until the Baldwin Locomotive Works delivered steam dummy No. 1 in 1886. The trains operated from a connection with Babcock's steam ferry line across San Diego Bay to the Coronado Strand, where Babcock completed his Hotel del Coronado in 1888. — *Historical Collection, Union Title Office, Title Insurance & Trust Co.*

Stripped of its usual horsecar body design, a typical Baldwin steam dummy looked like this. — *Collection of H. L. Broadbelt.*

During the 1870's the Baldwin Locomotive Works built a number of four-wheel dummies of the type shown here for street railway service. The Ferro-Carril Urbano One-Spot is seen on what was evidently a trial run over a Philadelphia horsecar line. The "apron boards," hung from the carbody to hide the side rods from the view of panicky horses, were a common steam dummy feature. — *Smithsonian Institution.*

Baldwin turned out this "soda motor" in 1886 for the Minneapolis, Lyndale & Minnetonka, a Minnesota steam dummy line that was getting complaints about the smoke and soot from its regular motive power. The soda motor's oversize boiler and complicated mechanism were concealed beneath a gaily decorated streetcar body. — *Both photos, collection of H. L. Broadbelt.*

The Connelly Motor Company tried this naphtha-powered streetcar at Elizabeth, N. J., in 1889. It was not a success. — *Collection of Howard E. Johnston.*

Rocks, Cliff House, and Adolph Sutro's Baths.

To overcome the objections to steam operation on the grounds of the smoke and cinders, a number of efforts were made to develop a "fireless engine" car. Typical of the attempts was the ammonia car developed by the Standard Fireless Engine Company of New Orleans in 1886. According to the claims of its inventors, it operated with "no fire, no smoke, no steam, and no heat." Ammonia gas was stored under pressure in an iron reservoir under the carbody and was supplied to a reciprocating engine identical to a steam engine. After use, the gas was exhausted into an air-tight water tank under the car which took advantage of the capacity of water to absorb 700 times its volume of ammonia. The gas was later recovered for reuse. At one end of the line, ammonia was pumped into the car at a pressure of 180 to 200 pounds per square inch, and one charge was sufficient to operate the car on a round trip between Canal Street and Carrollton. Fuel consumption was reported to be two gallons of liquid ammonia per car-mile.

A few years later a slight variation of this design appeared in a car which used liquid anhydrous ammonia. The ammonia was contained in a tank surrounded by an outer tank charged with warm water. Heat from the water expanded the ammonia, which passed through a reciprocating engine and was then absorbed by the water in the outer tank. The diluted ammonia was withdrawn, and new charges of warm water and anhydrous ammonia were placed in the tanks at a charging station. One charge was claimed to be good for 30 miles of operation.

Another attempt at a fireless locomotive was the "soda motor." One of these was constructed by the Baldwin Locomotive Works in 1886 for the Min-

neapolis, Lyndale & Minnetonka, a Minnesota steam dummy line. This particular contraption was based upon the discovery by Moritz Honigmann, a German, that a strong solution of caustic soda increases in temperature when water is added. The soda motor employed a large boiler that was charged with soda at a temperature of 329 degrees Fahrenheit at the beginning of a run. Tubes within the boiler contained pure water which evaporated to produce steam for the cylinders. As the steam was exhausted it passed into the soda chamber, where it condensed and reacted with the soda to increase the temperature and produce more steam.

A perennial objective of "fireless engine" inventors of the 19th century was to produce a workable compressed-air car. Most such efforts simply used large storage tanks mounted on the car from which air was released to power a reciprocating engine. The tanks were replenished at a charging station at the end of the line. A rather complicated variation of this basic idea was developed by George A. Clarke of Cincinnati in 1885. Clarke's compressed-air system for street railways employed double metal bottoms on the cars as air chambers; these were charged with air at a pressure of 80 pounds per square inch. A "simple contrivance," unexplained by the inventor, utilized the motion of the car to partially replenish the air supply. To provide additional replenishment, an air line, charged by a 12 h.p. compressor at each end of the line, was laid underground parallel to the track. Every few miles the cars were supposed to stop and tap the line for more air by means of special surface fittings.

Still another attempt to develop a mechanical streetcar was the Connelly gas motor car, powered by a rudimentary internal combustion engine fueled by naphtha gas. This car was tried out in Brooklyn

Compressed air was another often-tried source of streetcar motive power that never worked out. The patented Hughes & Lancaster's low-pressure compressed-air tramcar was tried in London. — *New York Public Library.*

34

Based on an early photograph, this drawing from an 1875 *Scientific American* depicts Hallidie's Clay Street cable line shortly after its opening, with Hallidie himself on the front platform of the trailer. — *New York Public Library*.

and Elizabeth, N. J., in the late 1880's. Naphtha and an absorbent material were placed in an inner tank surrounded by a water-filled outer tank. Pipes connected this outer tank with the water jacket of the car's two-cylinder engine, heating the water and evaporating the naphtha. Air drawn through the inner tank produced a combustible mixture of air and naphtha gas; this passed to the cylinders where it was compressed and ignited by an electric spark generated by a small dynamo attached to the machine. The engine ran at a continuous speed, and the speed and direction of the car were controlled by an "ingenious arrangement" of levers. Like almost all such efforts, the Connelly car was not a success.

Of all the inventions and ideas that were brought forth in the effort to mechanize the street railway, only one achieved any degree of success in the years before the electric street railway became a practical system. This was the remarkable cable railway invented by a London-born San Francisco businessman named Andrew S. Hallidie in the 1870's.

Hallidie, a manufacturer of the "wire rope" invented by his father, had noted the extreme difficulty with which horsecars negotiated the city's notori-

Here is a cross-section view of the screw-type grip developed by Hallidie for his pioneer cable railway. — *Collection of Stephen D. Maguire*.

One of the few significant improvements to Hallidie's original cable car design was this lever-type "California Street grip" developed by Henry Root. — *Smithsonian Institution*.

35

Among lesser cable lines in San Francisco was Frederick O. Layman's Telegraph Hill Cable Railroad, which extended from Powell Street up Greenwich Street hill to an ornate resort operated by Gustav Walter. The single-track line was provided with a turnout at midpoint, necessitating simultaneous starts from top and bottom. — *Collection of Roy D. Graves, from LeRoy O. King.*

From the horsecar days of the 1860's until completion of the San Francisco-Oakland Bay Bridge in 1936, the focal point of San Francisco's surface transportation was the Ferry Building at the foot of Market Street where transbay commuter and transcontinental traveler alike arrived aboard the steam ferries of the Southern Pacific Company. Horsecars and cable cars both can be seen in this 1888 scene. — *Southern Pacific Company.*

In the 87 years since this 1880 stereopticon view was taken of the California Street hill, the venerable California Street Railroad has remained an unchanging part of the Nob Hill scene. The line, opened in 1878, has long since succeeded to the title of the world's oldest operating cable railway. — *Historical Collections, Security First National Bank, Los Angeles.*

ous hills. Indeed, some of the hills were so steep that no horsecar could even attempt them. One rainy winter night in 1869 Hallidie had witnessed a cruel horsecar accident of a sort that was all too common. A heavily overloaded car drawn by four horses was struggling up a hill. About halfway up, one of the horses slipped and fell. The driver quickly wound up his hand brake, but the chain which set the brakes snapped and the car, out of control, rolled back down the hill, dragging the unfortunate horses across the cobblestoned pavement and injuring the animals so severely that they had to be destroyed.

The tough steel cable manufactured in Hallidie's San Francisco plant was already being used in such applications as elevators and several long aerial tramways that brought gold and silver ores down from the inaccessible heights of California's Sierra Nevada. Why, he thought, couldn't the same idea be applied to the street railway?

Organized by San Diego alderman John C. Fisher in 1889 to replace an unsuccessful electric street railway project, the San Diego Cable Railway was one of the most ill-starred of cable railway ventures. On opening day, June 7, 1890, cable car No. 2, *El Escondido*, was decorated with palms and the national ensign and carried a brass band. The line, a financial failure, operated under cable power for little more than 2 years. In 1896 it reopened as an electric line. — *Collection of Frederick W. Reif, from Eric Sanders.*

Among the rolling stock of the San Diego Cable Railway were a dozen exceptionally handsome semi-open cars designed by the company's chief engineer, Frank Van Vleck, and constructed by the Stockton Combine, Harvester and Agricultural Works. Interiors of the closed sections were finished in rare woods, stained glass was installed in the transoms, and the windows were richly curtained. Exteriors of the exquisitely lettered cars were finished in maroon and gray. In 1890 the company's car No. 3, *Las Penasquitas*, posed with its proud designer, Van Vleck, standing at left with arm raised. — *Collection of Frederick W. Reif, from Eric Sanders.*

In later years of cable railway operation Seattle adopted double-truck cars of the semi-open pattern in preference to the original grip-car-and-trailer arrangement. No. 52 operated on the Lake Washington line. — *Washington State Historical Society, from Robert S. Wilson.*

Chicago's cable railway mileage was second only to that of San Francisco. The Windy City's first cable line was a route of the Chicago City Railway on State Street between Madison and 21st opened early in 1882. By the time this view of State Street, at Madison, was taken around 1890, the street had become the scene of intense cable car activity. By the early 1890's the Chicago City Railway was operating as many as 300 cable cars simultaneously during rush hours. — *Chicago Historical Society.*

Between 1888 and 1891 the North Chicago Street Railroad converted three of its principal routes between downtown Chicago and the North Side to cable operation. In this view from the early 1890's, a Lincoln Avenue line grip car and trailer are northbound on Dearborn Street at Washington. — *Chicago Historical Society.*

The greatest day's traffic in the history of the Chicago City Railway came on October 9, 1893, when the company hauled some 700,000 passengers — almost all of them on its cable lines — to the Chicago Day celebration at the World's Columbian Exposition in Jackson Park. A virtually endless parade of cable trains, jammed almost beyond belief, accommodated the unprecedented traffic. — *Chicago Historical Society*.

To provide a through service into downtown Chicago, cable trains of the Chicago City Railway's Wabash Avenue and State Street lines picked up trailers from several of the company's horse-car routes. Because the city refused to permit installation of trolley wire in Loop streets, the arrangement was continued even after electrification of the connecting horsecar lines. In this 1905 view a State Street train is seen northbound at Adams Street with an Archer Avenue trolley car in tow. — *Chicago Historical Society*.

In order to avoid the frequent drawbridge delays occasioned by water traffic on the Chicago River, cable trains of the North Chicago Street Railroad used the La Salle Street tunnel, which had been built in 1871 to provide an uninterrupted crossing for vehicular traffic to and from the North Side. In a 1906 view at the south end, a southbound train from the Wells Street line is emerging from the tunnel, while a northbound Clark Street train is entering. To supply illumination for the cars while in the tunnel, the company installed an overhead trolley wire and placed trolley poles on its grip cars. A metal "pan" at each portal automatically raised and lowered the poles. Cable operation ended less than a year after photo was taken. — *Chicago Historical Society*.

Hallidie's scheme was simplicity itself. An endless wire rope, powered by a steam engine at a central power plant, could be pulled through a trough placed between the rails and below the street. Streetcars attached to the cable would be drawn through the streets, using the almost limitless energy of the central power plant to surmount the steepest of hills. A special contrivance with which the operator could grip the cable or release it at will would permit the car to be stopped at any point.

Joined by three close friends, Hallidie organized a cable railway company in 1872 and obtained a franchise to construct a line on the Clay Street hill, a route which included grades of more than 12 per cent. Development of the various mechanical devices required for the system proved difficult; con-struction of the line itself proceeded at a slow and laborious pace; and not until the final day for expiration of the franchise, August 1, 1873, was all in readiness for the trial run. At five o'clock on that historic morning the first car, with Hallidie himself at the controls, successfully made its way down the Clay Street hill and back up again. Later in the day, the Clay Street line's first revenue run — attended by such San Francisco notables as Mayor William Alvord, Fire Chief David Scannell, and the city's beloved eccentric, Emperor Norton I — was made to fulfill the franchise requirements.

Placed in regular service a short time later, Hallidie's cable railway proved to be a sensational success. In 1877 a second cable line was opened on Sutter Street, and the next year a splendid new

This ornate grip car for Cincinnati's Walnut Hills Cable Road was constructed by car-builder John Stephenson. — *Smithsonian Institution.*

Pulling what was undoubtedly a former horsecar, a grip car of the Baltimore City Passenger Railway Company's North Charles Street line rattled past Calvert Station about 1893. — *Collection of LeRoy O. King.*

Soon after Congressional legislation of the late 1880's hurried the departure of horsecars from the streets of the nation's capital, cable cars were clanging down principal Washington thoroughfares. In this mid-1890's view from the steps of the Treasury Building, cable cars of the Capital Traction Company share the broad expanse of Pennsylvania Avenue with a leisurely pedestrian, bicycle, and horse traffic which characterized that unhurried time.

Cable railway operation on the Avenue ended abruptly on the night of September 30, 1897, when fire destroyed the company's power plant at 14th and Pennsylvania, immobilizing 15 miles of cable lines. By that time electric traction had long since proved itself, and the company's directors decided to electrify their lines rather than re-equip the road for cable operation. — *Collection of Le-Roy O. King.*

47

In the place of its birth the cable railway survived to become a unique symbol of a city. This young group rides a car of the California Street line, a durable San Francisco institution now in its 89th year. — *San Francisco Convention & Visitors Bureau.*

cable railroad costing nearly a half million dollars was constructed on California Street by a group of powerful San Francisco capitalists that included Mark Hopkins and Charles Crocker, two of the original "Big Four" who had built the Central Pacific Railroad. The California Street Railroad was opened to service on April 10, 1878, amid civic festivities that included an address by Gov. Leland Stanford, and achieved no less a success than that of the pioneer Clay Street line. Other systems soon followed, and by the late 1880's San Francisco was served by an extensive network of cable lines comprising some 112 miles of track operated by eight separate major companies.

Other cities were quick to follow San Francisco's example. Even without hills to conquer, cable railways afforded numerous advantages over animal railways. Their average speed of around 9 or 10 mph was almost double that of a typical horsecar line. Despite the high cost of cable railway construction — many lines came to well over $100,000 a mile to build — the elimination of the many expenses associated with animal traction made cable lines much more profitable than horsecars had ever been. Cable cars were clean and quiet, and proved

immensely popular with the public. Real estate values increased rapidly along cable lines. In Chicago it was found that property values increased 50 per cent to 200 per cent in a single year following the construction of cable railways.

Chicago was the second city to adopt Hallidie's invention. Officials of the Chicago City Railway, searching for something more effective than horse traction for their large network of street railway lines serving Chicago's South Side, traveled to San Francisco in 1880 to study the several cable lines already in operation there. Plans were quickly formulated for conversion of the company's lines on State Street and Wabash Avenue. Construction started the following summer, and by January 1882 the first line, extending along State Street from Madison to 21st, was ready for operation. Appropriate ceremonies marked the opening of the line on January 28. A special train made up of two grip cars and seven trailers was assembled at Madison Street. The Lyon and Healy band climbed aboard the first grip car, a group of street railway officials boarded the second grip, and the seven trailers were filled by assorted civic dignitaries. With the band playing, the inaugural run proceeded proudly down State Street to the company's powerhouse at 21st Street, where a brief ceremony was held.

During the next 10 years the Chicago City Railway extended its cable lines far out into the South Side, and the West Chicago and North Chicago street railway companies constructed an extensive network of lines serving the West and North sides. By 1893 Chicago's street railway companies had invested an estimated 25 million dollars in a cable railway system totaling 82 miles, over which some 710 grip cars were operated. Next to that of San Francisco, it was the largest cable railway system in North America.

Philadelphia got its first cable line in 1883, and during the same year cable-powered cars began operating over the Brooklyn Bridge. Conversion of horsecar lines in the nation's capital was hurried by 1888 Congressional legislation requiring that some form of mechanical propulsion be substituted for horse power; and by 1894 the major lines of the city's principal street railway companies had been converted to cable operation. St. Louis, with 55 miles of cable line, had one of the largest systems. Denver, with 44 miles, was not far behind.

Cable railway construction in the latter city was enlivened by a rivalry between two companies, and at one point this reached an intensity reminiscent of the competition that on occasion had characterized steam railroad construction in Colorado. In 1889 the two rivals, the Denver Tramway Company and the Denver City Cable Railway Company, became embroiled in a dispute over which one would construct cable track on Lawrence Street between 15th and 19th streets. The Tramway Company dramatically settled the argument on the night of December 18, 1889, when it marshaled a force of 1600 men; brought in the necessary ties, rails, and cable equipment; and by dawn had laid down four blocks of cable railway. Ironically, the company's cable cars never did use the track!

By the early 1890's cable railways were serving some 28 American cities, and cable systems constructed under American supervision were functioning in cities in the British Isles, France, Australia, and New Zealand. By 1894 cable railway mileage in the United States had reached a peak of 662 miles, nearly 5000 cable cars were in operation, and cable railway traffic was in the vicinity of 400 million passengers a year.

Throughout the era of cable railways the mechanical details of their operation changed but little from those contrived by Hallidie for his original Clay Street line in 1873. To provide a conduit for the cable, the rails were supported by a series of cast-iron yokes, usually firmly set in concrete. The cable ran through the opening formed by the yoke and was supported at intervals by rollers or sheaves attached to the yokes. The yokes curved inward to cover the top of the conduit and supported continuous steel members that formed a narrow slot in the pavement.

One of the most intricate parts of the cable-car mechanism was the grip with which the car was attached to the cable. Hallidie's original line used a screw-operated grip mechanism operated by a handwheel. A considerably improved grip mechanism was created a few years later by Henry Root, the engineer in charge of construction for the California Street Railroad. Root's device was operated by a long grip lever on a quadrant arrangement, resembling a brake handle. This "California Street grip," or a similar design, was used on a majority of cable railways, and constituted the principal deviation from Hallidie's original system. Any number of inventors applied themselves, without any degree of success, to improving the grip mechanism. In 1882 the *Street Railway Journal* was said to have on hand copies of over 1000 patents for cable railway systems. In each of them the grip mechanism was the important feature.

The cable itself was a wire rope of anywhere from 1½ inches to 1¾ inches in diameter, ordinarily consisting of six strands made up of 16 to 19 steel wires each. It was lubricated with linseed oil, and a hemp center provided flexibility. The cable was guided around curves by arrangements of sheaves or pulleys, and reversed its direction at the end of a line by means of a huge horizontal sheave under the street. The cable entered a powerhouse at right

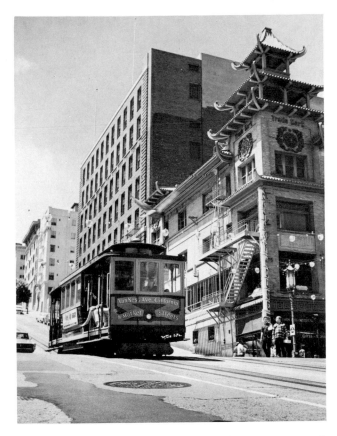

Halfway up the steep grade between Market Street and the top of Nob Hill, cable cars of the California Street line intersect the Grand Street "main drag" of San Francisco's Chinatown, a hallmark of the city only slightly less noted than the cables. — *William D. Middleton.*

angles to the track and was wound several times around a huge driving wheel 10 to 25 feet in diameter powered by a reciprocating steam engine. Before leaving the powerhouse the cable passed around a large-diameter vertical sheave mounted on a movable carriage. A counterweight attached to the carriage served to maintain a constant tension on the cable and helped to compensate for changes in its length brought about by variations in temperature and load or the age of the cable.

Usually several cables, each serving a particular line or section of line, were operated from a single power plant. Sometimes the individual cables reached extraordinary lengths. Probably the largest single cable railway power plant was that constructed in 1889 at Lawrence and 18th streets in Denver by the Denver City Cable Railway Company. All of the company's cable lines were powered from this single plant by means of five separate cables totaling almost 30 miles in length. The longest of them was approximately 7 miles long.

The life of a street railway cable varied considerably, depending upon the traffic and the amount of curvature on a line. On some heavily traveled Chicago lines a cable lasted less than three months; on

49

other lines a cable might last for more than a year.

In construction and appearance, cable cars were little different from the horsecars they replaced. Most cable systems used small four-wheel "grip cars," equipped with the grip mechanism, to haul one or more trailers through the streets. Quite often, these trailers were no more than former horsecars. In later years a number of lines developed large double-truck cars for cable service. In order to provide the gripman adequate visibility from his location near the center of the car, the early grip cars almost invariably were built as open cars. When double-truck cars were introduced they most often were built to the "semi-open" pattern, in which one end of the car was closed and the other, where the gripman was located, was open.

In several larger cities the Post Office Department found the speedy cable cars useful in providing more rapid mail distribution to branch post offices. New York was one of the earliest cities to get cable-car mail service when a Railway Post Office was inaugurated on the Third Avenue Railway on October 1, 1895. Ten special trailer cars, painted white and bearing the legend UNITED STATES MAIL RAILWAY POST OFFICE in blue, were constructed for this duty. The cars were loaded on a special siding on Mail Street at the General Post Office and were drawn by horses to the running tracks of the Third Avenue line; there they were picked up by cable trains. Mail was sorted in the Railway Post Office cars en route to the branch post offices. This particular route lasted only until 1897, when it was replaced with a pneumatic tube system. A similar service was started on the Cottage Grove-Wabash line of the Chicago City Railway in 1896. San Francisco and Cincinnati were among other cities with cable-car mail service.

Whatever its advantages over the horsecar, the cable railway had more than a few inherent shortcomings of its own. Because of the great weight of the cables, a disproportionate share of the energy delivered by a powerhouse was absorbed just by the moving parts of the system. A study made in San Francisco in 1888 estimated that 57 per cent of the power generated was devoted to moving the cable itself, 39 per cent to moving the cars, and only 4 per cent to moving passengers.

Cable systems were vulnerable to a wide variety of breakdowns and mishaps, most of them involving either the cable or the grip mechanism. One of the most spectacular mishaps would occur when a broken strand from the cable became entangled with the grip, making it impossible for the gripman to release the cable. As the car sped unchecked through the streets, bell clanging furiously, the passengers usually "joined the birds" while the conductor ran for the nearest telephone to call the powerhouse and have the cable stopped. To avoid an inevitable collision, cars ahead of the runaway would join the dash through the streets, and sometimes five or six cars, all clanging noisily, could be seen racing along pursued by the runaway. New York's Metropolitan Railway had special boxes set in the pavement at intervals which a conductor could open to pull a wire that would stop the cable. San Francisco cars were equipped with a "slot brake," a steel wedge that could be driven into the cable slot to bring a car to a halt when all else failed.

Gripmen had to be alert to release the cable at junctions or wherever it passed through a series of sheaves or pulleys, such as at curves and similar locations. Failure to do so was a cardinal sin for a gripman and almost always resulted in wrecking a grip and "cutting the rope." When this happened a line would be immobilized for 2 to 6 hours while the cable ends were located, pulled together with horse-drawn grips, and spliced.

The moving cable was often irresistible to small boys, who learned how to fish for it with a wire or string. A box or wagon could then be attached and dragged through the streets to the peril of pedestrians and other street traffic.

Sunday afternoon finds the Aquatic Park terminal tranquil as a car of the Powell & Hyde streets line is swung on the turntable by its crew in preparation for the return trip to Powell and Market. — *William D. Middleton.*

Inbound to Market Street, a Powell & Hyde car surmounts the harrowing Hyde Street hill against a spectacular backdrop of San Francisco Bay, Alcatraz, and the Marin County hills. At this same point in the fall of 1964 a car bound up the hill broke loose from the cable and rolled backward down the hill out of control. Tragedy was averted only by use of the last-resort slot brake. — *William D. Middleton.*

Cable systems were relatively indifferent to the hazards of winter weather, since they gave no trouble from slipping wheels regardless of the condition of the tracks. When all other means of transportation were tied up by heavy snow, the cable cars could often be found operating as usual. The greatest hazard of winter to cable systems was the problem of snow and ice accumulating in the cable tube. Chicago understandably had a great deal of trouble from this source and installed steam pipes at many points to melt the accumulation of ice. A horse-drawn steam boiler was brought to the site of the obstruction to fill the steam pipes.

Even as the cable railways began to displace animal traction on major street railways throughout the United States, a host of inventors and tinkerers were coming closer and closer to success in their effort to perfect a rival means of power that would supplant horsecars and cable railways alike. As early as 1883, when the cable car boom had hardly begun, President H. H. Littell of the American Street Railway Association proclaimed in an address at Chicago, "I see in the recent subjugation of the subtle and hitherto elusive force of electricity to the needs of man boundless possibilities for the world's three great requisites of advancement: heat, light, and motion." But even Littell had little idea of how swift or complete would be the triumph of electric traction.

51

A Time of
Trial and Triumph

Opening of one of the pioneer electric lines of the 1880's was invariably the occasion for a gala civic celebration. This dignified Los Angeles crowd attended the January 4, 1887, opening of the first electric road on the West Coast, a Daft system line built on Pico Street by the Los Angeles Electric Railway Company. Like most of the Southern California trolleys that followed it, the Pico Street line was built to promote a real estate venture, the "Electric Railway Homestead Association Tract." Within three days of the opening the tract was sold out. — *Historical Collections, Security First National Bank, Los Angeles.*

EVEN as the first horse-drawn streetcars began their historic journey along New York's Bowery in 1832, the first of the long series of inventors and tinkerers had begun the half century of experimentation that was eventually to lead to the overwhelming triumph of electric traction.

What might be described as the first step on the long road to development of electric transportation was the work of the distinguished English physicist, Michael Faraday, who in 1821 discovered that electricity could be made to produce mechanical motion. Faraday's principle of electromagnetic rotation, as it was called, was fundamental to the later development of the electric motor.

By far the most important of the early electric railway experimenters was a young Brandon (Vt.) blacksmith named Thomas Davenport. His accomplishments were all the more remarkable in the light of his limited education. Davenport was born at Williamstown, Vt., in 1802 and at the age of 14 was apprenticed to the village blacksmith. In 1833 he began the study of electromagnetism and in 1835 exhibited at the Rensselaer Institute in Troy, N. Y., and the Franklin Institute in Philadelphia a battery-powered rotary engine driven by electricity. Later the same year Davenport constructed a small circular railway driven by his electromagnetic motor. During the next few years he built over a hundred different motors of various types; one of them he used to power the world's first electric printing press on which he published a newspaper, *The Electro-Magnet*. In 1846 Davenport started work on the application of electric current to the strings of musical instruments and was preparing a patent application for what might have been the first electric guitar when he was stricken with a fatal illness and died in 1851.

The next important step in electric traction development was taken by Robert Davidson of Aberdeen, Scotland, who about 1838 constructed a 7-ton electric locomotive powered by a 40-cell iron-zinc sulphuric acid battery. Davidson's locomotive made several successful trips on the Edinburgh-Glasgow Railway, but then was wrecked by steam locomotive engineers and firemen who were fearful of the rival means of propulsion.

In 1847 Prof. Moses G. Farmer of Dover, N. H., operated a small experimental electric locomotive that pulled a car capable of carrying two people around an 18-inch-wide track. A 48-cell Grove nitric acid battery provided the power. Three years later Farmer, aided by Thomas Hall, exhibited a small electric railway at Boston — the first known use of the rails to carry the power supply to the car from a stationary source.

In 1851 Prof. Charles G. Page of the Smithsonian Institution, with $30,000 appropriated by Congress, constructed a battery-powered electromagnetic locomotive propelled by a 16 h.p. reciprocating electric motor of his own design. By reversing the polarity, a hollow solenoid and core produced a reciprocating motion which was applied to the flywheel by a crankshaft, much like a steam engine. Page's locomotive reached speeds as high as 19 mph on a 39-minute 5-mile trip between Washington and nearby Bladensburg, Md., over the Washington

THOMAS DAVENPORT

Thomas Davenport (1802-1851), a Brandon (Vt.) blacksmith, inventor, and classic example of the resourceful Yankee mechanic, built a model electric railway that was an important early step toward practical electric transportation. — *Smithsonian Institution.*

Davenport's circular electric railway of 1835, now on display at the Smithsonian Institution, was driven by a rotating electromagnetic motor. A crude battery provided the power. — *Smithsonian Institution.*

Professor Farmer's battery-powered electric train was a remarkably sophisticated-appearing machine for its time. "My father used the apparatus in 1847 when lecturing on electricity," his daughter later recalled. "He laid the rails around the hall and ran his car carrying four children." — *Smithsonian Institution*.

MOSES G. FARMER

Prof. Moses G. Farmer of Dover, N. H., built an electric train in 1847 that could actually carry two adults. Twenty years later, Farmer was one of the first to operate an electric car with power obtained from a dynamo. — *Smithsonian Institution*.

little further progress was made in the advancement of electric traction.

One of the first attempts to operate an electric car with generated power was made by Professor Farmer in 1867 utilizing a crude dynamo, but the first person to successfully operate an electric locomotive with power drawn from a dynamo was a German named Ernst Werner Siemens. Siemens, who was born at Lenthe in Hanover in 1816, had made

CHARLES GRAFTON PAGE

Prof. Charles Grafton Page (1812-1868) of the Smithsonian Institution operated an experimental car which attained 19 mph on a round trip between Washington and Bladensburg, Md., on April 29, 1851. A 100-cell battery provided the power. Congress put up the money for the venture. — *Smithsonian Institution*.

& Baltimore Railroad. The trip was not a complete success, for Page's pottery battery cells cracked at the slightest jolt, and by the time the return trip was completed the battery had been entirely destroyed.

If the early experimentation proved anything, it was that batteries were an unsatisfactory and uneconomical source of electricity for an electric railway. Consequently, until the development of a satisfactory dynamo, or generator, between 1860-1870

A year after his Lichterfelde line opened, Siemens electrified the horse railroad between Spandauer Bock and Charlottenburg. This early drawing shows the two-wire overhead system and four-wheel troller favored by Siemens after the use of running rails for power supply proved inadvisable. — *Smithsonian Institution*.

ERNST WERNER VON SIEMENS

Dr. Ernst Werner von Siemens (1816-1892), German electrician and inventor, built the first successful generator-powered electric railway in 1879 and the first commercial electric line in 1881.—*Siemens Archive, Munich*.

a number of important electrical discoveries and inventions, and, with J. G. Halske in 1847, had founded the Siemens & Halske electrical firm at Berlin. Even today the firm represents one of the foremost electrical undertakings in the world. At the Berlin Industrial Exhibition in 1879, Siemens & Halske constructed a small electric railway operating around an oval track about ⅓ mile long. A

locomotive which drew its power from a third rail between the running rails was capable of hauling three trailers accommodating 18 passengers at a speed of about 8 mph.

In May 1881 Siemens opened the world's first commercial electric railway at Lichterfelde, near Berlin. A car capable of carrying 26 passengers and of operating at a speed of about 30 mph was operated over the 1½-mile line. A single motor mounted beneath the carbody and connected to the axles by wire cables powered the car. Initially, 100-volt power was drawn from the running rails, an

Siemens' pioneer dynamo-powered electric railway at the 1879 Berlin Industrial Exhibition whisked passengers around an oval track at 8 mph. Some 80,000 passengers were transported. — *Siemens Archive, Munich*.

arrangement that was later changed to an overhead system after some rude experiences by horses and pedestrians. A year later Siemens electrified a horse railroad between the Berlin suburbs of Charlottenburg and Spandauer Bock.

At the Paris Exposition in 1881 Siemens displayed an electric car equipped with one of the earliest attempts at an overhead trolley system. Two years later, under the direction of Dr. Werner Siemens' brother, Sir William (a naturalized Briton who managed the company's branch in England), the Siemens firm installed at Portrush, Ireland, a 6-mile electric line notable for the first use of a hydroelectric power supply.

In the decade following the Siemens success at the Berlin Exhibition, increasingly rapid progress was made in electric railway development in both Europe and the United States. About 1879 Stephen D. Field, a son of Cyrus Field, promoter of the first successful transatlantic cable, developed plans for an electric railway taking its power from a third rail mounted in a slotted conduit. During 1880-1881 Field constructed and operated an experimental electric locomotive at Stockbridge, Mass. At about the same time, Thomas A. Edison began experimenting with electric traction, and in 1880 Field, Edison, and Siemens all applied for similar patents within three months of each other.

Edison's electric railway experimentation began in the spring of 1880 when a short loop of narrow-gauge track was installed at the inventor's Menlo Park (N. J.) laboratories. One of Edison's electric lighting dynamos was used as a motor for a small locomotive which drew its power from the running rails. Initially, the motor was connected to the wheels through a system of friction pulleys. When this proved impractical, a belt drive was installed.

With financial backing from Henry Villard, president of the Northern Pacific Railroad, Edison constructed an improved locomotive the following year. Villard had plans for electrifying some of the Northern Pacific's branch lines in the wheat regions of the northwest, but the Northern Pacific's bankruptcy a short time later brought an end to the work. Other railroadmen expressed little interest in electrification, and Edison soon turned his energies to other projects.

In 1883 Edison's interests were joined with those of Field to form the Electric Railway Company of the United States. Edison himself took little part in the work of the new company, which was managed by Field. By June 1883 the Edison-Field firm had completed an experimental 3-ton locomotive, *The Judge*. This engine pulled a passenger car along ⅓ mile of narrow-gauge track laid in the gallery of the main building at the 1883 Exposition of Railway Appliances at Chicago. It reached speeds as high as 12 mph and carried approximately 27,000 passengers.

About this time several important new inventors entered the electric railway field. Late in 1883 a British-born inventor named Leo Daft, who had been experimenting with electric traction since 1881, constructed the *Ampère*, a 2-ton electric loco-

Dr. Siemens' one-car mile-and-a-half line opened at Lichterfelde in 1881 and provided the world's first regular fare-paying electric railway service. These two views depict the line before a double-wire overhead system replaced the original method of current distribution through the running rails some 12 years after the line opened. — *State Historical Society of Wisconsin (right); Siemens Archive, Munich (left).*

Thomas A. Edison's Menlo Park electric railway of 1880 (left) zipped around the track at speeds as high as 40 mph, and the inventor delighted in carrying visitors on high-speed joy rides over the line. On at least one occasion a party of dignitaries was hurled into a ditch when the little locomotive derailed on a curve. A larger, improved model (right) constructed the following year with financial backing from the Northern Pacific was equipped with a huge cowcatcher, headlight, and cab, giving it a remarkable resemblance to a steam locomotive. — *Smithsonian Institution (left); Duke-Middleton Collection (right).*

Steam locomotive architecture obviously influenced the builders of the experimental Edison-Field locomotive, *The Judge*, built for the Exposition of Railway Appliances at Chicago in 1883. Power was obtained from a center third rail. — *Smithsonian Institution.*

motive that was successful in hauling a standard railroad coach carrying 75 people up a grade of almost 2 per cent on the Saratoga, Mt. McGregor & Lake George Railroad. After installing several successful exhibition lines, Daft was engaged in 1885 by Thomas C. Robbins, general manager of the Baltimore Union Passenger Railway, to electrify the company's 2-mile suburban line to Hampden. The conditions for a trial of the Daft system could hardly have been worse. Grades on the line were as steep as 6.6 per cent, and curves had a radius of as little as 40 feet.

Skeptical directors of the company specified that payment would be made for the installation only after it had been in satisfactory operation for a year; and even at that, they almost backed out of the deal when an "eminent scientist" called in to look over the line declared, "The man who undertakes to operate this section by electricity in the present state of the art is either a knave or a fool." Only General Manager Robbins' threat to resign deterred the directors from canceling the contract then and there.

Daft installed a powerhouse and a third-rail distribution system, and by August 10, 1885, the line

LEO DAFT

Leo Daft (1843-1922), British-born inventor who constructed several successful exhibition lines in the early 1880's, electrified at Baltimore in 1885 America's first commercial electric railway to operate for any appreciable length of time. — *Smithsonian Institution.*

Two of these little four wheel electric "tractors," as inventor Daft called them, pulled former horsecars over Baltimore's 2-mile Hampden line. Each of the 12½-foot locomotives was powered by a single 8 h.p. motor. — *Smithsonian Institution.*

After several unfortunate encounters between street traffic and the third-rail system on his Baltimore installation, inventor Daft was forced to erect an overhead power arrangement wherever the line crossed major streets. Here, with its crude pole raised to the gas pipe overhead, is electric dummy *Faraday.* — *Smithsonian Institution.*

was ready for regular operation. Standard 16-foot horsecars were pulled by two four-wheel dummy-type locomotives, the *Morse* and the *Faraday*, both capable of a speed of 10 mph with two trailers. The company soon reported that power costs for the line were only $7 a day, even with twice the former traffic; previously it had cost $18 a day to maintain the line's mules. After a year of reasonably satisfactory operation, the equipment was formally accepted; Daft was paid in full; and two more locomotives, the *Ohm* and the *J. L. Keck*, were ordered. Ultimately, however, the line reverted to horse power.

A Daft system line opened on Pico Street in Los Angeles in 1887 by the Los Angeles Electric Railway Company was powered by electric dummy locomotives almost identical to those used on Daft's historic Baltimore electrification 2 years before. The Pico Street line was equipped with a two-wire overhead system and troller current collection instead of the third-rail system used on the Baltimore installation. Dummy operation continued until a June 1888 boiler explosion at the powerhouse and subsequent bankruptcy put the company out of business. Pico Street electric operation was resumed in 1891 by a new company and continued until early 1963. — *Title Insurance & Trust Company, Los Angeles.*

Inventor John C. Henry of Kansas City, Mo., supplied electrical equipment for San Diego's Electric Rapid Transit Street Railroad Company, which opened for business late in 1887. Despite glowing initial accounts of the performance of the Henry equipment, the Electric Rapid Transit, like most of the early electric car ventures, was less than a complete success and operation ended by mid-1889. — *Herbert R. Fitch, from Eric Sanders.*

During the next few years Daft constructed several other small electric lines, none of them particularly successful. After repeated difficulties with third-rail current collection, Daft switched to a two-wire overhead system. Current was collected by a little four-wheeled carriage that rode on the wires and was connected to the car by a flexible cable. The device was called a "troller" after the manner in which it was towed behind the car; and from this the term, "trolley" eventually evolved. One reported disadvantage of the troller was its tendency occasionally to jump the wires and come crashing through the roof of the car, an occurrence that must have done little to promote feelings of ease or confidence among Daft line passengers.

Probably the most successful of the early Daft installations was the Sea Shore Electric Railway at Asbury Park, N. J., which opened with eight cars on September 19, 1887, and ran continuously until abandonment in 1931. The Daft "troller" system originally installed, however, was replaced only a year later with pole trolleys.

The earliest use of overhead current collection in the United States had been made by Prof. John C. Henry, a former Kansas City telegraph operator, who built an experimental line in 1884 that employed a two-wire overhead system using a troller for current collection similar to that later adopted by Daft. Henry, as a matter of fact, charged that the Daft overhead system was an infringement of his patents.

In 1885 Henry moved his experiments to the tracks of the Fort Scott & Gulf Railway, and during the following winter arranged to electrify a mile of track for the East Street Railway Company, a Kansas City horsecar line. Four motor cars were each equipped with a 25 h.p. motor which projected through the floor of the car so that all working parts were in full view of the motorman. The cars were noisy but the inventor was able to glibly explain this failing. "The buzzing of the motors is easily overcome," wrote one newspaper reporter, "but at present Mr. Henry prefers to have the noise as a notice to people on the streets."

Although Henry's Kansas City line operated reasonably well, it was not a commercial success and went bankrupt after a short time.

In 1887 a group of promoters in San Diego, Calif., who had organized the Electric Rapid Transit Street Railroad Company to construct what was proposed to be the largest electric street railway in the country, engaged Henry to install his system of electrification on their new line. Cars for the new venture were constructed locally, and the Henry Electric Railway Company supplied motors and other electrical equipment. Instead of using the two-wire system employed in his Kansas City experiments, Henry set up a single overhead wire and utilized the rails for the return circuit. Power was transmitted from the motor to the wheels of the cars through a friction clutch and differential gears.

The first line of the new company was placed in operation late in 1887 over a 4-mile former steam dummy line between San Diego and Old Town, and San Diegans marveled at the new electric cars. "The San Diego Electric Rapid Transit Railway is a success," proclaimed the San Diego *Union* a few days later. "The rapidity of motion is entirely under control. It surmounts almost incredible grades. It starts, stops, and moves promptly and smoothly." Stated another contemporary account, "The only noticeable noise was that caused by the electricity as it passed around the wheels."

Only a few weeks later, though, the San Diego *Sun* was reporting on "the baleful effect of the current on watches by the dynamos." "The finer classes of watches are injured," proclaimed the *Sun*. "A watch that has fallen under the electric influence may not show the effects right away, but it is liable to stop at any time and prove unreliable. A respected citizen says the company should never be permitted to run the electric motors without a car attached. It would be well for persons having fine watches to keep off the motors when riding over the electric road." For a short time a lively business was done by enterprising merchants who offered to demagnetize watches, but a few weeks later the company announced that Dr. Gochenauer (one of the promoters) had perfected a new motor "properly enclosed in glass" that would not injure watches.

Hardly had the company opened when it was in trouble. After a falling out with the Old Town steam dummy line over which the electric cars operated, the company discontinued service and dismantled the electric overhead less than a month

The Observatory Hill Passenger Railway at Allegheny City, Pa., was opened on January 1, 1888, the second in a series of unsuccessful attempts by the Bentley-Knight Company to perfect the underground conduit system of current collection. The underground system was installed on about a mile of the line, while a two-wire side-mounted troller system powered the remainder. Ultimately, a conventional system of overhead trolley wire was installed. Four cars, each powered by two 15 h.p. motors, operated over the line, which included grades of almost 10 per cent. — *Library of Congress.*

The first important Van Depoele installation, a mile-long line powered from an underground conduit, was built at the Toronto Industrial Exposition in 1884. For a bigger and better installation the following year, Van Depoele devised a crude pivoted beam arrangement (above) to take power from an overhead wire. It was probably the first use ever made of the underrunning trolley pole. — *Both photos, Toronto Transit Commission.*

CHARLES J. VAN DEPOELE

Charles J. Van Depoele (1846-1892), the son of a master mechanic for Belgium's East Flanders Railway System, gave up a successful art furniture business in Detroit to devote his time to electrical experimentation. He installed the world's first completely electrified street railway system in Montgomery, Ala., in 1886. — *Smithsonian Institution.*

after service was started. Grandiose plans were announced for other routes, and on New Year's Day 1888 a new line was opened on Fourth Street in San Diego. Operation continued for a year and a half, but the Henry equipment proved to have numerous weaknesses and the line was frequently shut down for mechanical difficulties. By June 1889 the company was losing $20 a day, and the Electric Rapid Transit quietly went out of business, to be replaced by an equally ill-fated cable railway venture {see page 39}.

Another approach to the problem of current collection was taken by Edward M. Bentley and Walter H. Knight, who electrified 2 miles of track on the East Cleveland Horse Railway Company in 1884. The Bentley-Knight line drew its power from underground conductors placed in a slotted wooden conduit between the rails. A "plow" placed on the cars was used for current collection. Although the line was not particularly successful, it operated until the fall of 1885.

In 1888 the Bentley-Knight Company electrified the Observatory Hill Passenger Railway at Allegheny City, Pa. About a mile of the 4-mile line was equipped with the conduit system, while the remainder used a side-mounted two-wire overhead

Among the early Van Depoele installations was this electrification opened on New Year's Eve 1885 to carry trains of the Minneapolis, Lyndale & Minnetonka, a steam dummy line, into downtown Minneapolis. Installed in response to protests against steam operation through city streets, the electrification lasted only a short time. A year later the line was experimenting with the soda motor {see page 33}. — *Street Railway Journal.*

Wheeling, W. Va., was among the earliest U. S. cities to receive electric traction service when a Van Depoele installation opened in 1887. After developing the first crude trolley pole in 1885, Van Depoele returned to the use of two-wire overhead systems and trollers dragged behind cars on a flexible cable for most of his subsequent installations. Clearly visible on *Evangeline's* front platform is the platform-mounted motor and chain drive Van Depoele favored, an arrangement that was to give endless trouble. — *Collection of LeRoy O. King.*

Proud citizens of Montgomery, Ala., flocked downtown to see the cars of the world's first all-electric street railway system. The 15-mile Van Depoele-equipped system, opened in 1886, brought the electric railway close to the point of commercial success. Reassuring the citizenry, the Montgomery *Advertiser* said, "There is more real danger . . . in a Texas mule's heels than in all the electric motor system." — *Smithsonian Institution.*

system. A conventional overhead trolley system was installed later.

During 1888-1889 the firm made a final attempt to perfect the underground conduit system in an installation on Boston's West End Street Railway Company. After six months of almost daily failures and troubles, the conduit system was abandoned and soon afterward the Bentley-Knight firm disappeared from the field.

Still another of the electric traction pioneers of the 1880's was Sidney H. Short, a professor of physics at the University of Denver. About 1885 Short conducted experiments, using an underground conduit system, with a small electric car operating over a loop of track installed on the university campus. The success of this trial installation led to the formation of the United States Electric Company, which constructed about 4 miles of electric railway in North Denver for the Denver Electric & Cable Company. Operation began in 1885 and continued until late 1887, when horsecars replaced the electric service.

The principal difficulties encountered in the Denver installation were created by the unusual "series" system of current collection devised by Short. In the Short system the power feed was installed in a conduit between the rails, with two iron plates forming a 1½-inch slot in the pavement. A series of contactors, or "circuit breakers," was installed in the conduit at a spacing of 17 feet. On arms projecting to the front and to the rear of the cars were metal shoes which slid along the slot. Suspended on hangers from the shoes was an 18-foot "brush" — a hickory slat on which were mounted brass strips wired to the motor. The arrangement was such that as the brass strips came in contact with the contactors in the conduit, a series circuit was completed through the motor. A switching coil box permitted the speed of the motor to be varied, and a means was provided for bypassing a stopped car. Otherwise, as with bulbs on a Christmas tree, if one car stopped, all of them would have had to do the same. The wide pavement slot permitted all manner of debris to fall into the conduit, aggravating the already formidable problem of maintaining the hundreds of circuit breakers installed under the pavement. In case of wet weather or malfunctions the iron plates forming the slot frequently became "hot" — creating a serious shock hazard to horses and pedestrians — since Short's series system required a much higher voltage than more conventional systems.

Foremost among the inventors who developed the electric railway to the edge of practicality during the mid-1880's was an immigrant Belgian cabinetmaker named Charles J. Van Depoele. After arriving in the U. S. in 1871 at the age of 25, Van Depoele con-

tinued the electrical experiments he had long pursued, and in 1881 his electrical manufacturing company began lighting the streets of Chicago utilizing a dynamo of his own invention. About this time Van Depoele became interested in electric railways. In the winter of 1882-1883 he constructed an experimental line at Chicago using an overhead system of current collection, and during the fall of 1883 he exhibited at the Industrial Exposition in Chicago a car which drew its power from an overhead wire.

The following year Van Depoele installed a 1-mile electric railway between a local horsecar line and the grounds of the Toronto Industrial Exposition. Drawing its power from an underground conduit, the little train that operated over the line could carry as many as 200 passengers a trip and was able to reach a speed of 30 mph. In the fall of 1885 Van Depoele was back at the Toronto Exposition with a bigger and better train. This time a motor car and a train of three cars were operated. The most important difference in the line from the previous year was the installation of an overhead wire power system. To draw current from the wire, Van Depoele devised a contact wheel, carried on a pivoted beam, that was held against the underside of the wire by spring tension. This was probably the first use of the trolley pole in substantially its permanent form. The train operated from 8 a.m. to 10:30 p.m. daily throughout the Exposition, carrying as many as 225 to 250 passengers a trip and over 10,000 people a day.

The second year of operation at the Toronto Exposition was a huge success, and Van Depoele soon found himself swamped with contracts for new installations. By November 14, 1885, a 1¼-mile Van Depoele installation was ready for operation at South Bend, Ind., and the line's four electric cars each carried 70 to 100 passengers during trial runs. Abandoning the trolley pole current collection developed for his Toronto line, Van Depoele used a carriage traveling on the overhead wires and connected to the car by means of a flexible cable, an arrangement more or less similar to the trollers employed by Daft and Henry.

Only a month after the South Bend line was completed, the Van Depoele forces opened a mile-long line, much like that operated a few months previous at Toronto, on the New Orleans Exposition grounds. Still another Van Depoele line opened on New Year's Eve 1885, when the Minneapolis, Lyndale & Minnetonka Railway, a steam dummy line, completed electrification of its route into downtown Minneapolis. By early 1886 other Van Depoele lines were under construction in Detroit, Mich., Appleton, Wis., and Montgomery, Ala.

By far the most ambitious electric railway installation up to that time was the Van Depoele electrification of the Capital City Street Railway Company at Montgomery. Construction work began early in 1886, and the first car operated over the line with the inventor himself at the controls in a secret test between midnight and 1 a.m. on March 25, 1886. Regular operation with two converted horsecars began on the company's Court Street line on April 15.

Initially, Van Depoele used a troller system for current collection on his Montgomery installation, but after experiencing repeated difficulties with it he switched to the trolley pole system he had developed the year before at Toronto. As on most of his earlier installations, Van Depoele mounted the electric motor on one platform of the car and used a chain drive to deliver the power to the wheels, an arrangement that proved the source of endless trouble.

If the Montgomery installation was still far short

After a winter storm draped the Richmond trolley wire with sleet and icicles, Pat O'Shaughnessy, Sprague's Irish mechanic, climbed atop the first car out of the barn and wielded a broom to clear the wire as the car moved through the streets. The event was depicted for *The Century Magazine* by Jay Hambidge. — *Virginia State Library*.

Atrocious trackwork and grades as steep as 10 per cent complicated Sprague's work in the Richmond electrification. This view, dating from about 1887, shows the long Franklin Street hill. — *Virginia State Library*.

of perfection, it did operate reasonably well over grades as steep as 7.5 per cent, and the electrification was gradually extended until some 18 cars were being operated over 15 miles of track, giving Montgomery the first completely electrified street railway system in the world. Except for a temporary return to mule power in 1888 after a fire leveled the company's powerhouse, the Montgomery system was at least successful enough to achieve permanent operation, something that no other line had yet been able to do.

Years of painstaking trial and error were finally bringing results, and by the late 1880's electric traction was showing real promise. At the start of 1888 there were 21 electric railway companies operating some 172 electric cars over a grand total of 86 miles of track. It was still a small beginning, representing scarcely 1 per cent of the total U.S. street railway mileage; but before the year was over, the dazzling

FRANK J. SPRAGUE

Frank J. Sprague (1857-1934), Naval Academy graduate and electrical inventor, applied a scientific approach to electric traction development. His electrification of the Richmond Union Passenger Railway Company in 1887-1888 was the first wholly successful installation of any consequence and set in motion a wholesale conversion of America's street railway systems to electric power. In later years he turned his talents to such notable developments as high-speed electric elevators and the multiple unit system of train control. — *Virginia State Library*.

triumph of a young former Naval officer and inventor named Frank Julian Sprague at Richmond, Va., was to set in motion a remarkable electric railway boom that would make electric traction supreme in the street railway industry in less than a decade.

Sprague brought to electric railway development a considerably more scientific approach than that of the majority of the inventors and experimenters then active in the field. Sprague was born at Milford, Conn., in 1857, and entered the United States Naval Academy in 1874. Even as an Annapolis undergraduate, Sprague had an intense interest in electricity. Following his graduation in 1878 he continued his electrical experimentation during off-duty hours.

During a Far Eastern cruise aboard the flagship U.S.S. *Richmond*, Sprague produced nearly 60 inventions covering a wide range of subjects. While assigned to the training ship *Minnesota*, the ambitious young ensign developed a scheme for installing incandescent light aboard the ship, utilizing an Edison dynamo and a disconnected single-cylinder boiler pump. When he failed to obtain the loan of a dynamo, Sprague had to call the project off.

In the spring of 1881 the *Minnesota* was ordered to Newport, R. I., where Sprague built a novel type of dynamo and tested it for Prof. Moses G. Farmer, then a government electrician at the Newport Torpedo Station.

After terminating his experiments at the Torpedo

Station, Sprague sought orders to attend the 1880-1881 Paris Electrical Exhibition. He was unsuccessful in this, but obtained a temporary assignment to the U.S.S. *Lancaster* — then going out as flagship of the European Squadron — with a three-month leave at his own expense on arrival. It was too late for Sprague to attend the Paris Exhibition, and he was ordered instead to the 1882 British Electrical Exhibition being held at the Crystal Palace in London. There he was made secretary of the jury testing dynamos and gas engines. Although he overstayed his leave by several months, Sprague regained the good graces of the Navy Department by submitting a voluminous report on the test results.

During his stay in London Sprague often rode on the city's pioneer steam-operated underground railway opened in 1863. For the first time he began to think seriously of the application of electric operation to railways and conceived the idea of an overhead power system using a type of underrunning

electric railway operation. The method of mounting electric motors had been the source of endless trouble to the early electric railway pioneers. Edison, Field, Daft, Van Depoele, and others all had placed the motors inside the car or on the platform and had connected them to the axles by means of belts, chains, or other flexible couplings rather than by some means of positive gearing. Bentley and Knight, in their 1884 installation at Cleveland, had placed the motors under the carbody — a considerable improvement — but had connected them to the axles with wire cables. Sprague developed a method of mounting that permitted the motor to be geared directly to the axle. In the Sprague arrangement, sometimes called a "wheelbarrow" mounting one side of the motor was hung from the truck frame on a spring mounting, the other was supported directly by the axle. Bearings in the axle side of the mounting permitted the motor to rotate slightly about the axle, thus maintaining perfect

An improved truck was developed by Sprague in 1888 for the pioneer Richmond system. Sprague's wheelbarrow electric motor mounting became almost universal on electric railways. Double reduction gears made it possible for the two 7½ h.p. motors to propel the cars up Richmond's 10 per cent grades. — *Virginia State Library.*

trolley. Charles Van Depoele was working on similar ideas at about the same time, and the two were later to become involved in a patent controversy over the matter.

Sprague returned to the United States in the spring of 1883. He resigned from the Navy and went to work as an assistant to Thomas Edison in connection with the latter's electric light business. Edison was uninterested in electric traction, and a year later Sprague resigned to form his own company and take up the development of his electric railway ideas. His first efforts were in the direction of elevated railway electrification, and in 1885 he devised a method of motor mounting and gearing which was to be almost universally adopted for

alignment between the gearing on the motor shaft and the axle, no matter how irregular the track or the motion of the axle.

In a paper presented to the Society of Arts in Boston in December 1885, Sprague outlined a detailed plan for the electric operation of the Manhattan Railway, and he devoted most of the next year to a series of experiments on a section of elevated track in New York. Among witnesses to one of the early tests were Jay Gould and members of the Field family — the principal owners of the elevated. Attempting an impressive demonstration of the experimental car's capabilities, Sprague opened the controller too abruptly, causing a fuse to blow out with a violent flash. Gould, who was standing

Derailments were a frequent occurrence during the early days of operation in Richmond. Artist Jay Hambidge pictured one of them for *The Century Magazine.* — *Virginia State Library.*

next to the fuse, was so startled by the report that he had to be restrained from jumping off the car. After this unnerving experience the financier abandoned all interest in electric traction. The stockholders and directors of the elevated company also took no further notice of Sprague's work, despite a number of highly successful experiments in subsequent months.

After he failed to develop any interest in his ideas for elevated railway electrification, Sprague turned his attention to the problems of electric operation of street railways. He seems for a time to have favored storage batteries rather than a central generating plant and an overhead distribution system as a source of power for street railways, and some of his first efforts, beginning in the spring of 1887, were a series of experiments with battery-powered streetcars at Boston, New York, and Philadelphia. Commented the New York *Sun* after one such experiment:

> They tried an electric car on Fourth Avenue yesterday. It created an amount of surprise and consternation from Thirty-Second Street to 117th

Street that was something like that caused by the first steamboat on the Hudson. Small boys yelled "dynamite" and "rats" and made similar appreciative remarks until they were hoarse. Newly appointed policemen debated arresting it, but went no further. The car horses which were met on the other track kicked without exception, as was natural, over an invention which threatened to relegate them to a sausage factory.

Despite the excitement they caused, Sprague's battery car experiments seem to have been inconclusive in their results. Batteries still were not the answer to the problem of street railway power supply. But even as the battery car experiments were being carried out, the Sprague Electric Railway & Motor Company was obtaining contracts for the electrification of street railways with an overhead power system in St. Joseph, Mo., and Richmond, Va.

The St. Joseph installation was to be a modest one, but the Richmond contract called for what was by far the most important street railway electrification ever undertaken. Backed by speculative New York investors, the Richmond Union Passenger Railway Company had obtained a franchise early in 1887 for construction of an entirely new system of street railways in competition with an already existing horsecar system. Conveniently, the franchise allowed operation by horse or mule power, "or such other motive power as may be hereafter allowed by the Council." A few months later the promoters quietly obtained permission to use electric power at about the same time they completed their contract with Sprague.

The contract was one, as Sprague himself observed later, "a prudent businessman would not ordinarily assume." It obligated the Sprague firm to equip a 375 h.p. central station power plant; to install a complete overhead power system on 12 miles of track, much of which had not yet definitely been located and none built; and to provide the motors and electrical appurtenances for 40 cars, each to be powered by two motors. As Sprague was fond of pointing out in later reminiscences, this was almost as many motors as were in use on all the cars throughout the rest of the world. The installation had to be capable of operating 30 cars at one time on a system with grades as steep as 8 per cent. All of this had to be completed within 90 days. Sprague was to receive a total payment of $110,000, provided the installation was satisfactory to the railway company.

From the viewpoint of actual experience, the Sprague firm had little more to its credit than the New York elevated experiments and a few battery car trials, and must have seemed ill-prepared indeed for a task of such magnitude. But Frank Sprague had an abiding faith in the rightness of his ideas and an almost reckless confidence in the abil-

Frank Sprague's Richmond trolleys represented the last word in 1887 municipal transportation. "All are modeled on the Broadway style and are gems of symmetry, finish, and convenience," proclaimed a Richmond *Dispatch* story, which went on to describe their electric lighting and heating systems and electric signal bell. Closed car No. 13 (above) and open car No. 6 (below) are shown not long after the system opened for regular operation in 1888. — *Both photos, New England Electric Railway Historical Society.*

Brilliantly lit by incandescent lamps, the new trolleys delighted Richmonders. This drawing by Jay Hambidge shows a lineup of cars surrounded by an admiring after-theater crowd. — *Virginia State Library.*

ity of his firm to successfully carry out the project. Before the contract was completed the Sprague firm had lost fully $75,000 on the job, but in its success had gained a reputation that was to prove almost priceless.

Things went wrong from the beginning. Hardly was the ink dry on the contract when Sprague was stricken with typhoid fever, removing him from active participation in the work for over two months. During Sprague's long convalescence, two energetic but inexperienced young assistants, both of whom had resigned from military service to join him in the promising electrical field, were left in charge of the work. Lt. Oscar T. Crosby, a West Pointer, did the overseeing at the firm's New York factory where the electrical equipment was being manufactured. The installation work at Richmond, where track construction had started late in May, was in the charge of Ens. S. Dana Greene, who, like Sprague, was an Annapolis man.

Upon returning to Richmond in early autumn to resume general charge of the work, Sprague found an almost appalling situation. The track installed by the promoters was, as Sprague himself described it, "execrable." Obviously none too strong financially, the line's promoters had built with an eye to economy rather than permanence. The rails were a flat 27-pound tram rail of antiquated pattern, poorly jointed, unevenly laid and insecurely tied,

and installed on an unpaved foundation of red clay. Curves were laid with a radius of as little as 27 feet and were provided with only one guard rail, thus permitting the rails to spread easily. The track was laid on grades as steep as 10 per cent, instead of the maximum 8 per cent for which Sprague had bargained. The longest grade was fully a mile long with a slope varying from 4 to 10 per cent.

As an article in the Richmond *Times* some years later put it, the combination of grades and curves was considered "insuperable," and "the average expert electrician of that day laughed in his sleeve as the work progressed." Fearful that the two 7½ h.p. motors he was installing in each car were inadequate for the task now demanded of them, even if a self-propelled car could maintain adhesion at all on such unprecedented grades, Sprague himself began to lose confidence; he set to work designing an electric motor-driven cable system to be installed in pits sunk beneath the track to haul the cars up the steepest hills.

But perhaps a car could climb the hills unaided after all, suggested Sprague's partner, Edward H. Johnson, at a conference called to consider the new crisis. There was only one way to find out, and late one evening in November, Sprague, Greene, and a picked crew, joined by Superintendent George A. Burt of the street railway company, took a car out of the Church Hill carshed at 29th and D streets to give it the acid test. With Sprague himself at the controls the car made its way up one hill and then another, easily swung through a sharp curve on a 6 per cent grade, and finally climbed steadily to the top of the long Franklin Street hill, where it came to rest amid an enthusiastic after-theater crowd.

It was a sort of Pyrrhic victory. Sprague knew the motors had been severely overheated, and a peculiar bucking movement when he attempted to restart the car told him that a motor had been disabled with a short-circuited armature, a difficulty that was to become all too familiar to Sprague before the Richmond project was completed. Announcing loudly that there was some slight trouble with the circuits, Sprague sent Greene for some instruments so that it could be located, turned out the car lights, and lay down on a seat to wait while the crowd dispersed. Finally, Greene returned with the "instruments" — a team of four sturdy mules — and the car was ignominiously dragged back to the shed from which its journey had begun a few hours earlier.

Having proven that it was at least possible to climb hills of 10 per cent or more, Sprague rushed back to his New York plant to try to come up with a solution to the remaining mechanical problem of getting a car up such severe grades without burning up its motors. Sprague's answer was an intermedi-

This old photograph depicts what was evidently a restaging of the historic lineup of 22 cars with which Sprague convinced President Whitney of Boston's West End Street Railway Company of the ability of his electric system to simultaneously start a large number of closely grouped cars. — *New England Electric Railway Historical Society.*

ate gear permitting a double rather than a single reduction between motor and axle. Tools and jigs were hastily made, new gears cast, and the cars altered.

During the next few months the cars ventured out on the line more and more frequently, but one difficulty after another plagued the installation. The motors were modified again and again as the severe strains of operation over the rough track revealed one weakness after another. Switches in the overhead work were giving trouble. No less than 40 designs for an underrunning trolley were tried before one of Sprague's draftsmen, Eugene Pommer, came up with one that worked reasonably well.

The company's promoters pressed Sprague relentlessly to begin regular operation, but when the 90-day limit expired Sprague still wasn't satisfied with his installation and had to agree to a reduced payment of $90,000 — half of it in the form of the company's bonds — in order to obtain a time extension. By January 7, 1888, the company was able to operate nine cars throughout the day, and several thousand delighted Richmonders were allowed to ride the cars free of charge. According to a report of the event in the Richmond *Whig,* no difficulties of any consequence were encountered, except for that presented by small boys who placed rocks on the curves. At one point three cars were brought to a halt for this reason. "It is hoped that some boy may be caught in the act and severely dealt with," commented the *Whig,* "for not only does it discommode the working of the line and endanger the property of the company, but also jeopardizes the lives and limbs of the passengers."

Two days later the company attempted to begin revenue operation with six cars. Motorman P. N. Grant and Conductor Walter Eubank took the first car, No. 28, out of the 29th and P streets carshed at 6 a.m., and a Church Hill resident, William A. Boswell, presented the first revenue nickel to Conductor Eubank. In order to avoid trouble from the inferior trackwork, a man was stationed at each curve with a brush, broom, and other appliances to keep the track clear. Operation continued sporadically throughout the day, but once again mechanical difficulties interfered and the cars were soon on their way back to the carshed for still more modification work.

A few cars continued to operate intermittently during the next several weeks, and by the end of

Bumping over one of the hose jumpers used to maintain streetcar service, one of the early Sprague cars passed a steam pumper of the Richmond fire department. — *New England Electric Railway Historical Society.*

71

A rare snowfall that cloaked the Virginia capital in white produced these views of the pioneer Richmond trolleys in the late 1880's. — *Both photos, New England Electric Railway Historical Society.*

January the company was ready to try regular operation once again — this time with about 10 cars. Crowds of children were carried without difficulty throughout the day on February 1, and the following day the line was again opened for regular service. Sprague's new gearing developed a disconcerting tendency to lock, and car after car suddenly stopped dead in the street. The crew would get off, remove the offending gear, and limp on with only one motor, if they could. Otherwise, the disabled car was simply hauled off the track so others could pass.

Sprague was convinced that the castings were faulty or the gears improperly cut, but one of his employees, an Irish mechanic named Pat O'Shaughnessy who had what Sprague himself termed "a most happy mechanical judgment," insisted the trouble was simply due to want of adequate lubrication. More oil was applied and the problem was soon remedied.

Motor difficulties continued to plague the line. Brushes on the motors were one of the most persistent trouble sources. Armatures were continually being grounded or short circuited, and commutators burned owing to arcing. Brushes made of copper, bronze, and brass in a wide variety of shapes and types were tried, but none seemed to work. As Sprague later described it, "The track soon looked like a golden path, for the rough commutator bars acted like a milling cutter, and shearing off the ends of the contact bars would send a shower of shimmering scales over machines and roadway."

At this point Sprague was using about $9 worth of brass daily just for brushes, and a car was unable to complete even half a trip without a stop for inspection and generally a change of brushes. The problem was finally solved by the adoption of carbon brushes, a proposal of Charles Van Depoele.

Armatures were disabled so regularly that replacements often had to be shipped from New York by express in order to keep the cars going. At times equipment was maintained in service only by borrowing parts from other cars. "Greene, this is hell," commented Sprague at about this point.

Despite all, the cars were kept moving, and gradually the difficulties lessened, even if new ones continued to present themselves. Little by little the number of cars in service was increased from 10 to 20. By the first week in May the number had been increased to 30, and for the first time the company was able to provide service over its entire system. Soon afterward, Sprague was able to operate 40 cars at one time, 10 more than he had contracted for. "It is almost needless to say that on that day we felt that we owned the street and the city as well," recalled Sprague in later years. "Fatigue and worry were all forgotten in what was to us a supreme moment."

But Sprague's finest moment at Richmond was yet to come. The West End Street Railway Company of Boston, then the world's largest street railway system, with a stable of some 8000 horses, was contemplating a change in motive power. The company had all but decided to adopt the then-popular cable system; but President Henry M. Whitney of the West End line, together with a party of directors and his general manager, was persuaded to visit Sprague's Richmond installation, stopping en route to visit the Bentley-Knight line at Allegheny City. Whitney was impressed with the Richmond line, but his general manager, Daniel F. Longstreet,

remained a firm advocate of the cable railway. Longstreet was pessimistic about the ability of the electric system to start a large group of cars that had become bunched within a short stretch of track, something that occurred frequently on a big city street railway.

Sprague decided to resolve the question with a dramatic display of electric traction's overload capacity. Late one night, after regular operation had ended, 22 cars were lined up platform to platform at the Church Hill carshed on a section of line designed for the operation of only four well-distributed cars at a time. The engineer at the power plant was instructed to load the feeder fuses, raise the voltage from the customary 450 volts to 500, and to hold on "no matter what."

Whitney and his party were roused from their hotel and taken to the carhouse to witness the test. At the wave of a lantern the cars started up, one after another, as soon as there was room. The line voltage dropped to barely 200 volts, and the car lights dimmed until they were hardly visible, but the cars kept moving. Gradually the voltage began to rise, the lights brightened again, and soon all 22 cars were merrily trundling out of sight.

Whitney was convinced, and promptly went before the Boston Board of Aldermen to obtain permission to electrify his system. Part of it was to be an underground conduit system; the remainder was to have overhead construction. Sprague motors were to be used on all cars.

The electric railway at long last had arrived. After Frank Sprague's "incredible adventure in Richmond," as one writer later termed it, the horsecar was an anachronism, and the cable railway boom would sputter to a halt in only a few more years. By the end of 1889 there were no less than 154 electric street railway systems in the United States, and within 2 years of the opening of the Richmond system the number had increased to more than 200 — well over half of them equipped by the Sprague firm.

The time of the trolley had come.

The coming of the trolley car was the cause for merry-making and rejoicing. This gala affair marked the opening of the Superior (Wis.) Rapid Transit Railway's line out Tower Avenue to South Superior on September 14, 1892. Following the arrival of the opening-day trolley caravan from downtown Superior, passengers and interested bystanders joined together in a big celebration and barbecue. Rarely has such excitement visited South Superior in the 75 years since. — *Collection of Wayne C. Olsen.*

The Time of the Trolley

WELL BEFORE the end of the 19th century, the trolley car had become an integral part of the urban American scene. Clanging noisily, ornately decorated electric cars rumbled through the city streets carrying Americans to and from their daily work. Balmy summer days brought out the breezy open cars, which hurried the cities' millions to beaches, parks, and other pleasure spots. Leather-lunged guides bellowed their spiels through megaphones as gawking tourists viewed the city from special trolley sight-seeing cars. Sparkling white-and-gold post office cars hurried through the streets, speeding the distribution of the U. S. Mail in America's great urban centers. Clad in dignified black, streetcar hearses rolled solemnly through the city to suburban cemeteries. In the golden age of electric traction the electric cars served almost every urban transportation need.

Rarely has America experienced anything quite equal to the great electric railway boom that fol-

A ceremonial first run was an indispensable feature of the opening of a new trolley line. Here two carloads of dignitaries have just completed an opening-day run over the Knoxville (Tenn.) Street Railroad Company's Lake Ottosee line on May 1, 1890. A similar affair marking the beginning of the Abilene (Tex.) Street Railway in 1908 wasn't quite as successful. The inaugural car derailed and landed in a ditch. — *Collection of Allan H. Berner.*

With Motorman Charles Sawyer and Conductor S. R. Nutbrown in charge, nine-bench open car No. 57 opened the Manchester (N. H.) Street Railway's Massabesic Lake line on August 3, 1895. The resort proved so popular that on the second day of operation each car carried an average of 100 passengers. — *Collection of O. R. Cummings.*

lowed on the heels of Frank Sprague's triumph at Richmond. In 1890, when the Department of Commerce and Labor first made a census of the street railway industry, only some 1262 miles of track were electrically operated. By the time the next census was taken in 1902, the mileage of electric lines had grown almost twentyfold to a total of nearly 22,000 miles.

Much of the growth of electric railways during the early years, of course, simply represented the conversion of horse and cable railways to electric power, but the industry itself was growing at a phenomenal rate too. By almost any index, the total size of the industry more than doubled in the dozen years from 1890 to 1902. Total track mileage increased to almost 3 times the 1890 level. The number of passenger cars and employees doubled. Investment in street railway systems leaped from less than 400 million dollars in 1890 to more than 2 billion dollars in 1902. In 1890 street railways carried slightly over 2 billion passengers. By 1902 they were carrying approximately 5 billion — more than 7 times the total number carried on the nation's steam railroads.

Practical electric transportation had arrived at an auspicious time. During the last few decades of the 19th century and the first few decades of the current century, the U. S. population was increasing at a rate of 10 to 15 million persons every decade; and the trend toward urbanization of the American populace was increasing rapidly. In 1880 less than 30 per cent of the population lived in urban areas; by the start of World War I fully half of the American population would be living in cities. Cities were becoming larger, too. In 1880 there were only 20 U. S. cities that exceeded a population of 100,000; by 1910 there were 50.

Except in those cities that had steam railroad commuter service to suburban areas, the extent of urban development was governed almost entirely by the practical radius of operation of the street railway companies. The horsecar had pushed the limits of residence out to about 4 miles, but its low speed made the animal railway impractical for much more. The faster cable car expanded the limits of urban growth considerably, but its exceedingly high construction costs limited the extent of its adoption. The electric railway, faster than either horse or cable railway and relatively cheap to construct and operate, changed the whole character of the American city.

Filling what a 1902 census report called "an imperative social need," the electric cars permitted the distribution of the burgeoning urban population over a much wider area than would otherwise have been possible. More than any other single development, the electric railways contributed to the growth

Few houses were in sight as the San Diego (Calif.) Electric Railway pushed this new line out University Avenue in 1907. — *Historical Collection, Union Title Office, Title Insurance & Trust Company, San Diego.*

of the metropolitan suburbs. Population growth followed the car lines, and a new trolley line extension invariably increased land values. Not infrequently, real estate syndicates built electric railways just to promote their developments.

In the early years, at least, electric railways were generally an enormously profitable venture. By roughly doubling the radius of practical street railway commuting, the electric cars generated a tremendous amount of new traffic; and the more attractive service provided by trolleys induced still further traffic growth in the form of pleasure travel. Between 1890 and 1902 the average number of streetcar rides per urban inhabitant increased from a little more than 100 a year to 177, and by 1917 had grown to some 260 rides a year.

In comparison with horsecar systems, electric lines were considerably cheaper to operate. The experience of the Lynn & Boston Railroad Company was fairly typical. In 1891, when the system was operated entirely with horses, the company's oper-

This specially decorated California car and the inevitable crowd of local dignitaries heralded the opening of a new suburban line at Fresno, Calif., on May 2, 1923. — *Collection of Allan H. Berner.*

ating expenses per car-mile averaged about 25 cents. In 1897, by which time the system was entirely electrically operated, expenses were averaging less than 15 cents per car-mile. During the same period, while gross earnings increased by not quite 1½ times, net earnings increased to almost 6 times the 1891 level.

In a 1907 census of street railways, 939 companies reported a total net income of over 40 million dollars on gross earnings of not quite 430 million, a profitable state of affairs that held true, more or less, until the beginning of World War I. Some of the greatest American fortunes of the turn-of-the-century period were made in street railway securities, sometimes under circumstances that would be considered highly questionable today. Perhaps the greatest street railway fortune of all was that assembled by Peter Widener, William Whitney, Thomas Ryan, and their associates, who in only 9 years between 1893 and 1902 netted a fortune of an estimated 100 million dollars through the systematic plunder of New York's Metropolitan Street Railway.

Street railway properties were such lucrative investments that scores of eager promoters rushed to construct new lines. In the early years of electric traction it was not uncommon for the larger cities to be served by a number of separate companies, frequently operating rival lines no more than a block or two apart. Even as early as the 1890's, however, an almost inevitable process of consolidation began, with the result that well before World War I street railway properties in most cities had been unified into a single system. What is probably some sort of record in this respect was set by the Pittsburgh

Railways Company which represented the amalgamation of some 114 underlying properties.

Municipalities customarily required some form of franchise for street railways. Understandably, the cities usually endeavored to extract the most favorable possible terms from the traction companies. All too frequently the traction men, in their eagerness to obtain the coveted franchise, paid too little attention to the fine print, or agreed to terms which were ultimately to prove almost ruinous.

In a minority of cases franchises were awarded which placed no particular requirements on the traction companies and entailed no compensation to the municipality. Popular opinion, however, held that the streets belonged to the people, and that a franchise for their use by a private corporation should be

Street railways were built largely with manual labor and animal power. This track gang laid a new line at Piedmont and Fifth streets on the Duluth (Minn.) Street Railway in 1910. — *Collection of Wayne C. Olsen.*

Horses used to build Duluth's East Ninth Street line rode to work in ease. — *Collection of Wayne C. Olsen.*

Street railway trackwork at major intersections was bewilderingly complicated. This 1897 view shows construction work at First and Broad streets on the Richmond (Va.) Traction Company.—*Valentine Museum, Richmond.*

awarded only for limited periods and with provision for compensation to the city. This prevailing viewpoint was expressed by the Mayor of Mansfield, O., who wrote in 1907: "The fact of the matter is that our city council has been too free in granting franchises for the occupancy of its streets by street railways. There are three streetcar lines now operating in our city, and not one cent has been paid, or asked of them, for a franchise, which to my notion is not what it should be."

Most often a franchise called for some form of payment to the municipality. Sometimes a lump sum was required at the time the franchise was awarded; but more often an annual payment, either a fixed amount or a percentage of the gross revenues, was required. Often franchises placed other requirements on the traction companies, such as street paving and cleaning, or snow removal. Some companies accepted "perpetual" franchises in which a fixed rate of fare — usually five cents — was established. Later on, as operating costs rose or municipal boundaries were extended, the companies found it impossible to operate profitably with a nickel fare and usually met with difficulty in attempting to obtain modification of the franchise terms.

Many cities and states required competitive bidding for franchises in order to obtain the most favorable possible terms. Sometimes the results were downright ridiculous. In New York, where the Cantor Act of 1886 required competitive bidding, the franchise for a new territory in the Bronx was

awarded to The Peoples Traction Company after the company had agreed to pay to the city 95 per cent of its gross receipts, in addition to the 3 per cent required by the state. It perhaps goes without saying that no lines were ever built or operated under this particular franchise.

Because of the enriching effect on real estate values, the construction of street railways was almost universally regarded with favor by property owners along the route of a new line. One electric railway construction engineer, though, told of a case where property owners took strong exception to installation of a trolley line along their residential street. One lady adamantly refused to allow the erection of a pole in front of her house. When construction men went ahead and dug a 5-foot hole for the pole, the lady jumped into it and refused to get out. The workers dug a new hole beside the first, installed the pole, and then gallantly hauled the lady out.

Sometimes, too, it was feared that the arrival of cheap electric transportation threatened the exclusive nature of a community. Such sentiment led to a bitter conflict in Montclair, N. J., in the early 1890's when an application for a trolley line franchise was filed. At a heated town meeting on April 5, 1892, one anti-trolley speaker declared that he "did not propose to make Montclair a dumping ground for Dutch picnics and sick baby excursions." Anti-trolley sentiment prevailed at this particular engagement, but eventually Montclair got its trolley line anyway. Even so, when a franchise was finally

Although details of this early Lexington (Ky.) photo are unknown, it may well represent the opening of the city's street railway system during the 1890's. Street paving was yet to come. — *Collection of William D. Middleton.*

granted in 1898 the cautious authorizing ordinance contained no fewer than 28 pages of regulations.

There were other, more serious, conflicts encountered by the trolley men. Ordinarily the purely urban trolley lines offered no competitive threat to the steam roads, but when the electric cars ventured into suburban territory they began to compete directly with the steam lines for suburban passenger traffic. In 1900, for example, the Pennsylvania Railroad announced that it was giving up its entire Chicago suburban service as a result of the competition offered by new trolley lines.

Occasionally the steam road men attempted to meet the trolley competition with rather forceful measures. A favorite tactic was to refuse the electric roads permission to construct grade crossings with the steam lines. One such attempt at Chicago in 1900 ended in a pitched battle between streetcar and steam railroad workers. The Western Indiana Railroad had obtained an injunction preventing the General Electric Railway from building a line across WI's tracks at 15th and Dearborn streets. After successfully appealing to the Supreme Court of Illinois, which dissolved the lower court injunction,

the electric line moved in a force of 500 men to seize the crossing and lay track. The steam line countered with a force of almost equal size, and 12 men were seriously injured in the battle for possession of the crossing. Superior numbers carried the day for the electric men, who gained control and proceeded to lay the crossing and begin running cars.

An even more violent fracas of this type was the celebrated North Abington (Mass.) riot of 1893, caused by the intractable opposition of the New York, New Haven & Hartford Railroad to construction of a crossing with its line at North Avenue in North Abington by the Rockland & Abington Street Railway. Initially, the New Haven moved to block the crossing by legal means. After a request for an

This is where the power for the cars came from. The generator in the Duluth (Minn.) Street Railway's 11th Avenue West powerhouse was driven by this massive Allis cross-compound condensing Corliss engine, which boasted a 96-ton, 28-foot diameter flywheel. — *Collection of Wayne C. Olsen.*

Street railway track required exceptionally heavy construction to successfully withstand the rigors of both trolley and street traffic. This Monongahela-West Penn Public Service Company line at Marietta, O., used heavy girder rail laid on wood ties, followed by a concrete slab and brick paving. — *Collection of F. W. Schneider III.*

injunction against the work was denied by the courts, the steam road men prepared to take other measures, resulting in what one historian described as the boldest attempt in the history of the Massachusetts Commonwealth of a corporation to defy the laws of the Commonwealth, the power of the state courts, the rights of the community, and the rights of another corporation.

Pending the outcome of the court litigation, Rockland & Abington construction forces had laid rails to within a few feet of the New Haven tracks on either side. Following denial of the steam line's request for an injunction, Maj. Edward P. Reed, president of the street railway company, announced his intention to install the crossing. New Haven Division Superintendent John C. Sanborn, backed by a force of 100 laborers, announced that he would resist the construction.

A temporary truce maintained the peace over a weekend, but on the following Monday morning the trolley men made their move. While the street railway forces laid their rails to within a foot of the New Haven tracks, Superintendent Sanborn and his force, now increased to a strength of 150 men, stood by watchfully.

On Tuesday morning the trolley men arrived at the scene to find that the trolley wire had been cut during the night. Repairs were made, but almost immediately a New Haven car was pulled over the crossing while an employee reached up to again cut the wire. The situation became increasingly tense

Sketch of 1893 North Abington (Mass.) riot. — *Courtesy* Transportation Bulletin, *Conn. Valley Chapter, NRHS.*

as three additional carloads of New Haven laborers arrived to swell Sanborn's "army" to 300 men. A crowd of some 1500 people was drawn to the scene by news of the prospective clash.

Affairs reached a climax on Wednesday, August 16. Seventy New Haven laborers, armed with shovels, patrolled both sides of the tracks. The 300 steam road men on the scene were backed by additional reserves held in nearby Weymouth. North Abington authorities deputized eight special officers to aid the four regular police officers, two special

Bound for a summer outing at Cape Porpoise, excursionists set out from Sanford, Me., over the Atlantic Shore Line Railway. — *Collection of O. R. Cummings.*

This party of trolley car tourists had just debarked from an open car of the Massachusetts Northeastern Street Railway for a visit to John Greenleaf Whittier's birthplace at Haverhill. — *Collection of LeRoy O. King.*

An outing at Fox River Park in Aurora, Ill., about 1915 brought this lineup of Aurora open cars on North Broad- way, where excursionists transferred from interurbans of the Aurora, Elgin & Chicago. — *Aurora Historical Museum*.

officers, and Road Commissioner Augustus H. Wright already on the scene; and an attorney was sent to Boston in an attempt to obtain a restraining injunction against the New Haven.

By noon a crowd of 2000 people had gathered at the scene, including a number of public officials and prominent citizens who repaired to the veranda of the nearby Culver House to watch developments in relative comfort.

At 1:15 p.m. the steam road men received word from New Haven headquarters in Boston to tear up the street railway tracks, and Superintendent San- born's crew, headed by blacksmith Angus Frazer swinging his shovel in pinwheel fashion, began the attack. Road Commissioner Wright and a deputy sheriff were manhandled in an unsuccessful attempt to halt the destruction, but two New Haven officials were arrested and hauled off to the local jail.

Commissioner Wright, who also doubled as the local fire chief, retaliated by calling out Hose Com- pany 2 to play two fire hoses on the New Haven forces. At this point the combatants began hurling paving stones, driving the dignitaries on the Culver House veranda to cover and smashing windows in the post office and a nearby store. Many store- keepers in the vicinity had prudently boarded up their windows when the situation had begun to get ugly during the morning.

After about 45 minutes of pitched battle the North Abington forces had pretty well stopped the attack with their fire hoses; but then the New Haven men rallied, cut the hoses, removed the nozzles, and

Riflemen ride a car of the Northampton Traction Com- pany at Easton, Pa. — *Collection of Howard E. Johnston*.

soon finished the job of tearing out the trolley rails.

About 4:30 p.m. Major Reed and Judge Kelley arrived with an injunction prohibiting the New Haven from interfering with the work. Both sides then met at Standish Hall for a peace conference and by six o'clock that evening the trolley rails had been relaid.

In the aftermath of the disturbance five New Haven officials were sentenced to terms of as much as four months in the House of Correction, and the railroad paid $15,000 in damages for injuries and property loss. As a final act of retribution, the New Haven erected a handsome new granite station building in North Abington.

On at least one recorded occasion a similar dispute occurred between two rival trolley companies. In Detroit, Mich., where there had long been antagonism toward the privately owned Detroit United Railway and agitation for municipal ownership, the city in 1920 established a street railway commission to build lines of its own and, ultimately, to buy out the Detroit United system. Early in 1921 the two rival trolley lines clashed head-on when the city set out to build a crossing with the DUR's Mack Avenue line for the first municipally owned trolley route.

When city forces made ready to install the crossing, DUR officials massed heavy equipment at the scene, including a snowplow, a wrecking train, and a number of trucks, in order to block the work. With the full resources of the city behind it, the street railway commission had a force of 200 policemen on hand to prevent any trouble.

As soon as work was started by city crews, a DUR man drove a heavy truck through the gang of workmen and abandoned it where it would obstruct traffic. DUR Assistant General Manager E. J. Burdick, who had been attempting to serve a restraining order issued by the courts to prevent the crossing, was promptly arrested by the city police when he appeared to be preparing to bring other equipment into action. While Burdick was taken to nearby Belle Island by policemen and detained there by the raising of the drawbridge to the mainland, the street railway commission men completed the disputed crossing.

Still another variety of dispute which ended in violence was represented by a 1913 conflict between the Borough of Sunbury, Pa., and the Sunbury & Susquehanna Railway Company. Frustrated in its efforts to get permission for a track extension from a hostile borough council, the street railway company decided to go ahead with the desired work regardless.

Moving in with a force of 15 men early on the morning of April 15, the streetcar men proceeded to tear up paving brick preparatory to laying the new track. Unable to obtain an injunction to stop the work because of the absence of the local judge who was on a fishing trip, Sunbury Chief Burgess S. H. McKinney took matters into his own hands. More than 60 bystanders and local citizens were deputized to act under orders of the Chief Burgess. Several fire companies were called out and their hoses were turned on the trolley men. A crowd of hundreds was quickly drawn to the scene.

Several fistfights broke out between trolley men and police, one trolley man cut a fire hose with an ax, and at several points the dispute threatened to develop into a full-fledged riot. The borough forces hauled ashes to the scene, which were dumped in the street in an effort to hinder the work of the trolley men, and later the borough's large road roller was brought into play in a further effort to disrupt the work.

Finally, tempers cooled and the trolley company withdrew to await a settlement in the courts. To ensure that the trolley men would refrain from further work, a Sunbury attorney made a dash by automobile to locate the judicial fishing party and obtain an injunction restraining the work. Eventually the matter was more or less amicably settled in the local courts, but the extraordinary affair managed to keep tongues wagging in Sunbury for days afterward.

A more celebrated dispute between a municipality and a street railway company was an event that

A unique trolley car outing around the turn of the century was a trip to "tent city" on the Coronado "Silver Strand" across the Bay from San Diego, Calif. Several hundred tents and palm-leaf-covered cottages were set up, a variety of recreation features were installed, and an old ferry boat was converted into a floating casino. An extension of the Coronado Railroad's Orange Avenue line delivered passengers from the Coronado ferry landing direct to the resort. — *Historical Collection, Union Title Office, Title Insurance & Trust Company, San Diego.*

Among the many trolley lines which derived a major portion of their traffic from pleasure travel was the Exeter, Hampton & Amesbury Street Railway of New Hampshire and Massachusetts. The line's principal attraction was Hampton Beach, N. H., where the company installed a large casino offering vaudeville and band concerts. One of the company's smart open cars pauses in front of the casino (above). In this later scene below, automobiles seem to be bringing most of the crowds, but Hampton Beach is obviously still an immensely popular resort. — *Collection of LeRoy O. King (above); Collection of F. W. Schneider III (below).*

Dressed up in their best bowlers and straw hats for a company picnic, employees of the Plainfield (N. J.) Street Railway posed at the Fourth Street carbarn in 1895. — *Collection of Howard E. Johnston.*

Portland (Me.) Railroad's 12-bench open car No. 125 waited for passengers at the company's Riverton Park casino, where facilities included private dining rooms and a dance hall. Other attractions were an open-air theater with vaudeville performances, a deer enclosure "for the edification of the public," and boating in the Presumpscot River. — *Collection of O. R. Cummings.*

took place at Toledo, O., in 1919. For more than 5 years following expiration of the Toledo Railways & Light Company's franchise in 1914 the city and the trolley company had unsuccessfully attempted to negotiate the terms of a new franchise. In the meantime the company had continued to operate without one. The dispute finally came to a head on November 8, 1919, when the city council passed an ordinance ousting the trolley company from the city streets. The trolley men promptly complied and by midnight had run all of the company's cars over an affiliated interurban line into Michigan, where they were safely beyond the reach of any injunction the city might obtain. For almost

a month, while the trolley cars languished in Michigan, Toledo struggled to get along with the stopgap transportation provided by a hastily assembled fleet of 2500 jitneys. Local business suffered severely and increasing pressure was brought to obtain a settlement. Federal Judge John M. Killits finally worked out a temporary agreement, and on December 5 the cars returned to Toledo. The judge himself, attired in a motorman's uniform for the occasion, ceremoniously piloted the first car back into the city.

During the golden age of the electric railway in the years before World War I, the trolleys represented far more than just a utilitarian means of home-to-work transportation. Among the many benefits brought about by electrification was a tremendous growth in pleasure travel, a trend which was quickly noted and assiduously promoted by the street railwaymen.

Whether for a family picnic, a church or social group excursion, a trip to a park, or other entertainment, the trolleys afforded an enormously popular outing. Even if people had no place in particular to go, they boarded the cars for the sheer pleasure of trolley riding. Huge fleets of open-air cars supplied respite from the hot summer weather, and as one early writer noted, "Trolley cars travel fast enough to produce a feeling of mental exhilaration, which is absent from, or scarcely felt by, passengers in horsecars." A ride on the cars was a cheap and popular way to court a young lady. Recalled a nostalgic Yakima (Wash.) newspaperman years later, "Marriages based on streetcar courtships seemed to stick."

There were many who claimed that trolley riding even had definite health benefits. In 1900 a prominent Louisville (Ky.) physician announced "after careful investigation" that streetcar riding was the best possible cure for insomnia. Advocating a 2-hour ride before bedtime, preferably on the front seat of an open car, the good doctor claimed, "An hour's streetcar riding scarcely ever fails to bring on a feeling of drowsiness, and it has actually been able to bring sleep to the most nerve-wracked of insomniacs by this simple device."

One of the most popular and successful implements of pleasure-travel promotion was a resort or park operated by a street railway company. At the time of the 1907 electric railway census there were some 467 parks or pleasure resorts operated by street railway companies, with an annual patronage well in excess of 50 million visitors. Since the streetcar parks were almost invariably located so as to require a trip on the cars to get there, it is reasonable to assume that more than 100 million trolley fares a year were collected from visitors to the "electric parks."

For many smaller lines, traffic to and from com-

Pleasure-seekers arrived at the popular Canobie Lake Park at Salem, N. H., aboard the open cars of the Massachusetts Northeastern Street Railway. — *Collection of LeRoy O. King.*

Open cars of the Concord (N. H.) Street Railway's Clinton Street line gathered outside the Concord State Fairgrounds in 1902 for the homeward rush. — *Collection of Carl L. Smith.*

pany-operated pleasure resorts represented a substantial portion of their total business. For example, in 1902 the Bridgeton & Millville Traction Company, a small New Jersey line, had 350,000 visitors to its summer park, and their travel to and from the park represented well over a third of the line's annual traffic of some 1.7 million passengers.

The streetcar parks offered an almost endless variety of diversions, and the pages of *Street Railway Journal* and other trade publications were frequently given over to detailed descriptions of the more successful parks or the latest fads in amusement devices.

The attractions afforded by Kennywood Park, operated by the Monongahela Street Railway Company, may be considered typical of trolley parks. Opened in 1899, Kennywood was located on an attractive site about 12 miles from Pittsburgh. Boating was available on a lake, and there were tennis courts, croquet grounds, bowling alleys, a general sports field, and a baseball diamond. Amusement devices included a merry-go-round and a three-way figure-8 toboggan slide. For musical entertainment

Rustic Otsego Park, on the banks of Otsego Creek not far from Oneonta, N. Y., was a big revenue builder for the Oneonta, Cooperstown & Richfield Springs Railway.

The splendid new amphitheater at Glen Echo Park, a trolley park near Washington, D.C., was ready for the opening of an 1892 chautauqua. — *Collection of LeRoy O. King.*

The handsome Wabash River steamer *Tecumseh* loaded Lafayette (Ind.) excursionists at the foot of Columbia Street around 1906. Naturally, everyone arrived aboard the local streetcars. — *Collection of Ed Hitze.*

In these two delightful drawings, artist F. Cresson Schell has captured the gaiety and excitement of a trolley excursion aboard Philadelphia's brilliantly illuminated "party" cars. — *Both prints, Library of Congress.*

there was a bandstand and an outdoor concert pavilion large enough to accommodate 200 musicians. A dancing pavilion was among the most popular features. Kennywood Park was extremely well-liked and drew a half million visitors in just its first season.

Regular vaudeville performances were frequently offered in outdoor theaters at the trolley parks. In New England, where street railway parks and resorts were probably more numerous than anywhere else, a number of street railways would frequently join together to form a vaudeville "circuit," permitting a different performance to be offered at each company's park every night.

Making the best of bad luck, one New England park, Nurumbega at Auburndale, Mass., even managed to convert a disaster to an advantage. Shortly after a 1909 fire destroyed the park's theater, dasher signs of the parent company's streetcars were inviting the public out to the park to view the ruins; and when the company elected to rebuild the theater in record time, a new set of dasher signs proclaimed "Come watch us build new theater in eight days."

Some of the most spectacular trolley park attractions were among those offered by the street railways of Chicago. The principal fascination at Ferris Wheel Park, operated by the North Chicago division of the Union Traction system, was the 250-foot-diameter Ferris wheel originally constructed for the 1893 World's Columbian Exposition. Passengers

The ornate trolley parlor car *Merrymeeting* of the Lewiston, Augusta & Waterville Street Railway in Maine seated 35 in plush upholstered wicker armchairs. The interior was finished in mahogany and the floor was covered with heavy green carpeting. Ornamental ironwork enclosed two observation platforms. The Briggs Carriage Company of Amesbury, Mass., built the car in 1899. — *Collection of O. R. Cummings.*

The Manchester (N. H.) Street Railway's parlor car *City of Manchester* was a vest-pocket version of the *Merrymeeting*. The interior appointments were equally luxurious, and the exterior was finished in royal blue and cream with intricate gold leaf ornamentation. An early account indicates that the car was originally equipped with a nickel-plated truck. Only $5 a day chartered the elegant vehicle. — *Collection of O. R. Cummings.*

were able to view the entire city from the top of the huge wheel, and on a clear day were even able to see the opposite shore of Lake Michigan, 50 miles away.

Sans Souci Park, operated by the Chicago City Railway Company, boasted the largest electric fountain of its kind in the world. The fountain, played twice each evening, was equipped with powerful electric pumps which discharged water at a rate of 150,000 gallons an hour through 2000 nozzles, reaching a height of as much as 150 feet, while 19 10,000-candlepower lamps produced a variety of colored lighting effects.

Daring Chicagoans flocked to ride the feature attraction at Chutes Park, operated on Kedzie Avenue by the Chicago Union Traction Company. Small boats were hauled to the top of the 90-foot-high chutes by an endless chain, then released to slide down a stream of water on a 325-foot runway, reaching a speed of 55 mph before splashing into the lake at the bottom.

Skating rinks were another favorite electric park feature. Duquesne Garden, a former carhouse converted into what was claimed to be the largest artificial ice skating rink in the world, was a popular attraction on the Pittsburgh Railways Company.

The Northampton Traction Company at Easton, Pa., and the Virginia Passenger & Power Company at Richmond, Va., were among a number of companies operating roller skating rinks.

An unusual difficulty experienced by the latter company at its roller rink in City Reservoir Park in Richmond was that of finding a band that could be heard above the continual thumping of falling be-

This trolley sight-seeing party toured Spokane, Wash., in a semi-convertible car of the Washington Water Power Company. — *Collection of LeRoy O. King Jr.*

91

These photos span a half century of trolley sight-seeing in Washington, D. C. In 1903 "Seeing Washington" cars operated 3 times daily at a fee of 50 cents (above). The *Silver Sightseer* introduced in 1957 (below) featured air conditioning, foam-rubber seats, and a uniformed hostess. The fare was 40 cents. — *Collection of William D. Middleton (above); Joseph P. Saitta (below).*

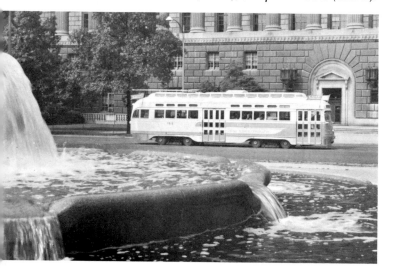

ginners. "A fife and drum corps were finally used with some success," reported the company's general manager, who noted that a 10-piece Italian band also seemed to work reasonably well.

Almost every trolley line derived extra income by offering its equipment to special parties at charter rates. Many systems operated de luxe parlor cars for the use of company brass and these were also made available for charter service. The luxuriously appointed trolley parlor cars were usually fitted with comfortable wicker or upholstered lounge chairs, heavy plush carpeting, plate glass windows, and draperies. Interiors were customarily finished in wood paneling and carvings, and the cars sometimes had brass-rail-enclosed observation platforms. Facilities for serving light meals and refreshments were frequently provided; and one such car, the *Bramhall*, operated by the Portland (Me.) Railroad, even boasted a special built-in ice-cooled wine closet.

Perhaps the ultimate in luxury trolley travel was proposed in 1900 by two Chicago men, who organized a special buffet car company. Their equipment was to be operated as trailers over the city's street and elevated railway systems under an arrangement comparable to that between the Pullman Company and the steam railroads. Each car was to be staffed with a porter in charge of a complete kitchen; and the service, it was assured, "will be conducted as well as any transcontinental dining car." Buffet car service, which was to be available for only a five-cent extra fare, would be just the thing, claimed the promoters, for someone who wanted to take guests or customers to luncheon while showing them the sights of the city, or for en-

Only a month after its completion by the Montreal Street Railway's Hochelaga shops, the first of the city's famous open-air sight-seeing cars posed at Mount Royal and Park avenues in June 1905 with proud company brass occupy-

ing the varnished observation seats. The car was finished in yellow and gold and generously supplied with ornamental brasswork. Two arches carried beaver emblems. — *Montreal Transportation Commission.*

Rebuilt from an old passenger car, the striped *Scout* of the Kansas City Public Service Company gave Kansas City sight-seers of the 1930's unrestricted visibility. — *Collection of Charles Goethe.*

joying a smoke and a late supper after the theater.

Sight-seeing by trolley was an attraction in almost every large city. Sometimes the trolley lines published guides for tourists making use of regular car services, but more often special sight-seeing services were offered. De luxe "party" cars were frequently used in this kind of service. In Detroit, for instance, the Detroit Citizens Street Railway operated its handsome party car *Yolande* in a regular "tallyho" service. Five times daily the car made a 2-hour sight-seeing excursion over principal lines of the Detroit system. A crack motorman and conductor were assigned to the crew, and a colored attendant looked after the wants of the passengers. Sight-seers paid only 25 cents for the de luxe tour.

A number of cities operated specially constructed sight-seeing cars. Several U. S. lines had roofless open cars — usually rebuilt from older equipment — for summer sight-seeing excursions. Surprisingly, this particular type of equipment enjoyed its greatest popularity in Canada, where special open cars with seats installed in a tiered arrangement were run in Montreal, Quebec, Calgary, and Vancouver.

In its golden age the trolley car played a part in almost every aspect of urban life. Before the automobile hearse usurped its place after World War I, the trolley funeral car was considered not only an acceptable but even a preferred means of transportation to one's final resting place.

Street railway funeral cars probably originated in Mexico City, where the horsecar system was operating 26 of them as early as 1886. The idea began to catch on in U. S. cities during the late 1890's, and almost every major city had one or more special cars operating to on-line cemeteries. The typical trolley funeral car was painted in suitably somber shades. Black was preferred in most cities, but St. Louis used chocolate brown and Buffalo a dark green.

The funeral service operated by the Baltimore & Northern Electric Railway, later the United Railways, was typical of that afforded by street railways. The company's luxurious funeral car *Dolores*, rebuilt in 1901 from an ordinary passenger car, was finished in black and silver, and fitted with enameled trucks. The coffin was loaded into a special zinc-lined vault through a large plate glass door. This gave onlookers a chance to view the costliness and detail of the coffin. A rack was placed above the casket for the display of floral pieces, which could be viewed through two elongated windows. Seats for members of the immediate family, arranged like two Pullman sections, were placed opposite the coffin and were separated from the rest of the car by a partition of carved mahogany and frosted glass. The main compartment was fitted with leather seats and folding chairs for the remainder of the funeral party. Window tops were etched with frosted drapes, and black shades and curtains could be drawn for privacy. Call bells summoned a conductor with ice water from a built-in cooler.

A trolley car funeral cost only $20, with an extra charge if it was outside the city limits. To avoid delaying regular cars, the *Dolores*, carefully waxed and attended by a company official arrayed in a silk topper, was scheduled to arrive at the street corner nearest the home of the deceased at an appointed

San Francisco's Market Street Railway served Mount Olivet cemetery, south of Daly City on the company's San Mateo line. Funeral car *Mount Olivet*, shown here at the cemetery office, was painted white instead of the usual black. — *Collection of Alfred E. Barker.*

time. The coffin was carefully lifted into its compartment, the mourners filed into the car, and the solemn cortege rolled through the streets to the cemetery. For large funerals, the *Dolores* was followed by one or more of the company's parlor cars, *Lord Baltimore, Maryland,* or *Chesapeake.* The greatest trolley funeral cortege ever assembled by the railway was that for Gen. John Mifflin Hood,

a former president of the Western Maryland Railway and chief executive of the street railway company at the time of his death in 1919. On this occasion the *Dolores* was accompanied by all three of the company's parlor cars.

Trolley car wedding parties were much less common than trolley funerals, but at least a few are on record. One such event took place at Minneapolis in 1944 when Frank P. Donovan Jr., a well-known Midwestern railway historian, writer, and trolley enthusiast, chartered a Twin City Rapid Transit streetcar for his wedding with Janice Goerner. Accompanied by 70 University of Minnesota students,

94

faculty members, and other friends of the couple, the wedding party rode through downtown Minneapolis singing folk songs and "The Trolley Song" to guitar and accordion accompaniment before being delivered to the First Friends Church for the Quaker ceremonies.

In addition to their primary role of passenger transportation, street railways often furnished a variety of other municipal services. One of the most common was street sprinkling or flushing. In many cities the electric lines were required to provide the service as partial compensation for franchise privileges. In a few cities this was done voluntarily; in others the city paid the trolley company to perform the service. Special gondola cars were operated over the street railways for ash removal or similar purposes in a number of cities. At Regina, Sask., the trolley company's work train hauled the city's garbage from a central collection depot adjacent to the carbarns to a disposal plant located 3½ miles west of the city.

The City of Duluth, Minn., operated a trolley car outfitted as a fire engine, and the Springfield (Mass.) Street Railway had a specially designed trailer for hauling the city's horse-drawn fire-fighting equipment. The Edmonton (Alta.) Radial Railway once

Baltimore's Loudon Park Cemetery had its own mile-long trolley line to transport mourners and visitors from a nearby line of United Electric Railway. Painted black with gold trim, the two former Baltimore city cars, *Linden* and *Loudon*, were used to operate the free service. — *Collection of Stephen D. Maguire.*

Trolley car weddings were rare. This one took place in Hamburg, Germany, in 1962 when tramcar enthusiast Reiner Zimmerman married Fraulein Helgard Voss. Two historic trams conveyed the newly-weds from the church to the reception. — *Conti-Press, from J. H. Price.*

converted a former passenger car for use as a mobile public library. Among other Canadian oddities were the two prison cars operated over the Montreal Tramways. Sheathed in steel and painted jet black, the cars bore the crest of the City of Montreal and the legend "Prison." With the nicest sense of the proprieties, the cars were divided into two compartments, separating accused from convicted prisoners. Twice a day during court sessions Montreal's trolley paddy wagons could be seen rumbling along St. Lawrence Boulevard on their route between the Champ de Mars courthouse and the city's Bordeaux Prison, a forbidding stone structure 7 miles from town.

In almost every major American city trolley car post offices sped the transportation of the U. S. Mail. The earliest use of the electric cars for mail service occurred around 1890, when closed-pouch mail was first handled by trolley on lines between St. Paul and Minneapolis and on New York's Dunkirk & Fredonia Railway. In 1891 Maj. James B. Harlowe, the postmaster at St. Louis, introduced a series of experiments with street railway mail handling, and late in the same year the first trolley Railway Post Office car was placed in operation on a suburban line between St. Louis and Florissant. Within a few years a network of 47 streetcar R.P.O. and closed-pouch routes was providing St. Louis with what one observer called "the best mail-collecting system in the world." A similar service was started in Brook-

Typical of trolley funeral cars was Chicago's No. 1. A special door facilitated loading and unloading of the coffin, and black curtains afforded privacy. — *Smithsonian Institution.*

lyn in 1894, and by 1908 trolley mail service was being operated in 14 major cities.

Trolley R.P.O. cars performed a number of postal tasks. Mail was carried between the main post office, substations, and steam railroad terminals. Mail was delivered to carriers along the route, and was picked up from substations, carriers, other R.P.O. cars, and letter boxes. The cars were fitted with a

work table, pouch racks, and letter cases; and Railway Mail Service clerks canceled and sorted the mail as the car rolled along its route.

The trolley mail cars, often converted from old passenger equipment, were painted white and generally lettered and trimmed in gold. Sometimes a handsome spread eagle seal was applied to each side of the cars as well as the usual "United States

Trolleys even carried the milk in Philadelphia. This Philadelphia Rapid Transit Company car was operated every morning from suburban Doylestown to a terminal at 15th and Huntingdon streets. — *Collection of Charles Goethe.*

Mail Railway Post Office" title. The white mail cars could be easily distinguished from regular passenger equipment, and ordinarily were allowed to run unmolested during street railway strikes. One Chicago line, suffering from labor troubles, attempted to paint all of its passenger equipment white in an effort to avoid interference from strikers. Postal authorities quickly put a stop to the practice.

In Canada, where both Ottawa and Quebec had trolley mail car service, the cars bore the proud "Royal Mail" title. Under Canadian law, any vehicle thus lettered had the right of way over all other traffic, and the Ottawa system is said to have taken advantage of its contract by applying "Royal Mail" to all sorts of equipment.

For the convenience of last-minute letter mailers, the trolley R.P.O.'s were customarily equipped with letter drops on each side. Several cities placed letter boxes on regular passenger cars, permitting people to mail their letters on the first passing streetcar. Arrangements were usually made for a postal employee to collect mail from each car as it passed the point nearest to the main post office.

Trolley mail cars permitted a tremendous improvement in urban postal service over that afforded by the horse-drawn mail wagons previously used. The R.P.O. cars followed regular schedules, which

were arranged so that cars from different routes would meet in the downtown area to exchange pouches destined for other parts of the city or the main post office. To further speed mail service, many cities had special trolley R.P.O. night circuits.

Trolley mail service proved to be an early victim of the motor vehicle. Increasing traffic congestion slowed the mail cars, and most post office departments soon found that trucks provided a more advantageous means of urban mail transportation. Despite rising costs, the Post Office Department proved reluctant to increase its three-cents-per-mile rate for the use of the trolley R.P.O.'s, so the traction companies found little financial incentive to continue the service. By 1915 trolley mail cars had ceased to operate in all but three cities. Baltimore, the last city to operate streetcar mail service, gave

This unique Duluth (Minn.) trolley fire car was installed in 1907 to provide fire protection on Park Point — a narrow strip of land separating the Duluth-Superior harbor from Lake Superior — whose only means of transportation was its street railway line. The trolley company furnished a special barn and a motorman for the fire car. The operation ended in 1930 when the city's famous Aerial Bridge, which joined the Point with Duluth, was remodeled to accommodate vehicular traffic. — *Collection of Wayne C. Olsen.*

In Cincinnati the mails went through aboard trolley mail car No. 215. White was the standard color for the street-car post offices. — *Collection of Barney Neuberger*.

Handsomely trimmed and lettered in gold, and bearing an official seal on each side, Chicago City Railway's trolley post office car No. 6 could not be mistaken as it rolled through Windy City streets on its important missions. The car was photographed in 1956 and now is part of a historic collection maintained by the Chicago Transit Authority. — *Stephen D. Maguire*.

Canceling and sorting mail en route helped trolley post offices speed mail service. — *Smithsonian Institution*.

up its trolley Railway Post Office operation in 1929.

Trolley cars almost always participated in holiday celebrations, parades, and similar affairs. An annual event in many cities was the appearance of a specially decorated Christmas trolley that trundled through the streets during the holiday season. Perhaps one of the most bizarre such cars was the "Santa Claus" trolley that took to the streets in Ottawa, Canada, the day before Christmas in 1896. The car was covered with imitation snow and icicles; replicas of reindeer, a sleigh, and Santa Claus were mounted on the roof; and both the sleigh and the trolley were filled with toys. The motorman and conductor were dressed as Icelanders, and an Eskimo stood beside the motorman and played a cornet throughout the trip. Huge crowds lined the Christmas trolley's route, and oranges were thrown to children along the way.

For New Orleans' celebrated Mardi Gras carnival in 1899, 20 special trolley car floats, all brilliantly illuminated by electric lights, were constructed for the big parade down Canal Street. A year later, 20 similar trolley floats were operated for a carnival in Milwaukee. Among the most spectacular floats at this particular affair were a reproduction of the battleship *Wisconsin* and a replica of a whale mounted on a 50-foot flat car and illuminated by 900 lights.

For the 1896 presidential campaign of William McKinley against William Jennings Bryan, the boys at the Fitchburg (Mass.) carbarn converted a 37-foot trolley flat car into the fearsome armored trolley cruiser *McKinley*, said to be patterned after the battleship *Brooklyn*, then the most powerful unit of the Great White Fleet. Two 6-pounders protruded from sponson mounts at each side of the *McKinley*'s massive ram bow, and a big 18-pounder was mounted on deck. A force of 22 soldiers, sailors, and marines in dress uniforms rode the decks of the armored trolley as it rumbled through the streets of

Street sprinkling and flushing was a service often provided by street railways. This trolley sprinkler operated on Cleveland Railways. More often than not the service was required by franchises. — *Collection of Charles Goethe.*

A more elaborate trolley sprinkler was this enclosed model built by the American Car Sprinkler Company of Worcester, Mass. It is shown during a demonstration at Worcester City Hall in 1919. — *Collection of Stephen D. Maguire.*

In the 1890's elaborate holiday street-car decorations were a popular Los Angeles custom, with cash prizes awarded for best trimmings. This Pico Heights car was all done up for the 1894 Independence Day celebration. Beneath all the finery was California car No. 106 of the Los Angeles Consolidated Electric Railway. — *Historical Collections, Security First National Bank, Los Angeles.*

Patriotically decorated open car No. 13 of the Oneonta, Cooperstown & Richfield Springs Railway rolled through the streets of Cooperstown with a capacity crowd. The occasion seems to be a Fourth of July celebration.

Fitchburg in support of the McKinley campaign.

The trolley car's participation in the everyday life of urban America was reflected by its place in the literature and entertainment of the period. Several early "business" novels of the pre-World War I era were set in the street railway industry. Meredith Nicholson's *The Main Chance* of 1903 involved a purely fictitious city and traction enterprise, but Theodore Dreiser's *The Titan*, one of the most celebrated novels of its time, was another matter. Dreiser's protagonist, Frank Cowperwood, was taken almost directly from the life of Charles Tyson Yerkes, the great "robber baron" of Chicago traction at the turn of the century. In fact, the library of the Peoples Gas Company in Chicago is said to have contained until recent years a copy of *The Titan* in which real names had been penciled in in place of fictitious names, and some of Dreiser's minor factual errors had been corrected. In a lighter vein, a more recent mystery novel, Ellery Queen's

Specially adorned Christmas trolleys were an institution in many cities. This one toured Seattle, Wash., streets in the 1930's. — *Courtesy of Railroad Magazine.*

The trolley car inspired many obscure musical efforts, one of which is represented by this sheet music cover. Only one, "The Trolley Song," achieved popular success. — *New-York Historical Society.*

The Tragedy of X, published in 1932, used a crowded 42nd Street Crosstown trolley in New York as the setting for a baffling murder.

The electric cars were frequent participants in films of the great era of silent screen comedy. The Keystone Kops, Laurel and Hardy, Harold Lloyd, and Buster Keaton were among the great comedians of the movies' early years who made frequent use of the cars as comedy props. What is perhaps the

William McKinley's successful campaign for the presidency in 1896 was aided by this gaily decorated trolley train which rolled through the streets of San Diego, Calif., shortly before election day. The significance of the Japanese lanterns was not explained. — *Collection of Frederick W. Reif, from Eric Sanders.*

most spectacular trolley car sequence ever recorded on film, however, was a chase scene in an obscure and long forgotten film of 1916 called *The Prince of India*. The plot of this early potboiler, produced by a Utica (N. Y.) motion picture firm, had the villain steal a precious jewel from the prince and make his getaway in a stolen trolley. The prince, pursuing by automobile, leaped to the rear platform of the speeding car and the customary hero-villain struggle followed. The villain, knocked unconscious, fell across

This Birmingham (Ala.) trolley promoted a Wallace Reid movie around 1928. As early as 1900 a few lines sold space on the exteriors of their cars for such advertising as patent medicine signs. The use of streetcars for advertising displays was relatively infrequent, however, for municipal authorities usually discouraged such efforts to develop extra revenues. Only in the trolley's declining years did the ad men have much success in getting their messages on the cars. On the other hand, the ubiquitous interior advertising car cards were an inescapable feature of streetcar riding from horsecar days onward. — *Collection of Stephen D. Maguire.*

the controls and front dash as the car ran out of control on a steep downgrade. At the last possible moment the hero prince jumped to safety as the car derailed and plunged off a bridge at high speed. To film the sequence, the moviemakers purchased a retired Ithaca trolley, staged the derailment on a high trestle of the Ithaca Traction Corporation, and actually sent the ill-fated streetcar on a 300-foot plunge into the ravine below.

Throughout the years before World War I the traction industry grew steadily in size and power. By 1917, when street railway systems reached the peak of their physical expansion, electric traction had become a giant industry. There were well over 60,000 streetcars in operation on some 26,000 miles of street railway trackage, and the electric railway industry, exclusive of rapid transit systems or interurbans, represented an investment in excess of 4 billion dollars. Street railway traffic was close to 11 billion passengers a year, and annual operating revenues were in the vicinity of 600 million dollars.

Virtually every city of any size or consequence had an electric railway — altogether there were well over 1000 companies in the U. S. and its possessions — and the trolley car had become an indispensable and universal part of the urban American scene. Throughout the land the trolley was supreme.

Los Angeles' "Flying Tiger" trolley recruited World War II "trolley pilots." — *Stephen D. Maguire.*

103

Despite a Knights Templar parade, the cars kept right on rolling on Elm Street in Manchester, N. H., around 1910. — *Collection of O. R. Cummings.*

In pre-automobile days the trolley dominated the urban scene. This view of heavy streetcar traffic was recorded at a downtown Indianapolis intersection about 1912. — *Collection of George Krambles.*

Although flivver traffic was beginning to get a little heavy in Washington, D. C., conduit-powered streetcars still had the upper hand in this scene at 15th and G streets, N. W., after World War I.—*Library of Congress.*

An extensive street railway network made possible the growth of suburban communities along the east shore of San Francisco Bay. Streetcars of the San Francisco-Oakland Terminal Railways rolled in procession down Oakland's Broadway in 1919.—*Collection of Erle C. Hanson.*

The Wonderful Trolley Car

IN the early years of electric traction the trolley car was little more than a horsecar adapted for electric operation, an arrangement that quickly proved to have serious deficiencies. Horsecar bodies were designed for the lightest possible weight, and axle bearings were generally carried in pedestals attached directly to the body sills, a combination that proved unable to withstand the heavy weight and strains imposed by electrical equipment. On some early cars the electric motors were mounted on the platforms or suspended directly from the carbody, and they quickly managed to shake the entire car structure apart.

One of the first inventors to recognize the insufficiency of horsecar design for electric operation was Frank Sprague, who devised a separate metal truck which supported the carbody and upon which the heavy electrical equipment was carried. Quickly adopted by carbuilders, the independent truck became almost universal in electric car construction.

Apart from the use of separate trucks and the adoption of generally heavier construction, the design of electric cars largely followed the practices that had been standard in horsecar manufacture. Until well after the turn of the century wood continued to be used almost exclusively for carbody

Electric cars of the late 19th century were ornate to a fault, but this Van Depoele car of the late 1880's outdid even most. Operating over the Lynn & Boston Railroad's Highland Circuit, the car was decorated in a Highland plaid. Open platforms left the motorman to the mercy of the weather.—*Smithsonian Institution.*

Outshopped during the 1890's by the Delaware Car Works of the Jackson & Sharp Company at Wilmington, Del., for the Perth Amboy Railroad Company of New Jersey, this handsome little four-wheeler was more or less typical of the early electric cars. The ornate striping, scrollwork, and gold leaf lettering required the highest order of paint-shop craftsmanship. — *Collection of Howard E. Johnston.*

fabrication. Seats were nearly always placed longitudinally and were finished in plain wood or in such easily cleaned materials as rattan, leather, or carpeting.

The exterior finish and ornamentation of the early electric cars was often lavish in the extreme. For a high quality finish as many as 15 hand-rubbed coats of paint and varnish were applied to a new car, followed by fancy scrollwork and lettering in colored paints or gilding. For even an ordinary finish a new car spent at least two weeks in the paint shop. The time was one in which individual pride of craftsmanship was at a height, and as an early treatise on car manufacture observed, the appearance of the finished product was largely dependent upon the skill and taste of the head painter.

The Robinson Radial Truck, developed during the 1890's, was a none-too-successful attempt to permit the construction of longer single-truck cars. The carbody was mounted on swiveling bolsters at each of the two end axles, which were connected by a linkage to a center axle that was free to move laterally according to the vagaries of the trackwork. The truck is shown on a car of the Rock Creek Railway at Washington, D. C. — *Collection of LeRoy O. King.*

Interior decoration was, if anything, even more elaborate. Such woods as cherry, maple, white ash, poplar, white oak, bird's-eye maple, red birch, and mahogany were usually chosen for interior finishes. Opalescent and colored glasses were widely used for decorative work. Ceilings were often ornamented with fancy stencilwork or stucco designs, or were decorated with such hand-painted designs as landscapes, figures of men and animals, wreaths

Interior accommodations of the early cars were usually rudimentary. The longitudinal benches and wooden slatted floor of this car, built by the American Car Company in 1893 for the Superior (Wis.) Rapid Transit Company, were typical. The rigorous winters of northern Wisconsin necessitated the bulky heating stove. Passengers either froze or roasted, depending upon their location in the car. — *Collection of Wayne C. Olsen.*

of autumn foliage, or spring blossoms and vines.

Lavish streetcar ornamentation was even considered to advance the public good. Pointed out one 1892 author in advocating fancy interior finishes, "Not only should a reasonable amount of decoration be provided in cars which are patronized wholly by a cultivated class of people, but in all cars, for by this means the comforts and solaces of fine art will be brought to a large number of lives and hearts that cannot afford to provide them in their own homes."

Initially, electric cars were no larger than their horse-drawn predecessors, which were limited by the pulling capacity of the animals to a length of not much more than 16 feet. The greater power available with electric operation, together with the demand for greater passenger capacity, soon led to a considerably larger car. So long as the single truck was retained, however, its inherent limitations restricted the maximum size of cars. Because of the sharp curves typical in street railway operation, the wheelbase of a single-truck car was limited to about 8 or 9 feet, and over-all car length was restricted by the tendency of carbodies with an excessive overhang to pitch or gallop. This had a devastating effect on even the most substantially constructed track. As a result, the single-truck car was confined to a maximum length of about 30 feet and a total weight of approximately 20,000 pounds.

Several attempts were made to develop a four- or six-wheel single truck with radiating axles which would overcome the length limitations inherent in a truck with axles fixed in a parallel position, but none was sufficiently satisfactory to win wide acceptance. Instead, the demand for an increasingly larger-capacity car led to the widespread adoption of double-truck equipment, thus permitting a substantial increase in the size of carbodies. Although the single-truck car remained in general use well into the current century, double-truck cars had become common even before the end of the 1890's.

Typically, the trolley car of the 1890's was a double-end vehicle with open platforms at each end and only a waist-high dash to protect the motorman from the elements. But by the end of the century an enclosed vestibule for the protection of the operator was becoming more and more common. In many cases its provision was hastened by state or local laws requiring vestibuling. In 1900 the president and the general manager of the St. Louis Transit Company were even ordered to stand trial for failing to equip their cars with vestibules.

The open trolley, a car type that had originated during horsecar days, became an immensely popular vehicle for summer joy riding, particularly in New England and the Eastern states. At the height of its popularity, shortly after the turn of the century, there were nearly 25,000 open cars in service on U. S. street railways.

The typical open car had a roof supported by posts, and canvas side curtains that could be lowered in case of rain. Longitudinal running boards permitted boarding at any point, and transverse benches the full width of the car afforded it a tremendous seating capacity.

Despite their great popularity, open cars had some serious disadvantages. The running board

This otherwise ordinary single-truck car of the Eckington & Soldiers' Home line in Washington, D. C., was notable for the use of an unusual surface contact system of current collection. The long metal "skates" under the car picked up current from contact plates mounted in the street, which were supposed to be energized by the action of magnets mounted on the car. Unfortunately, the contact plates weren't always dead when they should have been, and complaints from owners of electrocuted horses soon ended the experiment.—*Collection of LeRoy O. King.*

One attempt to solve the problem of obtaining the greatest possible traction from a single-motor truck was the Eickemeyer-Field truck, here applied to a double-truck car of Boston's West End Street Railway. Power was transmitted from the motor to both axles by a side rod arrangement reminiscent of that of a steam locomotive. A similar truck was available for single-truck cars. The design disappeared from the market soon after its debut in the early 1890's. — *Collection of O. R. Cummings.*

arrangement was the source of frequent boarding and alighting accidents. Some traction companies solved this problem by screening in the lower part of the sides and installing a conventional arrangement of vestibules and a center aisle. Still another problem was presented when the tight hobble skirt became fashionable, and women found it almost impossible to board the ordinary single-step open car. J. G. Brill, one of the leading carbuilders, came to the rescue with its patented two-step "Narragansett" open car.

The greatest drawback of the open car, though, was the enormous investment represented by a duplicate set of equipment that was used only during the summer season, and traction companies early set out to develop a summer car that could be used the year round. One approach to this problem was the combination or "semi-open" car which was divided between open and closed sections. This design was favored chiefly in California, where weath-

Double-truck electric cars began to appear during the early 1890's. This model was constructed for the Chester, Darby & Philadelphia Railway Company around 1893 by J. G. Brill and featured Brill's famous "maximum traction" truck. The truck, developed in 1891, provided greater traction with a two-motor car. By means of an offset center bearing, as much as three-quarters of the weight was placed on the large-diameter wheels, which were powered. Because of the unequal weight distribution, the small wheels had a tendency to derail at the slightest provocation, thus making the maximum traction truck unsuited for high speeds. — *Collection of Howard E. Johnston.*

er changes were often sudden and temperatures were relatively mild throughout the year.

Another approach was the "convertible" car, which was little more than an open car equipped with removable side panels so that it could be changed into a closed car for winter operation. Originally developed during the 1880's for a New York cable line, the convertible arrangement enjoyed only a modest success. Among its chief drawbacks were the nuisance of having to store the removable side panels during the summer season and the inability to quickly enclose the car in case of sudden weather changes. A few carbuilders attempted to overcome these deficiencies with convertible car designs in which both window sash and side panels slid into pockets in the roof of the car. These cars proved expensive to construct, however, and few were built.

By far the most popular variety of year-round car was the "semi-convertible" design. This represented a compromise between open and closed car arrangements. The semi-convertible was fitted with window sash which disappeared into various types of wall or roof pockets, while the side panels below the windows remained fixed in place. The storage problem of removable sash was eliminated and the cars could be quickly enclosed in the event of a sudden rain.

Except for the change to double-truck equipment

Plain lines and an impressive air of solidity characterized the trolley car of the pre-World War I era. This sturdily constructed and commodious double-trucker of the Manchester (N. H.) Street Railway was delivered in 1913 by New Hampshire's Laconia Car Company. It seated 40 passengers and provided standing room for 60 more. — *Collection of O. R. Cummings.*

111

A commonly required trolley car appurtenance of the earlier years of electric traction was some form of safety fender designed to scoop up wayward pedestrians. Above is the popular Eclipse Life Guard model applied to a car of San Francisco's Market Street Railway Company. The Duluth (Minn.) Street Railway car shown below was equipped with a much simpler model. — *Collection of Alfred E. Barker (above); Collection of Wayne C. Olsen (below).*

The interior arrangement of this roomy car turned out by J. G. Brill in 1911 for the People's Street Railway Company of Nanticoke & Newport (Pa.) was typical of much of the equipment of the period. Transverse "walkover" seats were upholstered in rattan. Hanging from the ceiling were the conductor's signal cord and fare register cords. — *Collection of Howard E. Johnston.*

and the conversion to steel construction in place of wood, which began soon after the turn of the century, one of the most significant advances in streetcar design during the early 1900's was the development of greatly improved interior arrangements.

Until early in the century trolley cars were almost always double ended with a platform at either end. Passengers boarded and alighted from the rear platform and fares were collected by the conductor as he passed through the car. Not only were a good many fares missed by this haphazard system, but the conflict between boarding and alighting passengers often slowed operation. The problems of this arrangement became increasingly serious as the size of cars was enlarged, and street railway managers began to search for improved methods of fare collection and control of passenger flow.

The earliest solution was the "Pay-As-You-Enter" or "prepayment" car developed by the Montreal Street Railway Company in 1905. Passengers entered at the rear platform, paid their fare to the conductor before entering the body of the car, and left at a front entrance controlled by the motorman. In some P.A.Y.E. cars there was an exit at the rear platform also, with a rail arrangement to separate incoming from departing passengers. In order to furnish ample room for passengers waiting to pay their fares, an extra-large rear platform was provided. P.A.Y.E. cars were almost always arranged for single-end operation only, requiring the installation of a loop or wye to turn the cars at the end of the line.

The P.A.Y.E. design was an enormously popular

Perhaps the most ungainly electric cars of the entire traction era were the boxlike models turned out by the short-lived Barber Car Company of York, Pa. This double-truck Barber car, nicknamed "Black Charlie" by the line's employees, operated briefly on Pennsylvania's Sunbury & Susquehanna Railway around 1915. Inadequate springing in the massive trucks caused the car to bounce alarmingly, and derailments were frequent. — *Collection of Gene D. Gordon.*

one. Not only was fare collection improved and service speeded, but most traction companies found that better control of boarding and alighting greatly reduced the number of accidents. In Chicago, for example, a 54 per cent decrease in accidents was reported after the introduction of P.A.Y.E. cars. Kansas City reported a remarkable 67 per cent reduction in platform accidents.

Following the success of the P.A.Y.E. car a number of other configurations were advanced for controlling fare collection and passenger movement. The "Pay-Within" car, evolved by the Philadelphia Rapid Transit Company, was a variation of the P.A.Y.E. arrangement in which the conductor was located within the carbody facing the rear platform rather than on the platform itself. Another type of car developed in Philadelphia was the "Pay-As-You-Leave" car. Passengers entered at the front only and left the car at the rear only, paying their fares to the conductor as they departed from the car.

Still another design developed by the Philadelphia Rapid Transit Company and widely used there,

Perennial efforts were made to evolve a satisfactory self-contained electric car for service on lightly traveled street railway lines. One solution that finally met with some degree of success after years of experimentation was the battery-powered streetcar. Even though battery cars were notoriously docile in performance, a mild flurry of interest in them arose around 1910, after development of Thomas A. Edison's alkaline storage battery and improvements to the lead-acid type storage battery made them reasonably practical. This 24-seat Brill model was operated by the Concord Street Railway in North Carolina. — *Library of Congress.*

113

Transverse benches the full width of the open car gave it a tremendous carrying capacity.
This was an early Baltimore (Md.) car. — *Collection of LeRoy O. King.*

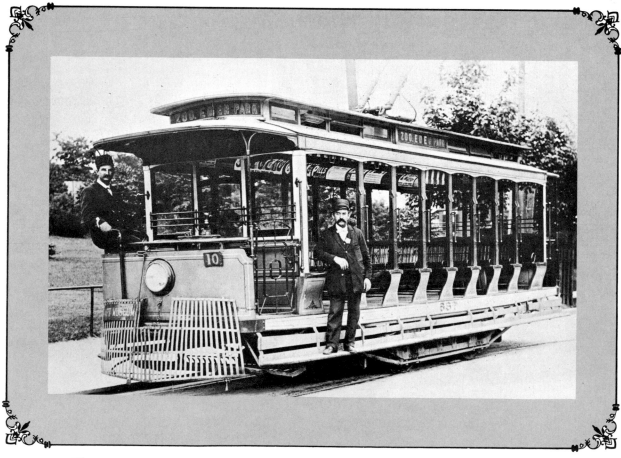

The open car was popular for summer trolley riding. This nine-bench single-truck model
carried Cincinnatians to Eden Park and the zoological gardens. The formidable fender
was an unusual Cincinnati characteristic. — *Smithsonian Institution.*

114

as well as in Chicago, Buffalo, and Atlantic City, was the "Near-Side" car. Large double doors, one for loading and one for unloading, were provided at the front platform; and the conductor, who was located directly behind the motorman, collected fares from passengers as they boarded the car. A small rear door was used only for emergencies. By placing control of the doors with the motorman, the possibility of accidents owing to misunderstanding of signals from the conductor was eliminated, and the Near-Side cars enjoyed a particularly good safety record. Philadelphia alone bought 1500 of them.

The Peter Witt, or "Pay-As-You-Pass," car, which appeared about 1915, was another popular model. Named for the Cleveland (O.) street railway commissioner who developed the design, the Peter Witt car was arranged for front entrance and center exit. The conductor was located at the center of the car and passengers paid their fare either when leaving the car or before passing to the rear half. By devoting the entire front half of the car to space for unpaid passengers, the Peter Witt eliminated delays caused by passengers waiting to pay their fares as they boarded.

New York's Third Avenue Railway, which made extensive use of battery cars on its lightly traveled lines, also experimented briefly with this GE gas-electric streetcar around 1910. Power was obtained from a gasoline-engine-driven generator mounted on the car. Although the builder enjoyed success with its gas-electric cars for steam railroad and interurban railway service, the gas-electric streetcar failed to attract repeat orders. — *Collection of Frank E. Butts.*

Open trolleys were phenomenal crowd swallowers. A 14-bench car such as No. 96 of the Boston & Worcester Street Railway could seat 70 passengers with ease and carry scores more on the running boards. The Newburyport Car Manufacturing Company of Massachusetts built the big car in 1903. — *Collection of LeRoy O. King.*

This 12-bench double-truck open car built by J. G. Brill in 1906 for the Cape May, Delaware Bay & Sewell's Point Railroad in New Jersey was typical of larger open cars. Gaily striped side curtains could be lowered for protection in the event of a sudden shower. — *Collection of Howard E. Johnston.*

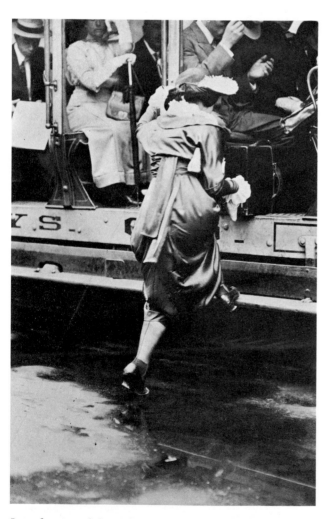

Introduction of the tight hobble skirt early in the century made it all but impossible for fashionable ladies to board the standard single-step open car. Witness this lady's technique in boarding an open car. J. G. Brill saved the day with the patented two-step Narragansett open-car design. — *Culver Pictures, from the Library of Congress.*

Yet another car pattern that was widely used was the center-entrance-and-exit car. One of the chief advantages of this type of equipment was that it permitted a depressed floor opposite the center doors, enabling rapid loading and unloading and materially reducing boarding and alighting accidents. One car of this type, developed by the New York Railways Company in 1912, provided a floor level between the car trucks only 7 inches above the rails. Officially termed the "public welfare" or "stepless" car, the New York cars quickly became known as "hobble skirt" cars because of the manner in which they facilitated boarding of ladies attired in the then-popular tight skirts. Within a few years 176 of them had been built for New York alone, and similar cars were operated in other cities throughout the United States. Confusion between boarding and alighting passengers was a disadvantage of the center-entrance arrangement, although some designs attempted to obviate this by supplying separate doors for entrance and exit. Their chief handicap, however, became evident during the 1920's when street railway systems began to convert to one-man operation. Most lines found that end doors could not be installed without costly alterations and the stepless cars were quickly retired.

Throughout almost the entire history of electric traction there was a continuing search by street railway managers for equipment designs which would allow greater passenger-carrying capacity without a corresponding increase in labor costs, or "platform charges," as they were usually termed.

One of the most persistent, and consistently fruitless, efforts in this direction was the attempt to develop a suitable double-deck car. In spite of its widespread adoption in Great Britain, Europe, and

One of the earliest designs for a convertible car was produced by the Heacock & Lovejoy Convertible Car Company of Portland, Ore., in 1891. This was one of five cars using the Heacock & Lovejoy system constructed for the Oakland, San Leandro & Haywards Electric Railway in 1894 by Carter Brothers of Newark, Calif. Window sash and side panels raised into the roof in a manner similar to that of an overhead garage door. — *Collection of Erle C. Hanson.*

This single-truck car built by Jackson & Sharp for the Bergen County (N. J.) Traction Company around 1900 featured the short-lived convertible car system developed by the Duplex Car Company of New York. Sometimes known as a "barrel" car, the design employed curved window glass and side panels built like the roll top of a desk which slid into the roof on a curved track. — *Collection of Howard E. Johnston.*

The combination open and closed trolley which, presumably, provided accommodations to suit everyone, enjoyed considerable popularity on the West Coast. One of the most common types was the "California" car, which had a closed center section and was open at each end. It is represented here by Los Angeles Consolidated Electric Railway 103 about 1894. The car's configuration, locating the motorman between back-to-back longitudinal benches in the open section, was virtually identical to that of the cable cars of San Francisco's California Street Cable Railroad, which gave the car type its name. — *Historical Collections, Security First National Bank, Los Angeles.*

117

The repair shops of a major street railway company were the scene of a fascinating variety of work. These views depict a few of the operations in the Harvard shops of the Cleveland Electric Railway shortly after World War I. (Right) One end of a car is lifted by an overhead hoist to permit replacement of a truck. (Center) The carpenter shop was capable of repairing or replacing almost any wooden part of a streetcar. (Far right) This formidable piece of equipment was a huge jack used to straighten bent car frames. — *All photos, collection of Charles Goethe.*

A less common variety of combination open and closed car was this design built by St. Louis Car Company in 1912 for the San Diego Electric Railway. The car was divided between open and closed sections, one on either side of a center entrance. No. 125, first of more than 100 San Diego cars of this arrangement, is at the entrance to Mission Cliff Gardens. — *Historical Collection, Union Title Office, Title Insurance & Trust Co., San Diego.*

elsewhere, the double-decker never caught on in North America. The earliest known electric double-decker was the *Columbia,* turned out for Pittsburgh's Pleasant Valley line in 1890. *Columbia* seated second-story passengers on longitudinal benches on the open roof. Its carrying capacity must have pleased the management — on one occasion the car was reported to have transported 160 passengers — but evidently the car was less popular with the public, for the design was not repeated. A year later the Pullman Palace Car Company turned out several single-truck double-deckers for the Highland Park & Fruit Vale Railroad, an Oakland (Calif.) horsecar line. These were converted shortly afterward to electric operation and remained in service until about 1898. Passengers reached the open upper level by means of an ornate cast-iron spiral staircase. During the next few years the Pullman works turned out several large double-truck double-deckers, one of which ran for some time on the Jamestown (N. Y.) Street Railway. Minnesota's Twin City Rapid Transit Company converted three large suburban cars to double-deckers during 1904-1906 but removed the upper decks within a few years.

Similar experiments were tried on a number of street railways, but none was ever successful enough to warrant repetition. Apparently the traveling public balked at having to climb a flight of stairs to reach the upper level. Moreover, the streetcar lines

Ready for shipment, a batch of single-truck open cars was loaded aboard flat cars at American Car's St. Louis (Mo.) plant, one of the principal carbuilders. During the great years of electric traction, city car production sometimes exceeded 4000 annually. — *Collection of Stephen D. Maguire.*

found that the double-deckers were extremely slow to load and unload.

Despite its record of consistent failure, the double-decker idea was briefly revived shortly before World War I when development of "low floor" car designs suggested the possibility of double-deckers of greatly reduced over-all height. In 1913 the New York Railways produced a double-deck version of its low-floor stepless car that was promptly christened the "Broadway Battleship." Similar cars were built shortly afterward for the Columbus (O.) Railway, Power & Light Company and for Washington, D. C. None were particularly successful, and all were taken out of service after only a few years of operation.

About the same time, the Pittsburgh Railways experimented with a somewhat similar low-floor double-decker design that held over-all height to 14 feet

After its development at Montreal in 1905, the "Pay-As-You-Enter" (P.A.Y.E.) car was widely adopted by street railway systems. Passengers paid their fare as they entered at the rear, and left the car by either end. By eliminating confusion between boarding and alighting passengers, the arrangement speeded service and reduced platform accidents. No. 501 was the first of an order for 100 P.A.Y.E. cars delivered to The Milwaukee Electric Railway & Light Company in 1911 by the St. Louis Car Company. — *State Historical Society of Wisconsin.*

The entire front half of the Cleveland-originated Peter Witt car, represented here by Cleveland Electric Railway No. 33, served as an area for passengers who had not yet paid their fares. A conductor at the center collected fares as passengers passed him on the way to the exit doors or to seats at the rear. — *Both photos, Smithsonian Institution.*

The "Near-Side" car, originated by the Philadelphia Rapid Transit Company in 1911, placed the conductor directly behind the motorman. Most Near-Side cars had both entrance and exit at the front, with a rear emergency exit. This model, photographed on Philadelphia's Route 42 about 1919, was provided with a center exit. — *Collection of Richard L. Allman.*

7½ inches. This trial was successful enough to encourage a repeat order for five double-deckers soon afterward, but the old problem of slow loading and unloading remained and the company finally took all six cars out of service in 1924.

The double-decker idea reappeared for the last time in the late 1920's when San Francisco's Market Street Railway produced a design for a car with a top deck that could be removed by a special lifting mechanism during periods of light traffic. Presumably the Market Street management took a look at the past history of double-deckers and promptly forgot the whole thing, for the unique removable-top double-decker never materialized.

Another recurrent approach to the desire for a high-capacity car that met with considerably greater success was the articulated car. Although several cars of this type were built during the early 1890's for Cleveland, the first important application of the idea was in a car constructed by the Boston Elevated Railway Company in 1912. This project took two old 20-foot single-truck cars, removed one platform from each, and suspended a center compartment between the two carbodies. Bostonians were soon calling the 62-foot 10-inch car "two rooms and a bath." Entrance was through the center compartment, which acted as a prepayment platform. The design not only provided a high-capacity unit operated by only a two-man crew and capable of negotiating Boston's sharp curves and narrow streets, but also permitted the company to recoup its considerable investment in a fleet of obsolescent but still serviceable single-truck cars.

So encouraging was Boston's experiment in articulation that during the next 3 years the company constructed 68 identical units from old single-truck cars, and between 1915 and 1919 built another 110 similar units from old double-truck cars. At least two other U. S. traction lines, the Portland (Ore.) Traction Company and the Virginia Railway & Power Company, built similar units; and the "two rooms and a bath" configuration also became popular in Europe, where its snakelike flexibility proved just the thing for narrow streets and sharp curves.

Several other large cities developed articulated equipment that employed two separate carbodies supported by a common truck at the center. Milwaukee and Baltimore rebuilt a number of old double-truck cars into units of this type. Milwaukee rebuilt its first car to this pattern in 1919 and had 33 of them on the streets by 1921. It found that the expense of the conversion was recovered in reduced labor costs in less than a year's time. During the late 1920's Milwaukee, Montreal, and Cleveland all ordered a number of three-truck articulated units seating a hundred or more passengers each. The record for the biggest streetcar of all, though, goes to an experimental four-truck, three-section articulated built for Detroit in 1924 by the Cincinnati Car Company. The 122-foot 8-inch monster seated 140 passengers and was run by a four-man crew.

A more common method of accommodating the crowds at rush hours or other peak periods was the operation of streetcar trains made up either of two or more motor cars operated in multiple unit or of a motor car and a trailer. Although train operation did not permit platform labor savings equal to those of articulated units, it avoided the costly investment represented by such specialized high-capacity equipment as the articulateds. Multiple-unit cars were

Brooklyn was among the many cities that employed the Peter Witt car design. Part of an early 1920's order for the Brooklyn City Railroad is shown on the erecting floor of J. G. Brill's Philadelphia plant. — *Duke-Middleton Collection.*

Double-decker No. 70 of the Terre Haute (Ind.) Street Railway boasted an almost incredible carrying capacity for a single-truck car. Shortly after the car was built in the late 1890's, however, the traction company removed the upper story. — *Collection of Howard E. Johnston.*

easily separated for individual service, and trailers were comparatively inexpensive units that could be stored during the off-peak periods.

Beginning with the general changeover to double-truck cars and the conversion to steel construction that started soon after the turn of the century, trolley cars had become increasingly large and heavy. Shortly after World War I, however, an entirely new type of car was developed which represented a complete reversal of the trend to larger and heavier

equipment. Beset by rising wage rates and other operating costs, and suffering from a small but growing competitive threat in the form of wildcat "jitney" buses and privately owned automobiles, the traction industry badly needed a car that could be more economically operated, particularly on lightly traveled routes.

The new streetcar was designed by Charles O. Birney, the engineer in charge of car design and construction for the Stone & Webster Corporation,

Devised by Frank Hedley and J. S. Doyle, general manager and superintendent of car equipment respectively for the New York Railways, the center-entrance "stepless" trolley had a floor only 7 inches above the rails. Aside from New York Railways itself, the largest user of the cars was the Southern Pacific Company, which purchased 36 of them from J. G. Brill in 1913 for service on several subsidiary electric lines in California. No. 31 was one of six stepless "dragons," as they were known in the West, operated by the Stockton Electric Railroad. — *Collection of William D. Middleton.*

New York Railways' experimental "Broadway Battleship" double-decker of 1913 was developed from the company's stepless car design. The extremely low floor, together with a novel interior arrangement, held over-all height of the car to less than 13 feet — little more than that of a conventional single-level car. The car was not particularly successful, though, and the New York Railways never repeated the experiment. — *Library of Congress.*

operator of a number of street railway properties in Texas, Washington, and elsewhere in the United States. Birney's concept called for a small, extremely lightweight car that could be worked at low cost with a one-man crew. Because of the low operating cost, Birney argued, more frequent service could be given, with a resultant increase in traffic.

The "Safety Car," as it was called, was a single-truck car averaging about 28 feet in length and seating approximately 32 passengers. Although the first experimental model, constructed by the American Car Company in 1915, weighed only about 5 tons, the standard production models were somewhat heavier, weighing anywhere from 7 to 9 tons. Even

The roomy double-decker *Columbia* of the Jamestown (N. Y.) Street Railway is pictured at Celoron Park about 1893. The design, built by the Pullman Palace Car Company, represented the work of George M. Pullman and H. H. Sessions. The motorman's upper deck enclosure resembled a pilothouse. — *Collection of Charles Goethe.*

at that, Safety Cars weighed only about half as much per seat as most of the heavier equipment they replaced. One of the car's novel features was its "dead man control," which automatically brought the car to a halt if the operator released the controller or a special foot pedal without first setting the brakes.

The first Birney cars, as they became generally known, were placed in service in 1916, and by 1920 over 4000 of them had been built. Ultimately, more than 6000 were in service throughout the United States as well as in a number of foreign countries. Their initial success was almost phenomenal. Operating costs proved to be little more than half as much as for older, heavier cars. Running the new cars on a more frequent headway, most street railway companies realized substantial traffic increases. The experience of the Chicago North Shore & Milwaukee Railroad, which re-equipped its city services with Birney cars, was typical. After installing the cars on its local lines at Waukegan and North Chicago,

Boston's "two rooms and a bath" car, made up of two permanently coupled single-truck cars with a suspended intermediate section, was just the thing for snaking through narrow Hub City streets. The center section (above) acted as a pay-as-you-enter conductor's platform. — *Collection of LeRoy O. King (above); Collection of O. R. Cummings (below).*

Ill., in 1919, the company was able to reduce headways from 15 minutes to 8 minutes. The improved service, together with reduced fares, brought a 39 per cent traffic increase in less than a year. The installation of Birneys on the North Shore's Milwaukee local line in 1923, along with a comparable increase in frequency of service, brought a traffic increase of 59 per cent and a revenue increase of 34 per cent in

only three months after the new cars entered service.

Even so, the standardized single-truck Birney proved to have its limitations. Because of the four-wheel design, the cars had poor riding qualities and were easily derailed. Propelled by only two 25 h.p. motors, the Birneys were notoriously underpowered. Several large cities that attempted to use Birneys on heavy traffic lines found the cars inadequate, and

124

A later articulated car, Boston Elevated 4200, made use of obsolete double-truck cars. — *Collection of Allan H. Berner.*

most were soon relegated to unimportant lines or were sold to small city systems. Most important, the lightly traveled lines for which the Birneys were best adapted proved the most vulnerable to a growing trend to bus substitution that began during the 1920's. After reaching a peak of 1699 cars built during 1920, Birney production declined rapidly, and the last one was constructed in 1930.

Despite the somewhat limited success of the single-truck Birney, many of its features were widely applied to other equipment. A larger, double-truck version of the Birney developed during the 1920's proved quite popular, and was turned out in quantity for a number of systems. The "Safety Car" features of the Birney were applied to thousands of older cars to permit the economies of one-man equipment.

The years following World War I were troubled ones for the street railway industry. Costs continued to rise, private automobile ownership was growing rapidly, and the motorbus was beginning to pose a serious threat to the supremacy of the electric car. A recurrent theme in industrial history is that times of adversity often produce some of the greatest and most rapid advances in technology, and the traction industry's troubled times spurred a continuing development effort that was to result in unparalleled advances in the efficiency, performance, and comfort of the trolley car.

Increasing use was made of such materials as alloy steels and aluminum to produce extremely lightweight cars. The development of new motors and controls improved performance characteristics.

Several builders turned out new types of trucks which incorporated roller bearings, rubber cushioning, worm drive motors, and other features intended to improve riding qualities and reduce noise. Such passenger comforts as rubber-tiled floors and individual leather upholstered seats were introduced, and greater attention was given to the appearance of equipment.

Several carbuilders developed standardized car designs which were built, with variations, for street railway systems throughout the U.S. The Cincinnati Car Company's curved-side lightweight car, although it was developed primarily for interurban service, appeared on several street railway systems. The St. Louis Car Company produced a modern car called the "Rail Sedan" for several systems. Easily the most successful of these "standard" cars was J. G. Brill's "Master Unit," a lightweight car of advanced design and modern appearance constructed in quantity between the late 1920's and 1934.

A brief attempt was made to revive the four-wheel car during the late 1920's. One of the most interesting efforts in this direction was that of the Twin Coach Corporation, a leading motorbus manufacturer, which introduced an "automotive-type" streetcar in 1928. Built from the same jigs used for the company's bus production line, the Twin Coach trolley looked little different from the company's standard bus, and even employed identical automotive-type brakes and leaf springs. The most novel feature of the design was the use of wheels that turned independently on automotive-type steering knuckles, permitting a low floor and a considerably

125

Cleveland's G. C. Kuhlman Car Company built 28 of these three-truck articulated cars for the Cleveland Railway in 1928. Each of the 101-foot, 40-ton monsters seated 100 passengers. Two conductors and a motorman operated each of the cars. — *Collection of Allan H. Berner.*

The biggest trolley of them all was this three-section articulated built for Detroit's Department of Street Railways in 1924. The 140-seat car was just right for auto plant rush-hour crowds but proved to be too large for off-peak services. — *Collection of Thomas J. Dworman.*

longer wheelbase for the car. This tended to eliminate the uncomfortable galloping motion that was characteristic of the usual four-wheel car. The company's promotional literature claimed that even though the bus-turned-trolley was hardly susceptible to flat tires, a wheel could be changed in a matter of minutes, just as on an automotive vehicle.

At about the same time, the St. Louis Car Company evolved a similar four-wheel "automotive-type" trolley, billed as the "New Birney," which carried the automotive treatment even to chromium-plated automobile bumpers. Neither the Twin Coach nor the St. Louis cars got beyond the demonstrator stage, however, and the four-wheel car idea was thereupon given up for good. The Twin Coach organization did make one further effort to invade the streetcar field the following year with a lightweight double-truck car of somewhat more conventional design. A single demonstrator operated for a few years in Brooklyn, but repeat orders never materialized and Twin Coach quietly retired from the streetcar business.

Throughout the 1920's the efforts to develop an improved streetcar were largely individual ones by equipment suppliers, carbuilders, or the traction companies themselves. But in 1929 an organization of street railway officials formed a new group — the Electric Railway Presidents' Conference Committee — to carry out an industrywide development program aimed at producing a new standardized streetcar design of radically improved appearance and performance. Headed by Dr. Thomas Conway Jr., one of the most noted executives in the traction industry, the Committee hired Prof. C. F. Hirshfeld, director of research for the Detroit Edison Company, as its chief engineer and authorized him to assemble a technical research staff and to proceed with development work.

Over a 5-year period more than a million dollars was spent on an exhaustive program of testing, research, and experimentation. A considerable amount of testing was carried out to develop the best possible lightweight body design. By experimentation the maximum acceptable rate of acceleration and other performance characteristics were determined, and such suppliers as General Electric and Westinghouse evolved the necessary motors and controls to meet the new specifications. Probably more at-

The single-truck "Safety Car" developed in 1915 by Charles O. Birney was a popular standardized streetcar. More than 6000 were built over a 15-year period. A 1920 modernization of The Milwaukee Electric Railway & Light Company's local lines at Racine, Wis., included 25 of them. — *State Historical Society of Wisconsin.*

tention was given to development of an improved truck design than any other feature of the new car.

The Committee's first car to take the rails, the Model "A" PCC (Presidents' Conference Committee) car, was a modern carbody borrowed from the Brooklyn & Queens Transit Corporation for the purpose of testing a new truck design and other electrical equipment. In 1934 an entirely new experimental car, the Model "B" PCC car, was ordered from Pullman-Standard. It incorporated an extremely lightweight streamlined carbody, spring suspended motors, eddy-current brakes, magnetic track brakes, "floating" type control, and improved heating, lighting, and ventilating systems. Employing newly developed high-tensile steel for carbody construction, the experimental car weighed only 31,000 pounds.

By the following year the Committee's work had advanced to the point where a specification for a production-model car could be presented to the carbuilders. The St. Louis Car Company was finally persuaded to undertake some of the remaining de-

velopment work and to manufacture the car. The resulting production-model PCC bore little resemblance to any previous streetcar. Utilizing a streamlined carbody of welded high-tensile steel, the standard PCC weighed about 33,000 pounds — far less than any previous car of comparable capacity and performance. Provided with comfortably cushioned seating and improved heating, lighting, and ventilating systems, and possessed of unparalleled riding qualities, the PCC represented an entirely new level of passenger comfort. The new trucks, featuring rubber-cushioned wheels and extensive use of rubber insulation, were remarkably quiet in operation. Four 55 h.p. motors provided the PCC car with the highest power-to-weight ratio in street railway history plus exceptional speed and acceleration characteristics. A dynamic braking system, which used the motors for braking action, supplemented by magnetic track brakes and air brakes, provided a comparable improvement in braking performance.

The PCC car won an immediate triumph with

127

Fresh from the paint shop, seven brand-new Birneys were lined up on a string of flat cars awaiting shipment to Brooklyn, N. Y., from the Philadelphia plant of carbuilder J. G. Brill. — *Duke-Middleton Collection.*

both car riders and the street railway companies. Great throngs inspected the new cars when they were placed on display, and soon after their introduction the traction companies were reporting traffic increases of as much as 33 per cent. Schedule speeds on PCC-equipped lines were increased by as much as 15 per cent, and most lines reported reduced accident rates, power consumption, and labor and maintenance costs.

The Brooklyn & Queens Transit Corporation, which had participated in much of the development work for the PCC, was the first system to purchase the new car, with an order for 100 placed in 1935. Major systems throughout the U. S. and Canada soon followed suit, and by 1940 some 1400 PCC cars were in service. Continuing improvements, most notably a change to all-electric operation, were made to the basic design throughout the more than 15 years that PCC cars were being turned out. The peak year for PCC orders was reached in 1946, when some 800 cars were constructed; and by 1951, when PCC car production ended in North America, nearly 5000 of them had been built. Toronto, the largest operator of PCC's, had 745, over half of which are still in service. Chicago and Pittsburgh each had nearly 700 PCC cars, Philadelphia had 559, and Washington had nearly 500. A few PCC's were built in the U. S. for overseas systems, and hundreds

Typical of the improved car designs of the 1920's was this lightweight suburban car for Wheeling, W. Va. — one of 15 delivered in 1927 by the Kuhlman works at Cleveland, O. Interior appointments included rubber-tile floors, seats upholstered in Spanish grain leather, and a Philippine mahogany finish. — *Collection of William D. Middleton.*

Following a disastrous car-barn fire in 1924, the Grand Rapids (Mich.) Railway sponsored a competitive trial of several new streetcar designs before ordering a new fleet of cars. The experimental car *Minnesota* was delivered by the short-lived Light Weight Noiseless Electric Street Car Company, which produced several orders during the mid-1920's in the Snelling Shops of the Twin City Rapid Transit Company at St. Paul, Minn. The car weighed 12 tons, and its truck design featured inboard roller bearings. — *State Historical Society of Wisconsin.*

more were built abroad utilizing various PCC car patents. Trucks and other components originally evolved for the PCC car were also used on a number of rapid transit cars.

Coincident with development of the PCC, several independent efforts were made to create a modern streamlined car. In 1934 J. G. Brill and Pullman-Standard each delivered an experimental streamliner to the Chicago Surface Lines. Both cars incorporated a number of innovations that were shortly to become standard on the production-model PCC, and the Pullman-Standard car was notable for the use of all-aluminum carbody construction. Neither car was sufficiently successful to warrant repetition,

however, and when Chicago Surface Lines commenced a large-scale equipment modernization program 2 years later, it was with PCC cars. Also in 1934, Detroit's Department of Street Railways constructed an extremely lightweight experimental streamliner in its own shops. The car was considered quite a success, but its technical features were nowhere near as advanced as those then under development for the PCC and the experiment was not repeated.

Impatient to begin an equipment modernization program, Capital Transit Company of Washington, D. C., divided an order for 20 streamlined cars between J. G. Brill and St. Louis Car Company in

An experimental rebuilding job by the Haselton shops of the Mahoning & Shenango Railway & Light Company at Youngstown, O., produced this ultramodern Birney car in 1928. Although the effort was not repeated, the exterior styling and such interior features as individual leather upholstered seating were applied to an order of "Master Unit" cars delivered a short time later by the G. C. Kuhlman Car Company. — *Collection of O. F. Lee.*

Another entry in the Grand Rapids design competition was this "Electric Coach" built by the G. C. Kuhlman Car Company at Cleveland. An exceptionally light-weight design, the car weighed less than 13 tons. The advanced truck design featured inside roller bearing journals, clasp band brakes, and rubber-cushioned wheels. The car was painted in Ohio State University's scarlet and gray colors. — *Collection of Charles Goethe.*

St. Louis Car Company's "Rail Sedan" was one of several standardized lightweight designs produced by car-builders during the late 1920's. No. 351 was one of five built in 1927 for the East St. Louis & Suburban Railway. Its advanced features included cushioned wheels and a load equalized braking system. In keeping with an emphasis on passenger comfort and appearance, the car was equipped with leather upholstered seats and finished in a snappy orange, cream, and red color scheme. The head-on pose with a Dodge sedan (above) was intended to show the utility of the Rail Sedan's automotive-type spring bumpers. — *Both photos, collection of William J. Clouser.*

1935. Although the cars were entirely satisfactory, and remained in service for more than 20 years, the PCC car marked such a radical advance that Capital Transit turned to the standard production-model PCC for subsequent orders.

When the PCC car went into quantity production in 1936, two builders — St. Louis Car Company and Pullman-Standard — were licensed to build it. Instead of taking up PCC car production, J. G. Brill of Philadelphia, which had been the leading street

New WEIGHT REDUCTION
An Epoch In Design

Automotive Practice
Arrives for Street Cars

Buslike styling of the experimental four-wheel "automotive-type" streetcar of 1928 was not coincidental. The builder, bus manufacturer Twin Coach, employed the same jigs used for bus production to assemble the car. A second Twin Coach experimental car built in 1929 (below) was a more conventionally arranged double-truck car but retained bus styling. Although neither experimental brought production orders, many features of the cars appeared in the PCC streamliner of the mid-1930's. — *Collection of Wayne C. Olsen (above); Collection of Stephen D. Maguire (below).*

Pittsburgh Railways experimental car No. 6002, built by the Osgood Bradley Car Company in 1929, represented one of the most advanced designs of the 1920's. Constructed largely of aluminum, the car weighed only 13½ tons. Timken-Detroit Axle Company trucks featured four 50 h.p. longitudinally mounted motors. Pedal-operated controls included dynamic braking.—*Collection of LeRoy O. King.*

railway carbuilder ever since the advent of electric traction, elected to go its own way with an independent modern car design. Convinced it could turn out a car superior even to the PCC, Brill produced the first model of a streamlined car called the "Brilliner" in 1938 for the Atlantic City & Shore Railroad, which a short time later increased its Brilliner fleet to a total of 25 cars. The Brill streamliner looked little different from the PCC car, but its performance was something else again. Aside from

Produced in quantity for systems throughout the United States, J. G. Brill Company's Master Unit car was the most popular of the standardized modern car designs that preceded the PCC streamliner of the 1930's. This double-end Master Unit was built for the Portland (Ore.) Traction Company. — *Duke-Middleton Collection.*

132

the Atlantic City orders, only five other Brilliners were ever built; and while St. Louis and Pullman busied themselves with record orders, Brill vanished from the carbuilding scene after filling an order for 10 suburban cars for a Philadelphia line in 1941.

Pullman-Standard built this Model "B" streamliner in 1934 as a test vehicle for the Presidents' Conference Committee. Most of its features, including welded high-tensile steel body construction, "floating" control, and magnetic track brakes, were later incorporated into the production-model PCC. The car's eddy-current braking system proved disappointing, however, and after brief periods of experimental operation in Chicago and Brooklyn the car was scrapped. — *Chicago Architectural Photographing Company, from Stephen D. Maguire (above); Courtesy Railroad Magazine (below).*

In 1935 the Brooklyn & Queens Transit Corporation was the first system to sign up for the new PCC streamliner with a 100-car order. No. 1001, the first production-model PCC, was delivered by St. Louis Car Company in 1936. After 20 years of service, the pioneer streamliner was retired to the Branford Trolley Museum at Short Beach, Conn., following abandonment of street railway service in Brooklyn. — *General Electric Company.*

PCC car production reached a peak in the years just after World War II. These standee-window, all-electric models were part of an order for 100 Philadelphia cars under construction at St. Louis Car Company in 1947. — *St. Louis Car Division of General Steel Industries.*

Chicago Surface Lines, which bought 683 PCC cars between 1936 and 1948, was one of the largest operators of the streamlined trolleys. No. 4063 was built by Pullman-Standard in 1947. Larger than standard PCC's, Chicago's cars were arranged for two-man operation. — *Collection of William D. Middleton.*

Blue-and-silver "Blue Goose" streamliner No. 4001 was built for Chicago Surface Lines by Pullman-Standard in 1934. The aluminum-bodied experimental had cushioned wheels, magnetic track brakes, and PCC-type control. The Blue Goose had a tendency to break down frequently, tying up the streets, and was removed from service in 1941 after only 7 years of operation.—*Ed Frank, from Robert W. Gibson.*

Detroit's homemade lightweight streamliner of 1934 incorporated such features as welded steel construction, foot-valve-operated air brakes, and indirect lighting. The 39-seat car weighed only 12 tons.—*Collection of Thomas J. Dworman.*

J. G. Brill's "Brilliner" streamlined car was an unsuccessful rival of the PCC car. Baltimore Transit Company, already the owner of a good-sized PCC fleet, took delivery of sample Brilliner No. 7501 in 1939. Performance failed to match that of the PCC's, however, and subsequent orders went to Pullman-Standard for PCC's. — *Collection of LeRoy O. King.*

135

America in the Time of the Trolley

Development of the one-man Birney "Safety Car" in 1915 provided a new lease on life for lightly traveled trolley lines and small city systems. An order of 18 Birneys from J. G. Brill in 1922 supplied almost all service on the Lafayette (Ind.) Street Railway until the end of rail operation in 1940. Two of them are shown on the State Street hill in West Lafayette, Ind., in 1928. — *J. C. Allen & Son*.

From the Pine Tree State to the beaches at Waikiki, a pictorial survey of the republic during the great years when electric traction ruled the urban scene.

The
New England
States

What greater pleasure could a balmy summer day hold than an open-car journey into town? Inbound from Gorham, Portland Railroad's 14-bench open car No. 155 loaded passengers near Westbrook, Me., on an August day around the turn of the century. — *Collection of O. R. Cummings.*

A trolley car outing to Riverton casino was a popular diversion for Portland citizens in the years before World War I. Piloted by a brass-buttoned motorman of irreproachable dignity, Portland open car No. 125 waited for passengers in front of the casino. The dash sign advertised the current casino attraction, "A Trip to the Sun," starring Harry Lander. — *Collection of O. R. Cummings.*

A trim four-wheel closed car of the Rockland, Thomaston & Camden Street Railway paused with a group of summer excursionists at Oakland Park, on the shore of Penobscot Bay, Me. — *Collection of Howard E. Johnston.*

140

Maine's shortest trolley line was the Norway & Paris Street Railway, which carried passengers over slightly more than 2 miles of track between the line's namesake towns in Oxford County, not far from the New Hampshire line. Despite the company's small size, it operated a traffic-building amusement park, known as Electra Park, midway between its two terminals. On one occasion a small orchestra was hired to play aboard one of the line's open cars in an effort to induce pleasure riding. All was to little avail, and the company went out of business in 1918 after only 23 years of operation. Single-truck open car No. 6, constructed by the Briggs Carriage Company of Amesbury, Mass., was one of the line's original cars. — *Collection of F. W. Schneider III.*

A handsome single-truck car, finished in the standard white prescribed for street railway equipment in the Railway Mail Service, posed with its proud crew before setting out to carry the mails to New Hampshire and Massachusetts points over the Exeter, Hampton & Amesbury Street Railway Company. — *Collection of LeRoy O. King.*

It was a big day in Goffs Falls, N. H., when the first trolley cars of the Manchester Street Railway arrived from nearby Manchester on June 10, 1901. A local photographer recorded the historic occasion after a ceremonial first run from the Manchester City Hall. — *Collection of O. R. Cummings.*

Crumbling old lime kilns in Woodford Hollow, not far from Bennington, Vt., were an interesting sight along the line of the Bennington & Woodford Electric Railway Company. — *Collection of Jim Shaughnessy.*

The interstate Hoosick Falls Street Railway rambled over the New England countryside between Bennington, Vt., and Hoosick Falls, N. Y. Open car No. 15 rolled through tree-shaded streets at Lincoln Square in North Bennington. — *Collection of Howard E. Johnston.*

By the time this 1890's scene was recorded on Tremont Street next to the Common, the triumph of electric traction was all but complete in Boston. The single Back Bay horsecar in the foreground shared the street with a steady parade of West End Street Railway electric cars. — *Collection of LeRoy O. King.*

THE dominant figure in Boston's early traction history was real estate promoter Henry M. Whitney, who organized the West End Street Railway during the 1880's to advance his Brookline property interests. By 1887, after engineering a consolidation with three other principal Boston street railways, Whitney presided over what was then the world's largest street railway system, with a stable of 8000 horses. Whitney journeyed to Richmond a year later to observe Frank Sprague's successful electrification of the Richmond Union Passenger Railroad, and soon afterward made his West End line the first major urban system to undertake wholesale electrification.

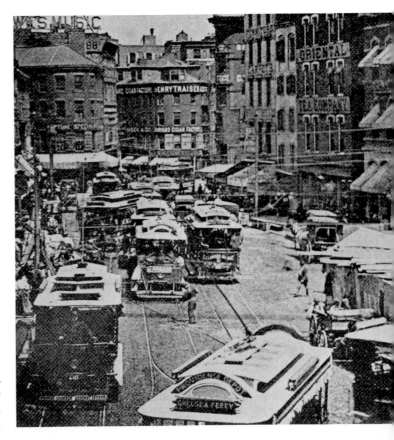

Scollay Square was the scene of intense streetcar activity. No fewer than 11 cars of the West End company and the Lynn & Boston Railroad Company are visible in this late 1890's view. — *Collection of LeRoy O. King.*

Boston's trolleys began operating through America's first subway on September 1, 1897, when the West End line opened its new Tremont Street surface car subway. (Right) In this opening-day scene, a helmeted policeman directs traffic. (Above) An open car loads at the subway's Park Street terminal. A month later subway operation was extended to Pleasant Street, where the station (below) was photographed. — *Collection of O. R. Cummings (above and right); Collection of LeRoy O. King (below).*

The Boston Elevated Railway, which took over the West End company by lease at the end of 1897, experimented with everything from trailers to multiple-unit operation to a fleet of home-built articulated cars in order to accommodate its heavy traffic. Car No. 529 leads a trailer through Copley Square. — *Collection of O. R. Cummings.*

Gen. William A. Bancroft, who became president of the Boston Elevated Railway in 1899, journeyed through Boston streets in unrivaled elegance aboard private car No. 101. Delivered from the G. C. Kuhlman car works at Cleveland, O., in 1904, the car was lavishly furnished with leather and wicker armchairs, heavy silk draperies and curtains, and oriental carpeting. The interior was finished in inlaid mahogany; bevel-edge mirrors were placed on the window posts; and the full Empire ceiling was elaborately embellished. A buffet and water cooler were also installed. The dark green exterior was intricately decorated in gold leaf designs. Such fripperies on the El were later regarded with disapproval by Boston politicians. — *All photos, collection of O. R. Cummings.*

The Boston Elevated and its 1947 successor, Metropolitan Transit Authority, became a major user of the streamlined PCC car following its development during the 1930's. Some 340 of the streamliners still operate over Boston's high-speed subway-surface trolley lines. This three-car lineup was photographed at Cedar Grove Cemetery along the Mattapan-Ashmont high-speed trolley line on a 1941 excursion. — *Loris J. Bass, from Richard L. Wonson.*

AMONG the least successful street railway ventures of New England was the 15-mile Blue Hill Street Railway, which connected the communities of Stoughton, Canton, and Milton with Boston. Constructed by the Stone & Webster utility firm of Boston, which usually did better with its electric railway ventures, the Blue Hill line opened in 1899 and folded after 21 years of unprofitable operation.

Initial equipment for the 15-mile Blue Hill line was a batch of five former Atlantic Avenue horsecars purchased from the Boston Elevated Railway. One of them is seen on Washington Street in Canton Corner in 1899. — *Collection of Carl L. Smith.*

Four years after its opening, the Blue Hill Street Railway completed a through route to a connection with the Boston El at Mattapan Square. Among the several hundred dignitaries who made this inaugural run from Mattapan Square to Stoughton on August 15, 1903, was Massachusetts Governor John Bates. — *Collection of Carl L. Smith.*

147

In a charming setting in the Pilgrim country of 19th century New England, a 10-bench open car of the Plymouth & Kingston Street Railway clatters down stone-block-paved Main Street in Plymouth, Mass., about 1898 en route to the company-owned Hotel Pilgrim. — *Collection of Carl L. Smith.*

One of the giants of New England traction was the Bay State Street Railway and its successor, the Eastern Massachusetts Street Railway. At the peak of its operations the Bay State system operated more than 2600 cars over nearly a thousand miles of track in Massachusetts, Rhode Island, and New Hampshire. This Bay State lineup is in North Andover, Mass. — *Collection of LeRoy O. King.*

Among the many predecessor lines of the Bay State Street Railway system were the affiliated Haverhill, Georgetown & Danvers and the Georgetown, Rowley & Ipswich street railways north of Boston in Essex County. A favorite spot for photographers was this trestle near Georgetown which carried the cars over a B&M branch. Open car No. 10 was on its way from Haverhill to Georgetown and Byfield. — *Collection of LeRoy O. King.*

One of the busiest spots on the Georgetown, Rowley & Ipswich was Governor Dummer Academy Junction, near Byfield, where routes for Haverhill, Ipswich, and Newburyport diverged. This view, photographed a few years after the line's opening in 1900, shows a flurry of activity as cars meet at the junction. — *Collection of LeRoy O. King.*

149

For several generations one of the première tourist attractions of the Connecticut River valley was the exhilarating journey up Mount Tom aboard the counterbalanced electric cars of the Mount Tom Railroad. Streetcars of the Holyoke Street Railway carried excursionists to Lower Station, in the company-owned Mountain Park, where a transfer was made to the mile-long incline. The two special incline cars, the *Rowland Thomas* and the *Elizur Holyoke*, were modestly described in the line's promotional literature as "models of taste and finish, excelling in size, proportions, and beauty all mountain cars in this country." The two cars were connected by a steel cable, which passed around an 8-foot sheave at the top of the incline. Each car was powered by two electric motors, and three different means of braking were provided. A turnout at the midpoint permitted the rising and descending cars to pass on the single-track incline. The three-story Summit House at the top boasted an observation room surrounded by plate glass windows. — *All photos, collection of William D. Middleton.*

Clattering along on a lush summer day, a little open car of the Warren, Brookfield & Spencer Street Railway paralleled a country lane. — *Collection of Howard E. Johnston.*

The New England trolley was generally a leisurely affair. From spring to fall the open car was supreme. In a classic scene of New England summer trolleying, a big open car of the Massachusetts Northeastern Street Railway hums past Lake Kenoza on casually laid side-of-the-road track not far from Haverhill. — *Collection of LeRoy O. King.*

o New England trolley road of any consequence felt at its equipment roster was complete without at least e handsome parlor car for the accommodation of such ecial traffic as theater parties and sight-seeing excur- ns. The boys in the shops of the Concord, Maynard & dson Street Railway in Massachusetts outdid them- ves in 1902 when they rebuilt the bodies of two gle-truck battery streetcars into the magnificent parlor Concord. The interior was finished in mahogany and ht blue and was provided with bronze trimmings and candescent lights fitted with "lily pattern" shades of ferent colors. Two tête-à-têtes and the customary sh-cushioned rattan lounge chairs supplied seats for passengers. Electric blue draperies with white cords d tassels were hung at the windows, and a figured vel- t carpet was laid on the floor. — *Both photos, collection O. R. Cummings.*

Around the turn of the century a lineup of closed and open cars of the Old Colony Street Railway waited for passengers at Newport (R. I.) station. — *Collection of LeRoy O. King.*

In a time when smoking was regarded as an uncouth and offensive habit, the Pawtucket (R. I.) Street Railway operated its open cars on special "workingmen's smoking trips" in all but the most severe weather. Smokers' open car No. 110, a former horsecar, was photographed in Pawtucket around 1900. — *Collection of Richard L. Wonson.*

152

New England's only cable railroad was a line installed at Providence, R. I., on which cable-drawn dummies hauled horsecars between Market Square and Red Bridge. After electrification, a portion of the cable line was rebuilt with a counterbalance system to assist electric cars up and down the steep College Street hill. Grip car No. 2 is about to uncouple from a car it has just brought down the hill. Although there were never any streetcar runaways on the hill, the weighted counterbalance car occasionally snapped its cable and ran downhill, tearing up the street at the bottom when it arrived at the end of its tunnel. — *Collection of Richard L. Wonson.*

Providence's College Hill tunnel, built in 1914 to replace the counterbalance cable line over the hill, was the scene of spectacular runaways in 1926 and 1942. In each instance a trolley car lost its brakes and plummeted down-hill through the tunnel, derailing on the sharp curve at the bottom and colliding with a building. United Electric Railways car No. 1875 emerges from the upper end of the tunnel in 1939. — *Loris J. Bass, from Richard L. Wonson.*

Among New England electric railways, the vast Connecticut Company system was second only to Massachusetts' Bay State Street Railway in size. Assembled under the control of the New York, New Haven & Hartford Railroad in 1910, the company at the time of its formation operated some 1800 cars over more than 800 miles of track extending to almost every point of importance in the state of Connecticut. The pride of the Connecticut Company system, and one of the most famous electric cars in New England, was the company's elegant trolley parlor car No. 500 constructed in 1904 by the J. G. Brill Company of Philadelphia. After 44 years of operation the car was retired to the Branford Trolley Museum at Short Beach, Conn., in 1948. It is shown along the shore of the East Haven River during a 1944 charter outing. — *George A. Roush.*

Long after the open-car era had ended elsewhere in the U. S., the Connecticut Company maintained a fleet of over 100 aged 15-bench open cars at New Haven for such extraordinary traffic loads as those imposed by football games at Yale Bowl. (Above) West Point cadets disembark from part of the fleet of 22 open cars that carried the corps from the New Haven railroad station to the bowl for the 1935 Army-Yale game. (Below) In the last year of operation, an open car bearing an almost unbelievable crowd turns into Chapel Street on its way to a football event at the bowl in 1947. — *Roger Borrup (above); John Stern (below).*

154

The Middle Atlantic States

Shortly after the turn of the century single-truck open cars of the Buffalo (N. Y.) International Railway Company rattled down the broad expanse of a Main Street that offered little in the way of vehicular traffic competition. S. Levyn's cigar store on the corner evidently served as a station for the International Railway's Niagara Falls and Lockport interurbans, which reached downtown Buffalo over the company's streetcar tracks. Hydroelectric power from the falls powered Buffalo trolleys. — *Library of Congress.*

For 40 years one of the most popular excursions available to Niagara Falls visitors was the spectacular ride over the Niagara Gorge Railway, which carried trolley tourists over a circular route covering both sides of the gorge for several miles below the falls. On the American side of the gorge the rails descended into the gorge itself, and falling rocks were hazards to the operation. The "Great Gorge Route" and some of its principal sights are shown in the above panoramic drawing from a 1927 promotional leaflet. Sights visible in the drawing include: (1) International Railway and Great Gorge Route terminals; (2) International Steel Arch Bridge; (3) Queen Victoria Park; (4) Table Rock and Scenic Tunnel; (5) Bridge Street and Railroad bridges; (6) Spanish Aero Car over the Whirlpool; (7) Niagara Glen; (8) Brock's Monument on Queenston Heights; (9) Queenston-Lewiston Bridge; (10) Lower Rapids and Devil's Hole; (11) Whirlpool; (12) Whirlpool Rapids; (13) Power plants of Niagara system; (A) City of Niagara Falls, N.Y.; (B) City of Niagara Falls, Ont.; (C) Village of Queenston, Ont.; and (D) Village of Lewiston, N. Y. The line's equipment included the luxurious private car *Rapids* (below and right), which was available for special tour parties. — *All photos, collection of Jeffrey Winslow.*

The first trolley line in Rochester, N. Y., began operating to nearby Charlotte, on Lake Ontario, in 1889. Two of the pioneer cars met somewhere along the line in this historic photo. — *Collection of Charles C. Robinson.*

In an effort to reduce downtown congestion, Rochester opened a streetcar and interurban subway in the abandoned bed of the Erie Canal in 1927. Interurban operation ended within 4 years, but trolley operation continued until 1956. Car No. 60 is shown leaving the canal bed shortly before the line's abandonment. — *Allan H. Berner.*

Two years after Rochester city cars began running to Charlotte, the Grand View Beach Railway opened a 7-mile line extending westward along the shore of Lake Ontario to Manitou Beach. Operated only in the summer, the line did a lively weekend business to resorts and summer cottages along the way. Open car No. 20 is crossing the 2000-foot Braddocks Bay trestle in 1905, by which time the company had been reorganized as the Rochester, Charlotte & Manitou Railroad. The long trestle, frequently buffeted by storms, was almost entirely destroyed during the winter of 1907-1908. The line ceased operation in 1925. — *Collection of Stephen D. Maguire.*

Hornell (N. Y.) Traction trolley No. 30 had the street to itself as it rolled down Broad Street past the Shattuck Opera House about 1914. — *Library of Congress.*

The Syracuse, Lakeside & Baldwinsville Railway, an 18-mile roadside trolley extending northward from Syracuse to summer resorts along the western shore of Lake Onondaga, was one of the few electric lines to make wide use of double-deck equipment. Each of the line's nine Jackson & Sharp open cars, known as "whales," seated 100 people. Two are shown on Clinton Street in Syracuse about 1901. — *Collection of William R. Gordon.*

The first trolley to run in Cooperstown, N. Y., rolled down Main Street on September 28, 1901. Trolley No. 3 of the Oneonta, Cooperstown & Richfield Springs Railway still bore the name of predecessor company Oneonta & Otego Valley. When the line had begun electric operation at Oneonta a few years earlier, the first car was halted by an undersheriff who served an injunction restraining further operation on grounds of electrical interference with the local telephone company.

Dominating the local transportation business in New York's Capital District was the United Traction Company, which through merger in 1899 assembled a formidable electric railway system. One of the company's trolleys rolls down State Street to Terminal Plaza in Albany. — *Collection of Jim Shaughnessy.*

A big center-entrance car, one of many rebuilt in United Traction shops from bodies of two single-truck cars, made a passenger stop on North Pearl Street in Albany in 1921. — *Collection of Jim Shaughnessy.*

A northbound Albany-Troy car stopped on Broadway in North Albany to discharge and load passengers at the carbarn. — *Collection of Jim Shaughnessy.*

Franklin Square in Troy, N. Y., was the scene of heavy trolley traffic in the summer of 1905. In the right foreground, a Hudson Valley Railway open car heads northward on a journey to Saratoga Springs, while at the left, United Traction city cars and a Schenectady interurban roll into the square. — *Collection of LeRoy O. King.*

One of the most delightful trolley car outings in the Capital District was afforded by the Troy & New England Railway, which reached neither Troy nor New England. The railway was originally planned to extend to Pittsfield, Mass., but contented itself with an 8-mile line from Albia, a Troy suburb, along Wynantskill Creek to Averill Park on Sand Lake. The little line did a brisk summer business until paved roads captured most of the traffic. Operation ended in 1925. Here a lineup of open cars loads at the Albia terminal. — *Collection of Howard E. Johnston.*

165

The Hudson Valley Railway, a Delaware & Hudson Railroad subsidiary, operated an extensive interurban and local electric railway system extending northward through the Hudson Valley from Troy to Lake George. Two cars met on a Glens Falls street around 1915. — *Pangburn Studio, Glens Falls, from George W. Walrath.*

Trolleys of the Fishkill (N.Y.) Electric Railway linked the village with the New York Central, the Newburgh ferry, and steamers of the Hudson River Day Line at nearby Fishkill Landing (now Beacon). This is open car No. 6 in 1913. — *Collection of Allan H. Berner.*

While a group of young locals lounged on the veranda outside the swinging doors of the Depot Square House, a trolley of the Westchester Traction Company rattled through the unpaved streets of Ossining, N.Y. Opened in 1893 as the Ossining Electric Railway, the line ran over a 2-mile route between the New York Central Depot and the Camp Meeting Grounds, with a short branch to Sparta Hill. During a 13-year career the line was sold to the town for unpaid taxes, reorganized, and finally torn up in 1906. — *Collection of Frank W. Schlegel.*

ALTHOUGH New York's unparalleled elevated railway and subway system has dominated Manhattan transportation since well before the turn of the century, the 22-square-mile island was also laced together with a network of nearly 300 miles of street railway track constructed by the New York Railways, the Third Avenue Railway, and their various predecessor companies. Lines on the principal crosstown streets connected the Hudson River ferry terminals, the bridges and ferries to Queens and Brooklyn, and a vast network of car lines in the Bronx with the north-south subway and elevated routes and the long surface lines that operated on almost all of the principal Manhattan avenues.

Herald Square, at the intersection of Broadway, Sixth Avenue, and 34th Street, was one of the busiest points on the New York street railway system. At one time it was claimed that more streetcars passed Herald Square every minute during rush-hour periods than any other street traffic point in the world. A dramatic night drawing by W. H. Crane for *Harper's Weekly* (right) shows horsecar and steam elevated action at the square in 1891. A later scene (above), photographed from the Sixth Avenue El structure about 1900, shows heavy car traffic on Broadway. — *New-York Historical Society (above); Collection of William D. Middleton (right).*

Two stages in history at 42nd Street and Park Avenue. The 19th and 20th centuries mingled in the turn-of-the-century scene at the left. The baroque façade of Commodore Vanderbilt's first Grand Central Terminal still towered over the intersection. A Metropolitan Street Railway electric car waited patiently to follow a horsecar down 42nd Street, and not a motor vehicle was in sight. By 1914 (above) the magnificent new Grand Central Terminal had risen in place of the old. — *Both photos, Library of Congress.*

The last New York trolley was the unusual Queensboro Bridge Railway, a remnant of the Steinway Lines system which once operated an extensive street railway system in Queens. Shuttling over a 1½-mile route between Manhattan and Long Island City, the bridge line provided a convenient service to the city's several public institutions on Welfare Island. In this 1954 photo, one of the former New Bedford (Mass.) Master Unit cars that served the line in its last years rolled high above the East River on its way to the Long Island City terminal. — *F. W. Schneider III.*

Everyone off to the races! Brooklyn Rapid Transit open car No. 2048 disgorged a capacity crowd at Brighton Beach racetrack. — *Collection of Jeffrey Winslow.*

Rush hour over, trolleys of the Brooklyn City Railroad, successor to the Brooklyn Rapid Transit, head into the carbarn during the late 1920's. Delivery of 100 of the front-entrance center-exit cars of this type in 1924 required re-education of a public accustomed to boarding by the rear platform. The distinctive sunburst/spiderweb design in red, yellow, and blue on the front dash identified the new cars. — *Collection of Jeffrey Winslow.*

John Roebling's durable Brooklyn Bridge has been an artery for Brooklyn-Manhattan commuters ever since its opening in 1883. In this view from the Brooklyn end about 1898, steady streams of open trolleys share the bridge with a cable-powered rapid transit train and horse-drawn wagon traffic. — *Library of Congress.*

173

IN the populous areas of northern and central New Jersey, street railway development began, as it did almost everywhere, with a myriad of small local systems. By the late 1890's the usual process of consolidation had grouped most of them into large individual systems serving the chief population centers. Then in 1903 a New Jersey state legislator named Thomas J. McCarter formed the new Public Service Corporation of New Jersey, which began a second round of consolidations that within a single decade had created one of the great North American traction empires. Made up of well over a hundred predecessor companies, the Public Service trolley network ultimately grew to a system of 900 miles of local, suburban, and interurban electric railway track extending to 147 different New Jersey municipalities. Nearly 2500 trolleys operated over the Public Service network, and at the peak of its development the system's cars were transporting over 400 million passengers a year.

A deterrent to the development of street railways connecting Hudson River ferries to New York with communities on the New Jersey side was the towering Hudson River Palisades. One of the first attempts to overcome this obstacle was the construction in 1874 of an inclined plane which hauled North Hudson County Railway horsecars — horses and all — to the top of the Palisades. A cable-powered elevated structure superseded the plane 12 years later, although the latter continued to operate as a public wagon elevator until 1928. The elevated was converted to electric operation in 1892 and remained in service as part of the Public Service system until 1949. Here a trolley climbs the 5½ per cent grade from the Hoboken ferry terminal. — *John Stern.*

Ferries of the New Jersey & Hudson River Railway & Ferry Company transported North Jersey commuters from 125th Street to this terminal at Edgewater, where the company's trolleys waited to take them to Bergen and Passaic county points. Car No. 25 loaded for the Fort Lee line in 1909. — *Collection of Howard E. Johnston.*

Public Service trolleys operating on the Newark-Paterson and Main Street lines rolled through Passaic, N. J., in 1908. A firemen's gathering was the occasion for the firehouse bunting. — *Collection of Howard E. Johnston.*

New Jersey & Hudson River trolleys scaled the Hudson River Palisades from their Edge-water ferry terminal by means of one of New Jersey's most spectacular stretches of trolley track. The original 1896 single-track line, with a switchback halfway up the Palisades, was replaced by double track and this famous horseshoe curve in 1900. Two open cars headed for the top in 1909. — *Collection of Francis J. Goldsmith Jr.*

Newark's famous "Four Corners" at Broad and Market streets, together with several other metropolitan points in the U. S., once claimed honors as the world's busiest trolley intersection. In 1910 (above) as many as 525 streetcars hourly passed through the intersection at the peak of rush period. Trolley traffic was so congested that sometimes as many as 20 cars at a time were backed up. In 1916 Public Service completed one of the world's largest off-street trolley terminals a few blocks away at Park Place, and Four Corners trolley traffic declined to a modest 326 cars an hour during peak periods. A decade or more later, when the Four Corners photo below was taken, intense flivver traffic competed for street space with the still-heavy trolley traffic. — *Collection of Howard E. Johnston (above); Duke-Middleton Collection (below).*

One of the largest New Jersey electric lines to escape the embrace of the sprawling Public Service Corporation was the Morris County Traction Company, which operated some 50 miles of meandering rural trolley line from Elizabeth to the popular summer resorts at Lake Hopatcong in North Jersey. On the way to Dover, the company's No. 2 was photographed beneath the Morris Canal viaduct at Landing, on Lake Hopatcong. A product of the Jackson & Sharp car works, No. 2 was one of a dozen Morris County cars mounted on the six-wheel Robinson Radial Truck. — *Collection of Stephen D. Maguire.*

EVER since the steam railroads made them readily accessible to the masses of New York, Philadelphia, and the large inland New Jersey cities, the beaches of the New Jersey coast have been the objective of throngs of summer visitors. Within the space of about two decades, beginning around 1890, almost every one of the principal Jersey coast resorts got its own little beach trolley line.

One of the principal routes to the beaches around Sandy Hook was the Jersey Central Traction Company. This line connected with Public Service trolleys and ferries from Staten Island at Perth Amboy, and with steamships from New York at several points along Raritan Bay. A crowd rushes for seats on a Jersey Central Traction Company open car at Atlantic Highlands in the summer of 1917. — *Collection of Howard E. Johnston.*

Among the most ill-favored of New Jersey's beach trolleys was the Monmouth County Electric Company, which wandered off from a connection with the Jersey Central Traction Company at Red Bank to the coastal towns of Long Branch and Oceanic (later Rumson). The little line was opened in 1896 and suffered an almost endless series of bankruptcies, carbarn fires, tax sales, and miscellaneous financial reverses before finally folding up for good in 1922. No. 26 is shown in front of the Oceanic Post Office about 1910. — *Collection of Howard E. Johnston.*

A splendid outing for Atlantic City vacationers was the long Atlantic Avenue trolley ride along the ocean shore from Inlet to Longport, on Egg Harbor inlet. Steam dummy operation over the route began in 1884, and electric operation started in 1893. Atlantic City Transportation Company No. 296, a former Fort Wayne (Ind.) car, visited Longport on a 1947 railway enthusiast excursion. Abandonment of the Atlantic City system came at the end of 1955 — *Collection of Howard E. Johnston.*

179

TRACTION EVOLUTION in Philadelphia followed the almost universal big city pattern of development by numerous independent companies and ultimate consolidation into a single massive system. Between 1854 and 1895 no fewer than 66 different street railway companies were incorporated in Philadelphia. By 1895 most of them had been combined into the new Union Traction Company, and in little more than a decade the process of consolidation had been completed by the organization in 1902 of the Philadelphia Rapid Transit Company, which united Union Traction with the city's remaining surface and rapid transit lines into a vast system dominating the entire urban Philadelphia area. A great era of growth began for Philadelphia Rapid Transit in 1911 when financier E. T. Stotesbury assumed control of the system and brought in noted street railway manager Thomas E. Mitten to direct a huge expansion and improvement program. "Mitten Management" extended PRT lines into new areas, reorganized existing routes to provide a more comprehensive service, and brought an enlightened labor relations policy that gave PRT an unprecedented period of labor-management harmony. An entirely new car design — the "Near-Side" car — was developed, and in only 3 years more than 1500 were in operation on the system. By 1923 Philadelphia Rapid Transit had grown into a system operating more than 3000 cars over nearly 700 miles of track and transporting over 900 million passengers a year. Even in 1967 the system, known since 1940 as the Philadelphia Transportation Company, remains one of the principal street railway operators in North America with nearly 500 cars running over 12 routes.

A jam-packed open car of PRT predecessor Union Traction Company rolled down Philadelphia's Frankford Avenue. — *Collection of LeRoy O. King.*

A Philadelphia trolley party group paused during a summer night's outing in 1898 while a local photographer recorded the event on a glass plate negative with a healthy dose of flash powder. The open party car *Defender*, together with the identical cars *Julia* and *Mascot*, was constructed by the Philadelphia Traction Company in its own shops the same year. The company was forced to contemplate discontinuance of party car service after receiving complaints about noise. — *Collection of Andrew W. Maginnis.*

Bound for the Delaware River waterfront, cars of the brand-new Philadelphia Rapid Transit Company headed down the narrow length of Chestnut Street in downtown Philadelphia early in the century. — *Library of Congress*.

Single-truck open car No. 520 of the Philadelphia Rapid Transit rattled along through bucolic scenery in 1909 on the grass-grown, side-of-the-road Doylestown-Willow Grove line. — *Collection of LeRoy O. King.*

THOMAS E. MITTEN

British-born Thomas E. Mitten managed street railway systems at Milwaukee, Buffalo, and Chicago before becoming general superintendent of the nearly bankrupt Philadelphia Rapid Transit Company in 1911. — *Collection of Stephen D. Maguire.*

Streetcars remained the backbone of Philadelphia's mass transportation through World War II. This lineup of Near-Side cars accommodated shipyard change-of-shift crowds at Richmond and Allegheny avenues in Port Richmond. — *Philadelphia Transportation Company, Collection of Richard L. Allman.*

Even the little Birney had a place on the far-flung Philadelphia Rapid Transit. Birney No. 1010 rattled over a
timber trestle near Swarthmore in 1937 on the scenic Fol-
som-Media line. — *Collection of Howard E. Johnston.*

Philadelphia's Luzerne Depot was the city's largest car-barn. (Above) Row upon row of the distinctive Philadelphia-originated Near-Side cars wait for assignments. (Below) In this twilight scene dating from World War II, PCC streamliners and standard cars are readied for the evening rush. — *Collection of LeRoy O. King (above); Philadelphia Transportation Company, Collection of Richard L. Allman (below).*

A unique Philadelphia institution was the Fairmount Park Transit Company, which operated an 8-mile trolley line entirely within the confines of 4000-acre Fairmount Park. The only Philadelphia line never merged into the PRT system, the quaint line was still running its original cars when it closed in 1946 after a half century of operation. One of them crossed Strawberry Bridge over the Schuylkill in 1941. — *John J. Bowman Jr., from F. W. Schneider III.*

The Lehigh Valley Transit Company of eastern Pennsylvania laced the Allentown-Bethlehem-Easton area of the Lehigh Valley with a network of local, suburban, and interurban lines, and joined the region to Philadelphia with its superb "Liberty Bell Route" interurban main line. Two of the company's big suburban cars met at Gauffs Hill Siding on the Allentown-South Allentown-Bethlehem run in 1941. — *Randolph L. Kulp.*

185

The big open cars of the Stroudsburg, Water Gap & Portland Railway did a brisk business transporting summer tourists to Delaware Water Gap resorts. (Above) Two cars load passengers at the trolley terminal in Delaware Water Gap, Pa. (Below) An open trolley parallels Delaware, Lackawanna & Western tracks along the Delaware River as the car heads northward toward the Lackawanna's great concrete arch viaduct near Portland.

Anyone for dancing at Flag Staff Park? Open cars of the Carbon Street Railway met in 1906 at a siding on the rural Mauch Chunk-Lehighton line in the anthracite country of eastern Pennsylvania. — *Collection of Allan H. Berner.*

A Wilkes-Barre (Pa.) Transit Corporation trolley rambled through verdant scenery not far from Glen Alden Colliery on the company's long suburban route to Nanticoke in the summer of 1950. Late the same year, Wilkes-Barre's cars made their last runs. — *John Stern.*

A Conestoga Traction Company trolley rolls down a Lancaster (Pa.) street around 1919. The company operated a network of rural trolley lines throughout much of Lancaster County. — *Collection of William D. Middleton.*

A handsome double-truck car, mounted on an early version of the maximum traction truck, led a three-car lineup in an unidentified dirt street in Lebanon, Pa., around 1900. — *Harry D. Lentz, from Howard E. Johnston.*

Hershey Transit's "Super Birney" car No. 30 was acquired in 1935 from Michigan's Grand Rapids Railway, which had dolled up the car with such extras as skirts and air horns as part of a 1920's experimental program to develop an improved streetcar design. After only a few years at Hershey, the car went on to the all-Birney system of Marion, Ind. — *Collection of Allan H. Berner.*

Among the most delightful of Pennsylvania's numerous country trolleys was the Hershey Transit Company put together by "Chocolate King" Milton S. Hershey to transport workers and milk to his plant in Hershey, a company town founded in 1903. Hershey Transit's One-Spot, an elderly Brill suburban car, traveled the Elizabethtown line in 1941. — *Bert Andersen, from Collection of Jeffrey Winslow.*

Trolleys were getting stiff bus and automobile competition by the time this photograph was taken at Third and Pine streets in Williamsport, Pa., in June 1929. Trolleys were gone from the Susquehanna Valley city by 1933. — *Collection of Allan H. Berner*.

On a summer day in 1939 a Johnstown Traction Company trolley raced along the banks of Stony Creek on an inbound journey from the Benscreek suburban line. The last small city system to run in the U. S., Johnstown Traction bought a fleet of PCC cars at the end of World War II and continued to run street railway service until 1960. — *Jeffrey Winslow*.

Oil City (Pa.) mail carrier and amateur photographer Arthur Cornell snapped a young lady with a bouquet of roses and the crew of Citizens Traction Company open car No. 7 during a layover at the end of the East Second Street line in 1907. — *Collection of Donald K. Slick.*

Tarentum, Brackenridge & Butler Street Railway Company No. 103, a single-truck car of almost interurban proportions, squealed around a curve in the hilly streets of Tarentum, Pa., in the coal country of Allegheny County. — *Bert Andersen, from Collection of Jeffrey Winslow.*

Pennsylvania's picturesque West Penn Railways was one of the few rural trolley systems to survive into recent years. It continued to operate a network of leisurely interurban lines and country trolleys until the early 1950's. One of the big orange cars paused at Vanderbilt one wintry day on a run from Dawson to Connellsville. — *J. J. Young Jr.*

REACHING a peak of over 600 miles of track and more than 1600 cars, the Pittsburgh Railways Company operated one of the half-dozen largest street railway systems in the United States, and undoubtedly afforded Pittsburgh a streetcar service more comprehensive than that of any other North American city of comparable size. Long after the electric cars had to a great extent been displaced elsewhere in America, Pittsburgh remained a trolley-oriented city. With over 400 cars in service on more than 30 lines as late as 1964, Pittsburgh Railways was one of North America's largest surviving traction systems until successor Port Authority of Allegheny County began wholesale abandonments in the mid-1960's.

Inbound from the Carson Street line about 1918, Pittsburgh Railways open car No. 1939 rumbled past the Pittsburgh & Lake Erie depot on its way across the Smithfield Street bridge. — *Collection of LeRoy O. King.*

Pittsburgh Railways was among the first street railway systems to develop a successful low-floor car design that helped to reduce loading and unloading time. The Pittsburgh design utilized wheels only 24 inches in diameter, as well as newly developed small motors. First of the distinctive designs entered service about 1912. Low-floor car No. 4872, shown in special colors honoring Carnegie Tech, was built by St. Louis Car Company in 1923. — *Pittsburgh Railways, from John Baxter.*

The steep Dravosburg hill and an unusually severe snow storm combined to the undoing of these Pittsburgh Railways trolleys on the McKeesport route in 1940. After one car stalled on the hill, 15 more piled up behind it. — *Pittsburgh* Sun Telegraph, *from John Baxter.*

Pittsburgh Railways was one of the first systems to order the PCC car, and ultimately bought 666 of them — a streamliner fleet that was exceeded only by those of Chicago and Toronto. PCC No. 1065, part of a 100-car order delivered in 1937, negotiated the scenic "Horseshoe Curve" between Dravosburg and Lincoln Place on the McKeesport line on a sunny June 20, 1959. — *F. W. Schneider III.*

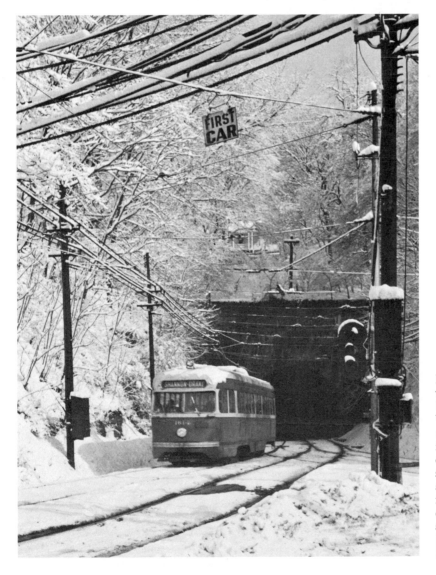

Favored by extensive private right of way and a fast exit from downtown Pittsburgh via the 3500-foot Mount Washington trolley tunnel, a network of Pittsburgh Railways routes provides fast trolley service for suburban residents south of the city. PCC No. 1614, specially equipped with roof headlight, air horn, and pilot for interurban service, emerged from the tunnel on a trip over the Shannon-Drake suburban run, a cutback of a former 29-mile interurban route southwest to Washington, Pa. — *John Baxter.*

Two big Wilmington (Del.) trolleys met at a downtown intersection during the 1920's.
Car at right was a Philadelphia-Wilmington interurban. — *Collection of LeRoy O. King.*

The South Atlantic States

Not a derailment, just a head-on view of a Wilmington "stepless wonder" trolley on the Oak Grove suburban line. Delaware Electric Power Company, which operated the Wilmington street railways, favored extremely low platforms. — *Collection of Allan H. Berner.*

Trolleys were a popular means of transportation for a summer's outing at a local park. A string of Baltimore Traction Company trolleys loaded crowds at Druid Hill Park around 1900. — *Collection of LeRoy O. King.*

A delightful Baltimore trolley outing was a journey aboard Baltimore Transit's big Brill semi-convertible cars on the Ellicott City suburban line. An outbound car (left) rattles through a deep cut near Ellicott City in 1948. A railway enthusiast special (below) rolls across the Patapsco River. — *John Stern (left); William Lichtenstern, from Jeffrey Winslow (below).*

Baltimore was among the earliest systems to order the new PCC car in 1936, and by 1944 had acquired 275 of the streamliners, a fleet that was exceeded in size by those of only a half-dozen U. S. cities. A bright yellow Pullman PCC glided through quiet residential streets on the way to Walbrook Junction in 1961. — *John J. Bowman Jr.*

An early view shows Washington trolleys at Delaware Avenue and B Street N. E. Congressional legislation passed about 1888 required the elimination of horsecars but prohibited the use of overhead trolley wires. The underground conduit system eventually adopted throughout most of the District of Columbia was not perfected until about 1895. — *Library of Congress.*

The first electric cars in Washington, D. C., began operation over the Eckington & Soldiers' Home Railway on October 17, 1888. A crowd gathered around one of the first-day cars at the line's New York Avenue terminal. — *Smithsonian Institution.*

This scene of electric car activity on Washington's Pennsylvania Avenue around 1908 provides an interesting contrast with the earlier view on page 47 of cable car activity from the same vantage point. — *Collection of LeRoy O. King.*

Another view of the cars on the capital city's ceremonial thoroughfare shows the portable wooden platforms used on Pennsylvania Avenue. These platforms could be easily removed for parades. — *Collection of LeRoy O. King.*

One of America's best-known scenic trolley rides was Washington's line from Georgetown to Glen Echo Park and Cabin John, operating over private right of way along bluffs overlooking the Potomac River. Capital Transit's standard car No. 766 was photographed near the Georgetown Reservoir in 1950. — *Herbert H. Harwood Jr.*

202

Late on the evening of January 27, 1962, a lone PCC trolley rolled up Pennsylvania Avenue from the Capitol building. It was the last night for trolleys in the nation's capital. — *Richard J. Solomon.*

The Glen Echo Railroad, an obscure line in Washington's Maryland suburbs, opened a short route between the D. C. boundary and Glen Echo Park in 1890. Scarcely 10 years later the company quietly folded up. No. 5 is shown at the Glen Echo terminal with an open trailer during the early 1890's. — *Collection of LeRoy O. King.*

203

A Richmond (Va.) trolley of the 1890's (above) laid over on the loop at the end of the Forest Hill Park line. Although only a few years had passed since Frank Sprague's triumph of 1888, the city's electric cars had already evolved into larger and more elaborate vehicles than the original Sprague models. In a summertime scene of perhaps a decade later (below), a pair of big open cars waited for passengers at the park. The trees shading the old stone building had grown noticeably larger. — *Both photos, Cook Collection, Valentine Museum, Richmond.*

A shop gang worked over a Richmond Traction Company Broad Street car in 1902. — *Valentine Museum, Richmond*.

Early in the century a big double-truck car of the Virginia Passenger & Power Company rolled past the statue of Gen. Ambrose Powell Hill, CSA, at Genter Park on the Boulevard in Richmond. — *Collection of Charles Goethe*.

By the mid-1920's the Virginia Railway & Power Company, which was operating the Richmond car lines as well as those in Petersburg, Norfolk, and Portsmouth, had fallen on hard times. The new Stone & Webster-managed Virginia Electric & Power Company took over in 1925 and quickly began a massive improvement program that included a fleet of new cars with luxury features such as leather upholstered seats, rubber-tile floors, and mahogany interior trim; wholesale refurbishment of older equipment; and greatly improved services. Within a few years the system had been restored to good health, and its achievements had won it the Charles A. Coffin gold medal. This lineup of new and modernized VEPCO cars was photographed at a Richmond carbarn in 1930. — *Virginia Transit Company.*

Residents of Newport News, Va., rode the trolleys of the Newport News & Hampton Railway, Gas & Electric Company to see World War I-era planes at the Atlantic Coast Aeronautical Station. — *Collection of H. Reid.*

Among the many VEPCO improvements under the new Stone & Webster management was a new line opened at Portsmouth, Va., in 1926 to serve Port Norfolk and Pinners Point. Here is one of the first cars on the line. — *Virginia Transit Company*.

Broad and Main cars carried Richmonders to Idlewood Park. — *Cook Collection, Valentine Museum, Richmond*.

An interurban-type pilot gave this Charleston (W. Va.) Transit Company streetcar of the 1930's an unusually authoritative appearance. Street railway operation in Charleston ended in 1938. — *C. W. Jernstrom.*

A Van Depoele system car of the early 1890's rolls past Atlanta's Southern Medical College on the Inman Park line of the Atlanta & Edgewood Street Railroad. — *Tech Model Railroad Club, M.I.T., from Charles C. Robinson.*

The Birney car was to be found almost everywhere in North America during the 1920's. Two of them rumbled down South Tryon Street in Charlotte, N. C., in 1928. — *Collection of John R. Hickman.*

The unusual stepped-roof design of Savannah (Ga.) Electric & Power Company trolley No. 478 readily identifies the car as one of the standard Stone & Webster-type cars built for the various street railway properties managed by the Boston-based utility firm throughout the U. S. In the background a single-truck Birney "Safety Car," a much more widely used design, heads through the intersection. — *Collection of Allan H. Berner.*

A new Tampa (Fla.) Birney car rattled over the Lafayette Street bridge in the early 1920's. Later Tampa Electric Company expanded its Safety Car fleet with some of the largest double-truck Birneys ever built. — *Collection of Allan H. Berner.*

A J.G. Brill battery car helped promote a real estate development at Everglades, Fla., during the hectic land boom of the 1920's. — *Collection of Stephen D. Maguire.*

The
North Central
States

A steady parade of trolleys rolled down the broad expanse of Cleveland's Superior Street early in the century. The car in the foreground was a Cleveland-Painesville interurban. — *Library of Congress*.

Tom L. Johnson, Cleveland mayor and traction tycoon, and his two sons were all set to hit the campaign trail in 1902 in Johnson's Winton "Red Devil." – *Cleveland Public Library.*

A LEADING FORCE in Cleveland's street railway development and one of the most colorful figures of the traction era was Tom L. Johnson. Johnson was born in Kentucky in 1854 and appeared on the Cleveland scene in 1879 when he purchased the city's Brooklyn Street Railroad and immediately set out to develop the little line into a major system. Johnson had an engaging personality and quickly became a public favorite. A series of flamboyant promotions drew patronage to his horsecar line from rival systems. His shop forces constructed a mammoth snowplow, and whenever snow began to fall Johnson would send the huge rig over the line behind 10 spans of prancing white horses. He bought a baseball park along his line and brought throngs of streetcar riders to the park with such stunts as hiring prize-fighting champion John L. Sullivan to pitch a game. Even more important, Johnson's car line offered excellent service. Other properties were gradually added to the Johnson system; and by the turn of the century, when Johnson retired from business to enter politics, his Cleveland Electric Railway, together with rival Cleveland City Railway backed by Marcus A. Hanna, dominated Cleveland traction.

Johnson was elected mayor of Cleveland in 1901 and won re-election on three successive occasions on a platform of "home rule, three-cent fare, and just taxation." Many of his energies during 8 years as Cleveland's mayor were devoted to securing municipal ownership and operation of the city's street

Top brass of the Cleveland Railway rode over the system in high style aboard parlor car No. 99. – *Collection of Barney Neuberger.*

214

Cleveland's Public Square was a center of street railway operations. A big center-entrance car and trailer loaded passengers in front of the Soldiers' & Sailors' Monument around 1920. — *Collection of Stephen D. Maguire.*

In a scene typical of single-track operation on scores of small city systems, two Lorain (O.) Street Railway Birneys met at a turnout in a quiet residential street during the 1930's. — *C. W. Jernstrom.*

With a band aboard the lead car, this parade of trolleys celebrated the opening of a new rural line of the Mahoning Valley Railway between Niles and Warren, O., in 1902. The photo was taken at the Mason farm, north of Niles. The line later became part of an important eastern Ohio interurban system. — *Collection of O. F. Lee.*

The Northern Ohio Traction & Light Company, one of the state's largest electric railway and power companies, operated street railway systems in Akron, Canton, and Massillon, as well as an interurban railway network in northeastern Ohio. This view was taken at company's Canton carbarn. — *Collection of Stephen D. Maguire.*

railway system. In 1903 the city's two systems were combined into the Cleveland Railway Company, and in 1908 Johnson was finally able to put into effect a plan under which the properties of the Cleveland Railway were leased to the new Municipal Traction Company. His promised three-cent fare was at last established, although many Clevelanders living in outlying areas found they were paying more than before because of supplementary fares for long distances. Partly because of the bitter struggle be-

Zanesville (O.) streetcar riders traveled in style aboard a fleet of these curved-side, single-truck cars from G. C. Kuhlman in Cleveland. — *Collection of Barney Neuberger.*

tween Johnson and the street railway owners, the three-cent fare experiment was unsuccessful; and the municipal system fell deeper and deeper into debt and was finally bankrupt. Following the turbulent years of three-cent fare and municipal operation, the Cleveland Railway was reorganized in 1910 under an unusual "service-at-cost" plan, which succeeded in providing the owners with a reasonable

return while supplying the public with good service and low fares. Stability restored, Cleveland Railway developed into one of the nation's most progressive street railway systems. At the peak of its rail operations in the early 1920's, the Cleveland system was operating approximately 1500 streetcars over some 415 miles of track and was transporting an annual traffic of about 87 million passengers.

Trolleys of the Pennsylvania-Ohio Electric Company load at the Youngstown (O.) Public Square in 1920 (left). Modernization of the Youngstown system during the 1920's took the form of new J. G. Brill Master Unit streetcars, one of which is shown (right) in a publicity photograph taken shortly after delivery of a 13-car order from Brill subsidiary G. C. Kuhlman in 1928. — *Collection of O. F. Lee (left); Collection of Charles Goethe (right).*

City service in many of the smaller Midwestern cities was operated by the interurban companies that passed through them. A Bellefontaine (O.) city car operated by the Urbana, Bellefontaine & Northern Railway turns the corner at Columbus and Main streets on the way from Silver Lake in 1905. — *Collection of Simon E. Herring.*

A Toledo trolley rumbles down Summit Street shortly after 1900. Visitors to the city were encouraged to see Toledo's many industries, parks, and handsome residences from one of the several "Seeing Toledo" trolley trips operated by the Toledo Railways & Light Company. For sightseeing trips around town or into the surrounding countryside over one of the company's affiliated interurbans, large parties could charter the elegant parlor car *Toledo*, complete with luxurious lounge chairs and large plate glass observation windows. — *Library of Congress.*

On a summer afternoon in 1905 a crowd of formally dressed Bellefontaine citizens stroll from the end of the local car line into the grounds of the popular Silver Lake resort. In the distance, a Big Four steam train unloads a similar group. — *Collection of Simon E. Herring.*

With pardonable pride, Laclede Car Company prominently displayed its name in the cast-iron steps at each end of the Cincinnati Street Railway's parlor car *Mahketewah.* Heavy drapes, wicker lounge furniture, plate glass windows, and two ornate observation platforms were features of the car, which was available for charter service in the early days of electric traction in Cincinnati. After a controversy with the telephone company over interference caused by stray return currents, the Cincinnati system installed a second overhead wire for current return. — *Collection of Stephen D. Maguire.*

One of the most incredibly dilapidated street railway properties of the Midwest must have been that of the Lancaster (O.) Traction & Power Company. Roof lines of the company's sagging No. 7, photographed during the late 1930's, betrayed probable horsecar origins. — *Van-Zillmer Collection.*

219

After the interurban system that operated local trolley service in Marion, Ind., abandoned its line in 1932, employees bought the streetcar system and continued to run it as an independent company until after World War II. Single-truck Birney Safety Cars were used exclusively. The company's Birney No. 1 is shown on the Soldiers' Home line. — *Collection of Frank E. Butts.*

A South Bend city car of the Northern Indiana Railway rolls through a trough of snow on its way downtown from the Notre Dame campus. — *Van-Zillmer Collection.*

A unique feature of the Cincinnati street railway system was the Mount Adams incline, which lifted trolley cars a distance of 270 feet by means of counterbalanced platforms. Two Corliss steam engines provided the necessary power. The incline opened in 1877 for horsecar traffic; later it was strengthened for use by electric cars and continued to operate until 1947. In the early view above, a single-truck car operating on the Fountain Square & Eden Park line is shown at the top of the incline. At the left, a curved-side lightweight car built by the Cincinnati Car Company climbs high above the Ohio River Valley in 1937. — *Smithsonian Institution (above); E. A. Seibel, from Collection of Jeffrey Winslow (left).*

A home game for the "Fighting Irish" always taxed the facilities of the South Bend system. This lineup of 37 Northern Indiana Railway cars waited for the crowd at Notre Dame stadium in 1937. — *Van-Zillmer Collection.*

STREET RAILWAY development in Detroit was distinguished by a long-standing battle between proponents of private operation and those of a municipally owned system. A multitude of predecessor companies were combined in 1901 into the privately owned Detroit United Railway which continued to operate until after the First World War. In 1920 the City of Detroit established its own Department of Street Railways and began to build its own car lines. Detroit United resisted the competition briefly but soon saw the handwriting on the wall and sold its entire system to the city in 1922. Municipal trolley operation continued until 1956.

Open cars were popular for summer trolley riding at Detroit in the early years. This view of open-car activity at Cadillac Square dates to about the time Detroit traction was consolidated under the Detroit United Railway in 1901. — *Library of Congress.*

After a brief and unsuccessful fling with Birney car operation, the Detroit municipal system settled on the Peter Witt car as its standard type and bought nearly 700 between 1921 and 1930. No fewer than 8 of them are visible in this 1949 scene of change-of-shift activity at the loading platforms of the Ford Motor Company's great River Rouge plant. — *John Stern.*

Street railway business was never very good on Michigan's upper peninsula, and single track was more than adequate for the trolley traffic on downtown Marquette's Front Street. The Marquette City & Presque Isle Railway provided service between Marquette and the Lake Superior & Ishpeming Railroad ore docks. In the line's last years, wages paid to its employees fluctuated with each day's fare-box receipts. — *Library of Congress.*

Kankakee (Ill.) trolleys didn't do quite the roaring business that this Court Street scene suggests. Evidently to facilitate transfers between lines, trolleys from the Kankakee Electric Railway's several local lines were scheduled to meet on Court Street between East Avenue and Schuyler every 20 minutes. — *Library of Congress.*

1882 he moved to Chicago and soon entered the street railway business; by 1886 he controlled all of the major North Side and West Side car lines. During the next 15 years Yerkes extended and entrenched his hold on the Chicago street railway system. Under Yerkes the city's street railways were unified, principal lines were converted to cable traction, and electrification was begun. Although Yerkes gave Chicago a superb transportation system, his legendary contempt for politicians, stockholders, and the public made him a singularly unpopular figure. Typical of Yerkes' disdain for public opinion was his famous reply to a request that he provide more cars during rush hours. "Preposterous," Yerkes is said to have rejoined. "It is the straphangers that pay the dividends."

Yerkes' devious financial methods created so bewildering a network of construction companies, operating companies, and holding companies that his street railway empire was known as the "Chicago traction tangle." Rival companies were ruthlessly dealt with, and Yerkes callously bought whatever

Elbowing their way through market-district traffic, two Ogden Avenue cars of the Chicago Union Traction Company traveled along Randolph Street between Halsted and Desplaines in 1905. — *Chicago Historical Society.*

CHARLES TYSON YERKES

Philadelphia-born financier and traction magnate Charles Tyson Yerkes assembled the world's greatest street railway empire in Chicago. — *Chicago Historical Society.*

OF the men who rose to positions of power and wealth in the turbulent boom years of electric traction development, the greatest street railway tycoon of them all was Chicago's Charles Tyson Yerkes. Notorious for his skill at financial sleight-of-hand, political bribery, and legislative manipulation, Yerkes was above all a superb organizer and developer and he, more than any other man, was responsible for shaping the greatest street railway empire in the world in Chicago.

Yerkes was born in Philadelphia in 1837 and began his career as a broker in his native city. By 1871 he had the financial life of the city almost entirely within his grasp. The panic which followed the Great Chicago Fire caught Yerkes overextended, and he went to jail on embezzlement charges. In

One of the busiest trolley crossings in Chicago was that at Milwaukee and Chicago avenues. The intersection is depicted with heavy horse-drawn-wagon and trolley traffic about 1910. — *Chicago Historical Society*.

Under the reform ordinances of 1907 both of Chicago's major operating companies were obligated to undertake massive equipment replacement programs. Chicago Railways Company adopted a roomy Pay-As-You-Enter car as its standard type and ordered 1000 between 1908 and 1910. No. 952 was built by Pullman in 1910.—*Smithsonian Institution.*

The commodious Chicago trolleys were great crowd-handlers. This lineup waited near Soldier Field to pile the crowds aboard after a speech by President Harry S. Truman on a cool, sunny April 6, 1946. — *Stephen D. Maguire.*

The Chicago Rapid Transit "L" terminal at 63rd and Halsted produced this scene of co-ordinated electric transportation in 1923. A row of Chicago Surface Lines trolleys and an interurban car of the Chicago & Interurban Traction Company connected with South Side elevated trains. — *Collection of Barney Neuberger.*

politicians he needed to safeguard his interests. In the rough-and-tumble business and political world of turn-of-the-century Chicago, he probably had no alternative.

Yerkes finally met defeat in the late 1890's when he set out to safeguard his long-term interests by attempting to secure legislation extending his street railway franchises for 50 years. A compliant state legislature soon produced the Allen Law, which gave city councils the authority to extend the franchises; but by the time Chicago's so-called "boodle aldermen" met to vote Yerkes what he wanted, a thoroughly aroused public would have none of it. A mob carrying guns and nooses surrounded City Hall, the aldermen got the point, and the measure failed to pass. The following fall the state legislators who had voted for the Allen Law were booted out of office to a man and the law was promptly re-pealed. Despite the alleged expenditure of a million dollars in bribes, Yerkes had been soundly beaten.

Following his defeat, Yerkes sold out his Chicago traction holdings in 1900 and went to London where he headed a syndicate organized to build the city's subway system. Five years later Yerkes was dead.

By 1907 stability had been restored to Chicago traction by a series of ordinances under which the two dominant street railway systems, the Chicago City Railway and the Chicago Railways Company, were granted reasonable franchise provisions. Under a unification ordinance passed in 1913, the two major operating companies were consolidated under the management of the Chicago Surface Lines. By the early 1920's CSL was operating a fleet of nearly 3500 streetcars over a surface lines network of some 1070 track-miles, and it was transporting nearly 1½ billion passengers annually.

Proving that Chicago traction afforded something other than intense urban activity, a Chicago Surface Lines trolley, No. 5337, rattled along rural single track on the Argo (Ill.) suburban line in the summer of 1947. The route was abandoned less than a year after the photograph was taken. — *Van-Zillmer Collection.*

The Illinois Power Company operated an unusually large fleet of single-truck Birneys on its Peoria street railway system. Here Birney No. 440 rattles over the Illinois River on the Illinois Terminal bridge on its way to the Caterpillar plant in East Peoria. The Peoria Birney fleet of 68 cars was built by American Car. — *Paul Stringham.*

Connecting with the Chicago Surface Lines and the elevated system, the Chicago & West Towns Railways operated an extensive service into Chicago's western suburbs. Chicago & West Towns' line car No. 15, a conversion from a veteran trolley of 1897 origin, paced a Baltimore & Ohio Chicago Terminal 2-8-2 on parallel track near La Grange in 1946. — *Gordon E. Lloyd.*

A Rockford (Ill.) trolley rolled down a nearly deserted street into a late-afternoon sun a half century ago. — *Collection of Charles Goethe.*

Westbound near Soldiers Home, a Milwaukee trolley headed for suburban West Allis in 1957. Milwaukee Electric interurbans once shared this private right of way with West Allis cars and the company's overhead power lines. Here a storage track for Milwaukee County stadium special cars has replaced one of the interurban tracks. — *William D. Middleton.*

John I. Beggs

Under the direction of John I. Beggs, a dominant figure in Wisconsin public utility development, The Milwaukee Electric Railway & Light Company assembled a powerful electric railway and power empire that included street railway systems in Racine, Kenosha, and Milwaukee. — *Stein of Milwaukee; State Historical Society of Wisconsin.*

Two Birney cars of the Eastern Wisconsin Electric Company loaded a crowd of passengers on a downtown Oshkosh street early in the 1920's. — *Collection of Frank E. Butts.*

Milwaukee's first trolley began operating in 1890 on the Wells Street line. Ornately decorated No. 41 was one of the first cars to run on Wells Street. — *State Historical Society of Wisconsin.*

Until 1903 the twin cities of Marinette, Wis., and Menominee, Mich., were served by independent traction companies whose cars met at the center of the Menominee River bridge to exchange intercity passengers. After a 1903 merger of the two systems as the Menominee & Marinette Light & Traction Company, cars such as No. 17 supplied an interstate through service. The little single-truck car was notable for a pair of Eclipse Life Guard fenders of generous dimensions and a heating stove — visible inside — of enormous size. — *Collection of Frank E. Butts.*

231

Two Twin City Rapid Transit gate cars ran past the Masonic Temple in Minneapolis in 1908. — *Library of Congress.*

AMONG the major street railway properties of North America there was probably none quite so individualistic as that of Minnesota's Twin Cities. Creation of the great Minneapolis-St. Paul traction empire was largely the work of a single dominant figure — Minneapolis lawyer and real estate dealer Thomas Lowry who first became prominent in the local street railway business when he was elected vice-president and general manager of the Minneapolis Street Railway a few years after its organization in 1873. By the late 1880's Lowry controlled horsecar systems in both St. Paul and Minneapolis

which operated a combined total of over 350 horsecars, about 2000 horses, and more than 100 miles of track. In 1891, soon after the two systems began the costly task of electrification, Lowry merged them into the new Twin City Rapid Transit Company and began an era of unprecedented growth and expansion. Ultimately TCRT grew to a system operating more than 1000 cars over 530 miles of track.

Twin City Rapid Transit individuality was perhaps best expressed in the company's predilection for home-built rolling stock. Having determined early in its career that the products of the standard

During the two winter seasons preceding the opening of the Duluth-Superior interstate bridge in 1897, the street railway systems of the two cities constructed this flimsy-looking trestle between Rice's Point in Duluth and Connor's Point in Superior in order to provide a connecting service between the two cities in competition with the Northern Pacific Railway. Car No. 126 of the narrow-gauge Superior Rapid Transit Company is on the trestle. A ferry made the connection during the navigation season. — *Collection of Wayne C. Olsen.*

232

The standard "gate car" design developed by Twin City Rapid Transit and built in its own shops is represented here by car No. 183 of the Duluth Street Railway, which depended almost exclusively upon TCRT shops for the manufacture of its rolling stock. Exceptionally heavy trucks and body construction characterized the Twin City cars. Both entrance and exit were from the rear platform, which was protected by folding gates under the control of the motorman. No. 183 was part of a 15-car order delivered in 1906. — *Collection of Wayne C. Olsen.*

One of the longest TCRT lines was the Como-Harriet route, which extended from downtown St. Paul through Minneapolis to Lake Harriet. A westbound car is shown at the viaduct in St. Paul's Como Park. The company's 40-mile "Twin City Sightseer" tour included this pleasant ride through Como Park. — *Library of Congress.*

233

In a region noted for the severity of its winter weather, Duluth's great storm of March 1892 is still a celebrated event. While temperatures hovered around the zero mark, winds of gale proportions drove a heavy snow into huge drifts. Communication lines were severed, steam railroads ceased to operate, and the trolleys of Duluth's two-year-old street railway system were stuck tight in the drifts.

The storm's fury is evident in this view (above right) taken at Third Avenue West and Superior Street. (Left) In a scene dating from about 1915, a big gate car bearing the unmistakable lines of Twin City Rapid Transit's Snelling Shops rolls westward on Duluth's Superior Street under more temperate circumstances. — *Both photos, collection of Wayne C. Olsen.*

carbuilders were inadequate to meet the demands imposed by the rigors of Minnesota winters and what it considered to be its own peculiar operating conditions, the company developed its own standard streetcar design and built almost all of its equipment in company shops. Only in its final years of

trolley operation did the Twin City system finally relent when, after careful testing of a sample model, company management determined that the standard PCC streamliner was indeed up to the demands of Twin Cities service and ordered 140 of them from the St. Louis Car Company.

A spectacular Duluth attraction was the street railway company's Seventh Avenue inclined railway, which provided a connection between the car lines on Superior Street, at the foot of the bluff, and an isolated line that served the Duluth Heights residential suburb at the top. The 2970-foot incline, installed almost entirely on a steel superstructure, lifted the two counterbalanced incline cars to a point 500 feet above the lower station. The Hilltop Amusement Hall built at the summit of the incline a year after its 1891 opening is shown on the occasion of an 1893 balloon ascension.—*Collection of Wayne C. Olsen.*

234

The capabilities of TCRT's Snelling Shops were nearly legendary. More than 1200 of the company's standard cars were built almost from the ground up, complete even to trucks in most cases. In 1906, when six express boats were needed for the company's steamer service connecting with the Lake Minnetonka suburban line, Snelling Shops built them. During the 1920's, when TCRT was deeply engaged in the development of lightweight equipment, the separate Light Weight Noiseless Electric Street Car Company was formed which utilized TCRT's Snelling Shops to construct orders for nearly a hundred cars for street railways as far removed as

A Duluth landmark which remains virtually unchanged to this day is the "Point of Rocks" outcropping towering above Superior Street, the city's principal thoroughfare. A westbound car rumbled past it in 1910. On at least one occasion a rock slide from the Point disrupted trolley traffic. — *Collection of Wayne C. Olsen.*

Chicago, Grand Rapids, and Chattanooga. Twin City Rapid Transit cars were among the most meticulously maintained in the entire industry, and every 5 years Snelling Shops took each car apart right down to the underframe and rebuilt it into what was virtually "like new" condition.

A 1938 view from the top of the incline shows Duluth's famous Aerial Bridge and the long sweep of the 9-mile Park Point spit which forms the Duluth-Superior harbor.

The incline car in the foreground was one of two built in 1911 by TCRT's Snelling Shops. Operation of both the incline and Duluth trolleys ended in 1939 — *Herman Rinke.*

235

What was more than likely the smallest interstate trolley line in the U. S. was the obscure Wahpeton-Breckenridge Street Railway, which operated two cars and a little more than a mile of track between its two namesake towns in North Dakota and Minnesota. Car No. 2 is at the Wahpeton terminus. — *Collection of Charles V. Hess.*

Westbound to downtown Des Moines, Ia., an old trolley of the Des Moines Railway approached the Chicago & North Western crossing on Locust Street. The Iowa state capitol is visible in the background. — *Frank E. Butts.*

The last word in Des Moines trolleys was a group of 40 cars delivered in 1931 by Cummings Car & Coach Company at Paris, Ill. One of them, No. 704, travels north on private right of way of the Fort Des Moines suburban line in 1948. — *John Stern.*

Wearing the latest thing in 1921 high fashion, a group of Davenport (Ia.) ladies waited to board a Tri-City Railway & Light Company car at Second and Main streets. A special dash sign invited attention to the new front-end boarding arrangement required for the just-introduced one-man operation. — *Collection of Paul Stringham.*

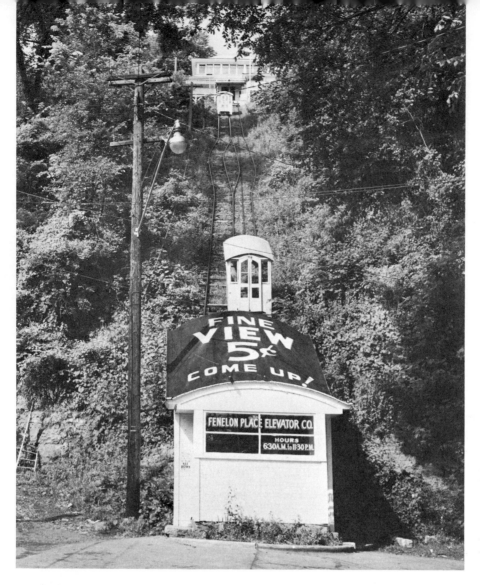

The little incline cars of the Fenelon Place Elevator Co. survive Dubuque (Ia.) streetcars by more than 30 years. The company provides transportation up and down the steep Mississippi Valley bluff that separates a portion of residential Dubuque from the remainder of the city. — *William D. Middleton*.

Union Electric Railway open car No. 71 delivered summer excursionists to the company's Union Park at Dubuque. — *Collection of Barney Neuberger*.

The Omaha & Council Bluffs Street Railway operated local service in both of its namesake Nebraska and Iowa cities, as well as an interstate service between them across the Missouri River bridge. Birney 1502 was one of the last cars to run in Council Bluffs local service, which ended with the interstate service in 1948. — *Frank E. Butts.*

Two early trolleys of the Kearney (Nebr.) Electric Company lined up on South Central Avenue outside the Buffalo County courthouse in the spring of 1891. — *Collection of William D. Middleton.*

The transition from cable operation to electricity often was a gradual one. Around the turn of the century this St. Louis electric car followed a cable car down one of the city's main avenues. — *Collection of Allan H. Berner.*

The Intramural Railway which looped through the grounds of the 1904 Louisiana Purchase Exposition at Forest Park in St. Louis afforded the hometown St. Louis Car Company an ideal opportunity to display its handiwork. Shown on the exposition railway are two trains made up of the distinctive Robertson System semi-convertible cars manufactured by the St. Louis plant. The cars were loaded from floor-level platforms. After the exposition, steps were added and the cars were sold to different street railways. — *Collection of William J. Clouser.*

240

Unusually large windows and the steel section running the length of the car at the base of each side were among the distinctive features of the St. Louis-built Robertson semi-convertible car. This one ran on the Kirkwood-Ferguson line of the United Railways of St. Louis about 1918. —*National Museum of Transport, from William J. Clouser.*

An exceptionally roomy front platform and a businesslike pilot were distinguishing characteristics of the Wichita (Kans.) Railroad & Light Company's trolley No. 201, shown here in 1910. — *Collection of Paul Stringham.*

The
South Central
States

In the 1890's a little open trolley rolled down Main Street in Lexington, Ky. The overhead banner evidently belonged to a political organization that took its name from Lexington's favorite son, John Cabell Breckinridge, who had been a member of the House of Representatives, U. S. Vice-President, proslavery presidential candidate, U. S. Senator, Confederate general, and Confederate secretary of war, in that order. Breckinridge had long since fled the earthly scene when this photograph was taken. — *Collection of William D. Middleton.*

En route to South Fort Mitchell, Ky., a trolley of the Cincinnati, Newport & Covington Railway—the "Green Line" — clears John Roebling's Ohio River suspension bridge of 1866 on the way out of Cincinnati in 1949. — *John Stern*.

The quiet of a summer afternoon in Kentucky was broken briefly by the rumble of a Green Line car crossing the Sleepy Hollow Road trestle at Park Hills on the South Fort Mitchell line. — *John Stern*.

Louisville, Ky., was an early convert to electric traction. In 1889, only a year after Frank Sprague's success at Richmond, the first Louisville trolleys were running on Green Street. By 1895 110 of the city's nearly 150 miles of street railway were operated by electric power. Two of the early electrics, converted from horsecars, are seen at the Highland and Baxter avenues carbarn around 1889 or 1890. Early in the century cartoonist Fontaine Fox was a frequent passenger on Louisville's Brook Street trolley, and the city claimed that the line's dilapidated equipment provided the prototype for Fox's "Toonerville Trolley" comic strip. — *Collection of George H. Yater.*

The ball game is over at Louisville's Parkway Field, home of the American Association's "Louisville Colonels"; and a string of Louisville Railway trolleys swings around the ball park loop to load homewardbound fans. The date: July 1926. — *Louisville Railway Company.*

Lexington's Kentucky Traction & Terminal Company pepped up its local business in 1922 with a fleet of single-truck Safety Cars of the distinctive curved-side design built by Cincinnati Car Company. No. 38 is seen in the colors of successor Municipal Street Railroad & Traction Company in 1929. — *Collection of William D. Middleton.*

A big J. G. Brill center-entrance car of the Chattanooga (Tenn.) Traction Company laid over on the loop at the end of the Signal Mountain line around 1916. Trolleys continued to run in Chattanooga until early 1947. — *Collection of William D. Middleton.*

Louisville Railway was one of many systems that tried the Master Unit car developed by the J. G. Brill Company in the late 1920's. Master Unit No. 100 was photographed in downtown Louisville in 1929. — *Duke-Middleton Collection.*

The most popular of Chattanooga's several scenic attractions was the incline railway journey up Lookout Mountain, where trolleys of the Lookout Incline & Lula Lake Railway took passengers for a 5-mile ride around the top of the mountain. One of the line's cars was festooned with icicles after a storm. *Collection of Alfred E. Barker.*

NATURAL BRIDGE. SUNSET ROCK. POINT LOOKOUT.

Birmingham (Ala.) Electric Company was one of the last operators of the four-wheel Birney car in North America. The Woodward Iron Works of Bessemer Steel provided an appropriate background for a trolley in the "Pittsburgh of the South." Birney No. 2837 worked the Rigby shuttle line in the late 1940's. — *Frank E. Butts.*

Shortly before World War II, Birmingham Electric acquired a number of lightweight cars from defunct electric railway properties and sent them to the Perley A. Thomas Car Works and the St. Louis Car Company for rebuilding into Peter Witt-type cars. Among them were 12 Cincinnati curved-side lightweights from Ohio's Stark Electric Railroad. One is shown on the North Bessemer line in 1951. — *John Stern.*

A New Orleans City Railroad single-truck car of 1898
Jackson & Sharp vintage pauses to load and unload passengers at the corner of Carondelet and Canal streets
around 1900. The car was outbound on the Henry Clay
Avenue route which terminated at the Louisiana Retreat,
an insane asylum. — *Library of Congress.*

The evening rush is over, and rows of trolleys pull into the storage tracks at the Canal carbarn. — *Allan H. Berner.*

One of the greatest of all "streetcar thoroughfares" in North America was New Orleans' celebrated Canal Street. Ever since horsecars of the New Orleans City Railroad Company began operating along Canal in 1861 the broad street has known some form of street railway service. In the great years of electric traction, almost solid rows of electric cars moved up and down the four-track boulevard in the center of the street, and a nine-track layover terminal at the foot of Canal Street accommodated the cars of 20 different lines. The days of glory were largely in the past on a rainy evening in 1959 as a lone trolley, No. 900, waited to depart from Eads Plaza at the foot of Canal Street for the 3½-mile run over the Canal-Cemeteries route. — *F. W. Schneider III.*

Cars running over New Orleans' remaining St. Charles route are repaired and serviced at the Carrollton shops and carbarn. This shop view dates to 1958. — *F. W. Schneider III.*

An unusual characteristic of many New Orleans car lines was the grass-grown "neutral strip" reserved right of way followed by the cars. Trolley No. 832 was inbound on the St. Charles line in the summer of 1958. Still operating, the St. Charles line is America's oldest surviving street railway; it has run continuously since 1835 behind horse, steam, and electric power. — *F. W. Schneider III.*

It was a great day when the Fort Smith (Ark.) Light & Traction Company opened its new line to South Fort Smith. The construction crew was all set to follow aboard the work flat as soon as the dignitaries set out in the semi-convertible car. — *Collection of Charles Goethe.*

While a crowd gathered outside a newspaper office to watch 1914 World Series bulletins, trolleys of the Bartlesville (Okla.) Street & Interurban Railway's Smeltertown line changed ends. — *Collection of Charles Goethe.*

During its last decade of operation, the Oklahoma Railway at Oklahoma City provided a refuge for a variety of modern street and interurban railway equipment from defunct Midwestern traction properties. In this 1946 view, former Flint (Mich.) city car 145 permits former Dayton-Xenia Railway car 234 to pass. — *Gordon E. Lloyd.*

For a number of years the Dallas street railway system was under the management of the Stone & Webster utility firm. A reminder of Stone & Webster days was Haskell Avenue car No. 181, which incorporated the curious stepped-roof design that was a characteristic of the standard Stone & Webster city car. — *George A. Roush.*

253

While waiting passengers looked on from their parked automobiles, a big Brill trolley of the San Antonio Public Service Company moved up a dusty hill on South Walters Street in 1928. Only 5 years later the San Antonio system became one of the first of the larger systems to convert to buses. — *Collection of Allan H. Berner.*

South of downtown Dallas, city cars of the Dallas Railway & Terminal Company and Texas Electric interurbans shared this massive viaduct across the Trinity River flood plain. — *George A. Roush.*

The annual Cotton Bowl game at Fair Park in Dallas brought out this trolley lineup at Second and Parry avenues in 1950 to accommodate the crowds. — *George A. Roush.*

A single-truck open car paused to load passengers on its way up Congress Avenue toward the pink granite Texas state capitol building at Austin sometime around the turn of the century. — *Library of Congress.*

The Mountain States

One of the most profitless street railway ventures surely must have been that in Billings, Mont. Operated with a small fleet of J. G. Brill storage battery cars, the Billings Traction Company opened in 1912. Barely 4 years later the bankrupt system closed. Two of the battery cars are shown on the city's main street. — *Collection of Allan H. Berner.*

A tranquil scene at Sixth and Main streets in Helena, Mont., around 1900 features two little trolleys rolling down a dusty Main Street that has yet to see pavement or motor vehicles. — *Collection of Allan H. Berner.*

By the time it was abandoned in 1951, the municipal trolley system at Fort Collins, Colo., had achieved considerable fame among the traction faithful. The last small-town, all-Birney system in North America, the Fort Collins street railway was run in a decidedly unorthodox manner. At peak periods three cars traveled over the single-track system that was made up of a long loop over Whedbee and College avenues and a route to City Park. All three cars met at a wye on the corner of Mountain and College avenues every 20 minutes, whirled past each other in a flurry of activity, then hummed off in different directions. — *Collection of Barney Neuberger.*

258

The San Francisco Opera Company, appearing nightly at Riverside Park, was a big attraction at Boise, Ida., in 1906. The businesslike motorman of Boise Traction Company semi-open car No. 45 wore leather gauntlets and shirt garters. — *Collection of Henry R. Griffiths Jr., from Donald Duke.*

A busy moment at Arapahoe and 15th streets in Denver. After an unsuccessful experiment with Professor Short's series system electrification during 1885-1886, Denver had a brief fling with cable railways but returned to electrification in 1889. — *Colorado State Historical Society, from Electric Railroaders' Association.*

With relatively few exceptions, Denver Tramways depended upon a local firm, Woeber Brothers Carriage Company, for the manufacture of its rolling stock. Typical of earlier Woeber Brothers cars was 221 built in the late 1890's. — *Collection of Alfred E. Barker*.

This "Seeing Denver" open observation car was popular with Denver tourists shortly after 1900. Operating twice daily from the Brown Palace Hotel, the car provided a 40-mile outing for 25 cents. — *Collection of Donald Duke.*

The final cars constructed for the 3-foot 6-inch Denver system were a group of 50 cars built in the tramway company's own shops in 1922. One of them is seen during the late 1940's. — *Collection of Donald Duke.*

Southbound on Broadway, a Denver trolley rolled past the Colorado state capitol in 1949, a year before the system's abandonment. — *John Stern.*

261

This elongated single-truck car of the Provo (Utah) City Railway worked the Brigham Young University line on a winter day around World War I. Niles delivered two of these to the Provo system in 1914. — *Collection of William D. Middleton.*

Two Phoenix (Ariz.) trolleys met on Washington Street near the state capitol in 1946. At the time of the capitol's construction in 1901, the territorial legislature became involved in a controversy with the street railway company, whose tracks passed through the projected site. Commented the Phoenix *Gazette:* "The Capitol commissioners are determined that the electric streetcar line shall not cross the capitol grounds. The *Gazette* is of the opinion that the legislature will rather like to leave it there as it lets off passengers at the Capitol door. This is especially agreeable during wet weather. . . ." Gen. Moses Sherman, the street railway's promoter, finally relented and moved his tracks. — *Alfred L. Haij.*

At Manitou Springs the CS&I trolleys afforded a connection with the lower station of the cog railway that carried tourists to the summit of Pikes Peak.—*Collection of Donald Duke.*

Trolleys of the Colorado Springs & Interurban Railway provided local service in the resort city as well as a connection with the mineral baths at nearby Manitou Springs. A Birney car headed down the main street in Colorado Springs from the Antlers Hotel early in the 1920's. Beyond, the Rockies dominated the scene.—*Courtesy of Railroad Magazine.*

A big trolley on the East Broadway route of the Spokane (Wash.) Traction Company headed down a still unpaved Main Street in Spokane around 1907. The Washington Water Power Company operated a rival street railway system until 1922, when both systems merged into the Spokane United Railways. — *Collection of LeRoy O. King Jr.*

The Pacific States

A few miles of cable railway continued to run in Tacoma, Wash., long after introduction of electric power. A trolley waited for a cable car to cross Pacific Avenue around 1915. — *Collection of Allan H. Berner*.

California-type car No. 4 of the Seattle Traction Company paused at a street corner on the University line during the late 1890's. Seattle Traction was one of a dozen independent street railways consolidated into the new Seattle Electric Company between 1900 and 1903. — *Washington State Historical Society, from Robert S. Wilson.*

A view of downtown Seattle's Second Avenue early in the century as two trolleys waited at the Yesler Way intersection for a Lake Washington cable car. — *Washington State Historical Society, from Robert S. Wilson.*

Seattle's Alaska-Yukon-Pacific Exposition, held during the summer and fall of 1909 on what is now the University of Washington campus, generated a considerable traffic for the trolleys. This special terminal built on the exposition grounds helped handle the crowds. — *Courtesy of Electric Railroaders' Association.*

Eleven big Seattle Electric Company trolleys made an impressive sight in this 1909 photograph of the company's Jefferson Station carhouse. — *Washington State Historical Society, from Robert S. Wilson.*

A Seattle trolley turned the corner into Jackson Street from Fourth Avenue South about 1913. The traction supremacy of the Puget Sound Traction, Light & Power Company, successor to Seattle Electric, was being challenged by an upstart municipal system, which was to swallow up the entire privately owned system in another 6 years. — *Collection of LeRoy O. King Jr.*

A Portland (Ore.) Traction Company Sunnyside route trolley paused at 33rd and Belmont streets on the Mt. Tabor line in the early 1920's. American Car Company of St. Louis built the semi-convertible car in 1911. The Portland system was constructed to a 3-foot 6-inch track gauge. — *Collection of Gary G. Allen.*

ONE of the finest scenic trolley rides in all North America was that afforded by the Portland Traction Company's route to Portland Heights and the wooded park at Council Crest, located nearly 1000 feet above the level of downtown Portland, Ore. Trolley excursionists to Council Crest Park were treated to a magnificent view of the Willamette and Columbia river valleys, virgin forests stretching toward the horizon, and the snow-capped summit of Mount Hood. Traction service part of the way up the Heights began in 1890 with the opening of a cable railway. The electric line to the summit which replaced the cable operation in the summer of 1904 required curves and grades of extraordinary severity. Grades as steep as 12 per cent were necessary at several points, and the cars passed through no fewer than 67 curves. The big Brill semi-convertible cars operated were specially equipped with magnetic brakes, and at several points the line was provided with safety derails designed to harmlessly bring the cars to a halt on the ground should a descending motorman fail to make the required safety stop. Despite the exceptional safety precautions, the line experienced several serious runaways. The trunk of one particular tree at South West 18th Avenue and Elizabeth Street had to be filled with cement during the 1930's after twice resisting the onslaught of runaway cars. Trolley operation to Council Crest ended in 1949, a year before all Portland city cars quit running.

The Council Crest views on this and the following page convey some idea of the attractiveness of Portland's famous scenic trolley ride. A Brill semi-convertible labors upward through the wooded park near the Council Crest summit. — *Alfred L. Haij.*

269

A car has halted on the west side of the Council Crest loop to permit its passengers to admire the view of the Tualatin Valley. — *Alfred L. Haij.*

In Council Crest's last year of operation an aging Brill trolley descending from the summit passed elegant Portland Heights residences. — *John Stern.*

The 11,920-foot Twin Peaks tunnel, opened in 1918, sped Municipal Railway service to southwestern San Francisco. Still in service, the tunnel is used by three of the five remaining Municipal Railway lines. Car 206, outbound on the Ingleside line, met streamliner 1004 at the south portal in 1951. — *William D. Middleton.*

TRACTION DEVELOPMENT in San Francisco was considerably more turbulent than in most other cities of comparable size. The city's extensive cable railroad system, operated by a number of independent companies, provided the backbone of San Francisco street railway service well into the current century. A slow transition to electric power was hastened by the events of that fateful day in April 1906 when the great San Francisco earthquake and fire smashed the cable system into ruins. Many of the cable lines found their conduits so badly damaged or clogged by debris that it was far more expedient to string trolley wire than to attempt the restoration of cable service. Much of the city's rolling stock — both cable and electric — was destroyed

in the flames, and the order books of the St. Louis Car Company were soon fattened by a contract for 200 new electric cars for the United Railroads of San Francisco. Another 50 cars under construction for the Chicago City Railway at the American Car Company plant in St. Louis were diverted to the San Francisco system to help replace fire losses. The United Railroads (succeeded by the Market Street Railway Company in 1923) became the principal San Francisco system during the era of consolidation and electrification after the turn of the century. United Railroads' dominance was challenged, however, by the new Municipal Railway of San Francisco, which was created by a 2-million-dollar bond issue in 1909. The first Muni line was opened on

The Ferry Building at the foot of Market Street was the center of San Francisco traction activity throughout almost the entire street-railway era. A two-car Market Street Railway train from the Valencia Street line swings around the loop in the Embarcadero in front of the Ferry Building. The cars were part of the 200-car order received from St. Louis in the aftermath of the 1906 fire. — *Collection of Jeffrey Winslow*.

Geary Street in 1912, with Mayor James Rolph Jr. at the controls of the inaugural car. Subsequent construction extended Municipal Railway service throughout most of metropolitan San Francisco. Although an effort at municipal acquisition of the Market Street Railway system was made as early as 1925, operation of the two rival systems continued until 1944, when the Market Street Railway system was finally purchased and merged with the Municipal Railway. Complete consolidation of San Francisco street railway service was not realized until 1952, when the privately owned California Street Cable Railroad, bankrupt and strikebound, finally became part of the municipal system.

Two ornate San Francisco electrics of the pre-earthquake era met at 30th Street and San Jose Road in 1893 on the run between the Ferry Building and Holy Cross Cemetery via Union Park (now Union Square). Although trolleys were beginning to appear on a few suburban runs such as this one, the cable railways would continue to reign supreme almost everywhere in the city until after San Francisco's shattering catastrophe of April 1906. — *Collection of Alfred E. Barker.*

A four-wheel California car of the Presidio & Ferries Railroad is about to depart from the Ferry Building for the Presidio via Union Street. A former cable line, the Presidio & Ferries converted to electric operation following the 1906 earthquake and fire. The line was taken over by the Municipal Railway in 1913. — *Collection of Charles Smallwood, from LeRoy O. King.*

A four-track trolley artery on San Francisco's Market Street supported what was claimed to be the heaviest street railway traffic in the world. Cars of the Market Street Railway used the two inner tracks while the outer tracks were employed by the municipal system. In 1929 the two systems were operating a combined total of over 4200 cars a day in each direction on the lower end of Market between Sansome Street and the ferries. A year after the Market Street system's 1944 merger into the Municipal Railway, declining trolley operation permitted a reduction to two tracks. — *Collection of Charles Smallwood, from LeRoy O. King.*

An unusual feature of the San Francisco street railway scene was the Market Street Railway's combination cable-trolley line on Fillmore Street. To negotiate two blocks of 24 per cent grade, the cars were attached to a cable system. The cable was unpowered, and the cars operated under electric power, with a descending car counter-balancing an ascending one. — *Collection of Gilbert H. Kneiss (above); R. Demoro, from Railroad Magazine (below).*

The venerable *San Francisco* began its long career as a United Railroads funeral car early in the century. It was used later as a parlor car, and finally was assigned to school and charter service. The car is seen here on a 1948 railway enthusiast excursion on the San Mateo line. — *Alfred E. Barker.*

Trolleys and cable cars shared four tracks in San Francisco's Columbus Avenue until the Municipal Railway's Stockton Street line was abandoned in 1951. In this prewar view, Muni "Magic Carpet" car No. 1002, a 1939 streamliner of modified PCC design, meets a Powell and Mason cable car of the Market Street Railway near the Crystal Palace Baths. — *Gerrard Graham, from Railroad Magazine.*

Among the earliest electric railways in the East Bay area of San Francisco Bay was the Oakland, San Leandro & Haywards Electric Railway Consolidated. The company's No. 100, the first electric locomotive on the Pacific Coast, was designed and built in the railway's own shops in 1893. — *Collection of Erle C. Hanson.*

A busy moment in downtown Oakland about 1906. By this time Oakland transit had come under the control of borax millionaire Francis Marion Smith, who had pyramided his mining fortune into a great East Bay real estate and transportation empire. By 1912 he had merged virtually all East Bay street railway properties into his giant "Key System" traction empire. — *Collection of Donald Duke.*

Key System trains met at Macdonald Avenue and 23rd Street in Richmond in 1920. The car at the left was one of 18 cars acquired secondhand from Pennsylvania's Lehigh Valley Transit Company in 1904 and known thereafter as "Lehighs." — *Collection of Erle C. Hanson.*

Rush-hour passengers in Richmond, Calif., board a lineup of California cars and an open trailer on Macdonald Avenue at the East Shore & Suburban Railway's 17th Street trolley terminal in 1907. — *Collection of Erle C. Hanson.*

Motorists and trolley riders stroll in the countryside near Santa Cruz, Calif. In the background is an electric car of the Union Traction Company. — *Collection of Charles Smallwood, from LeRoy O. King.*

To comply with franchise requirements, Central California Traction Company, which operated a 53-mile interurban railway between Sacramento, Lodi, and Stockton, was obliged to provide local trolley service over its interurban trackage between Eighth and J streets and the Colonial Heights section of Sacramento. No. 105 worked the run in 1910. — *Collection of Alfred E. Barker.*

Narrow-gauge trolley No. 27 lays over at the Alum Rock Park terminal of the San Jose & Santa Clara Railway. The 8-mile line from San Jose to the park was opened in 1896 as a steam dummy line. — *Collection of LeRoy O. King.*

Two Stockton Electric Railroad trolleys rolled down Main Street around 1925. The slatlike fenders on all sides of the cars were a safety device common to many California lines. — *Collection of Gary G. Allen.*

Double- and single-truck Birneys of the Fresno Traction Company breasted heavy flivver traffic on Fulton Street in downtown Fresno during the late 1920's. The 42-mile system was one of the Southern Pacific Company's many electric subsidiaries. — *Collection of LeRoy O. King.*

Seven of these center-entrance semi-convertible cars, delivered by J. G. Brill about 1911, supplied all trolley service to the Spanish-founded city of Santa Barbara, Calif. — *Collection of Gary G. Allen.*

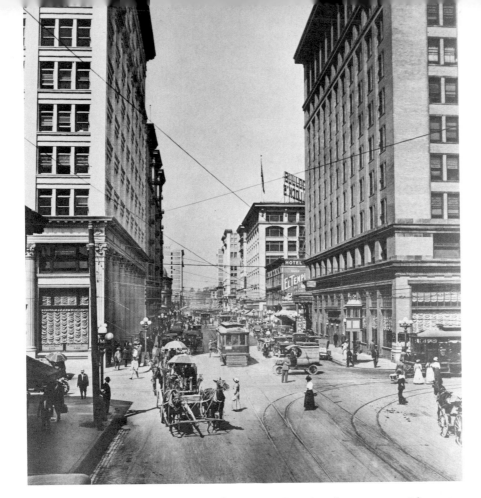

Horse-drawn wagons still shared downtown Los Angeles streets with motor vehicles and trolleys in this scene at Seventh and Spring streets around 1915. — *Title Insurance & Trust Company, Los Angeles.*

DURING the boom years of the 1890's and the first decade of the new century, Los Angeles became the center of an unrivaled Southern California electric railway network. The earliest efforts at the development of a consolidated Los Angeles street railway system were made in the early 1890's by financiers Eli P. Clark and Gen. Moses H. Sherman, who had developed the extensive Los Angeles Railway system before the turn of the century. Rivaling the Sherman-Clark system was the powerful Los Angeles Traction Company formed by Midwestern banker William S. Hook. As the two systems struggled bitterly for traction supremacy, a new figure appeared on the scene in 1898 in the person of Henry E. Huntington, the wealthy nephew of the Southern Pacific's Collis P. Huntington. Backed by SP money, Huntington soon swallowed up both rival systems and set in motion a vast construction program that was to lace all of Southern California together with a great electric railway network. Two closely allied properties whose development was always carefully co-ordinated with the comprehensive Huntington real estate interests made up the great Huntington empire. Street railway operation in Los Angeles itself became the almost exclusive province of Huntington's Los Angeles Railway, while his Pacific Electric Railway assembled a huge

HENRY E. HUNTINGTON

Traction tycoon Henry E. Huntington shaped an incomparable Southern California trolley empire. — *Historical Collections, Security First National Bank, Los Angeles.*

interurban network radiating from Los Angeles with extensive local operations in the cities reached by its interurban lines. By the time Henry Huntington retired from active management of his traction properties in 1910, the "Huntington System" represented the world's greatest electric railway empire.

279

Pacific Electric trolleys on Santa Monica Boulevard waited for cross traffic in 1922. — *Historical Collections, Security First National Bank, Los Angeles.*

At the peak of its rail operations in the late 1920's the narrow-gauge Los Angeles Railway operated 1250 cars. Type "H" car No. 1238, a steel-bodied California type, represented the last word in LARy trolleys of the period. St. Louis Car Company delivered 250 between 1921 and 1924. Multiple-unit controls permitted train operation. — *Collection of Gary G. Allen.*

Between 1937 and 1948, Los Angeles Railway and its successor, Los Angeles Transit Lines, acquired 165 PCC streamliners. One of 40 built by St. Louis Car Company in 1948 lays over on the Pico line. — *Donald Sims.*

280

Around 1912 the trend to the hobble skirt put pressure on the Los Angeles Railway to develop a "stepless" car that would facilitate tight-skirt boarding and alighting. The company's South Park shops experimentally rebuilt an old car into a drop-center center-entrance car. An additional 106 old cars were similarly rebuilt, and St. Louis Car delivered another 76 — all known as "sow-bellies." In 1946 sow-belly 51 rolls along on the "A" line. — *Donald Duke*.

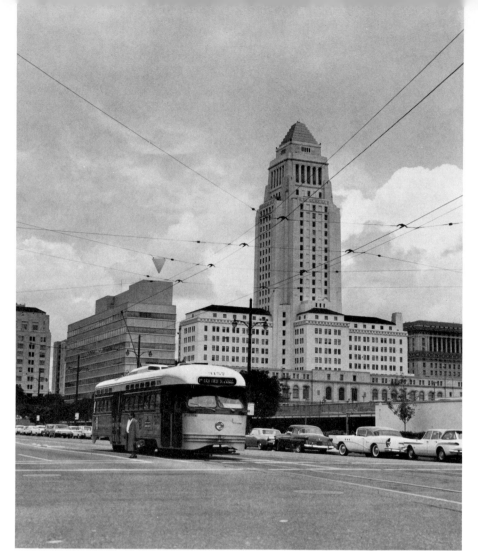

In the declining years of Southern California rail operation, the two Huntington traction properties were finally united in 1958 under ownership of the Los Angeles Metropolitan Transit Authority. Former LATL PCC No. 3157 wears the Authority's green and white colors not far from the Los Angeles City Hall shortly before the end of all Los Angeles electric railway service on March 31, 1963. — *Donald Duke.*

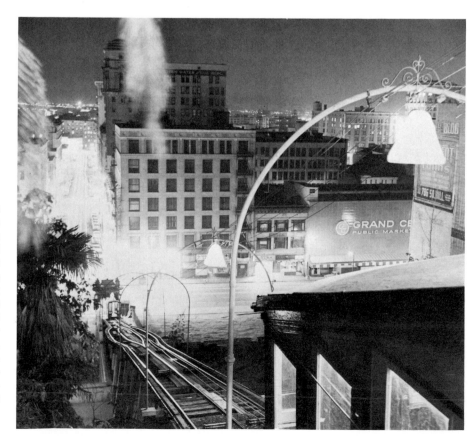

In 1967 a lonely remnant of the traction era still clung to the side of Bunker Hill in downtown Los Angeles as the orange and black incline cars of the Angel's Flight Railway continued to shuttle between their terminal at Third and Hill streets and the top of the hill. The 335-foot, 33 per cent grade cable railway opened on New Year's Eve 1901. By 1967 Bunker Hill urban renewal threatened its future. Illuminated Christmas bells decorated the line's overhead arches on a December evening in 1964. — *William D. Middleton.*

282

Two double-deckers and a single-truck California-type car congregate at the corner of Fifth and H streets in San Diego about 1893 — *Collection of Frederick W. Reif, from Eric Sanders.*

JOHN D. SPRECKELS

San Francisco sugar and shipping magnate John D. Spreckels invested heavily in the future growth of San Diego — most notably in the city's street railway system. — *Historical Collection, Union Title Office, Title Insurance & Trust Company, San Diego.*

San Diego's trolley builders pushed their lines far out into open countryside, confident that real estate booms would not be far behind. The Adams Avenue line opened in 1907. — *Collection of Charles Smallwood, from LeRoy O. King.*

By 1912 downtown San Diego had developed a decidedly metropolitan air. The big California-type cars were recent products of the San Diego Electric Railway's own shops. — *Collection of Eric Sanders.*

Beginning with a 24-car order in 1912, the center-entrance trolley became a popular San Diego car type. Additional orders in 1913-1914, delivered in time to accommodate the heavy traffic to the 1915 Panama-California Exposition in San Diego's Balboa Park, increased the center-entrance fleet to more than 100 cars. Two-car trains loaded racetrack crowds on M Street about 1916.— *Collection of R. V. Dodge, from Eric Sanders.*

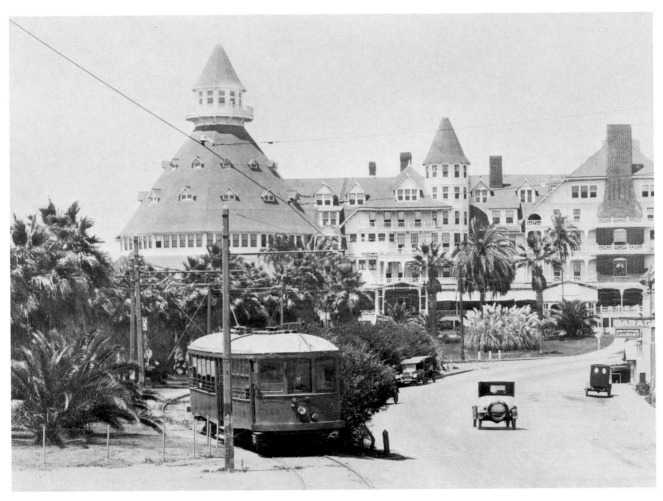

Outwardbound to the Coronado "tent city," a center-entrance car left the grounds of the Hotel del Coronado about 1920. — *Collection of R. C. Brandt, from Eric Sanders.*

San Diego Electric Railway completed a magnificent new interurban line to Mission Beach and La Jolla in 1924, long after electric railway construction had virtually ceased elsewhere. Fifty new lightweight cars were ordered from the American Car Company to operate the service. Multiple-unit controls permitted operation of the cars in trains of as many as six cars. Pantographs were fitted for current collection from the catenary overhead system. Car No. 435 is shown at the mission-style terminal at La Jolla in June 1925. — *Historical Collection, Union Title Office, Title Insurance & Trust Company, San Diego.*

Until the end of electric car service in 1949, San Diego trolleys coursed through the city's Balboa Park on private right of way. No. 426 rumbled over one of the park line's high steel trestles in 1948. — *Donald Duke.*

An inbound interurban train from Ocean Beach passed two city cars at Third and Broadway in downtown San Diego about 1925. — *Historical Collection, Union Title Office, Title Insurance & Trust Company, San Diego.*

Not the least of the many Balboa Park attractions was this outdoor pipe organ, donated by San Diego traction tycoon John D. Spreckels. Following a dedication concert on New Year's Eve 1914, President Woodrow Wilson pressed a button in Washington that formally opened the Panama-California Exposition in Balboa Park. — *Historical Collection, Union Title Office, Title Insurance & Trust Company, San Diego.*

The San Diego system was among the first street railways to adopt the PCC streamliners, with orders for 28 cars delivered in 1937-1938. Two are shown at the Santa Fe depot in 1948. Following the end of San Diego trolley operation in 1949, 20 of the PCC cars were sold to the El Paso City Lines. — *Donald Duke.*

A King Street car of the Honolulu Rapid Transit crosses a bridge over Nuuanu stream. The car was one of eight convertible cars featuring the Duplex Car system of windows and side panels which slid up into the roof to convert to open cars. — *Bernice P. Bishop Museum, Honolulu.*

Honolulu street railway service was inaugurated in 1888 by mule cars of the British-financed Hawaiian Tramways, Ltd. The firm failed to modernize its service and was crowded out soon after 1900 by the U. S.-backed Honolulu Rapid Transit & Land Company. HRT&L 33 is shown on Hotel Street near Iolani Palace. — *Bernice P. Bishop Museum, Honolulu.*

During the early years of Honolulu traction, cars were lined up for a company photograph at the Alapai Street car-barn. Company offices were to the left, the powerhouse was in the rear. — *Collection of Robert A. Ramsay.*

Boat day at Honolulu's Fort Street docks brought a line-up of cars and carriages. — *Collection of Roy S. Melvin.*

Honolulu trolley crews were elegantly attired in the early days. — *Bernice P. Bishop Museum, Honolulu.*

Inbound from the Queen Emma Street line, a Brill open car rolled down King Street on a summer afternoon around 1920. — *Collection of Robert A. Ramsay.*

Peter Witt No. 2790 paused at the intersection of Adelaide and Bay streets in Toronto in 1927. To the north is the City Hall tower. — *Toronto Transit Commission.*

Traction in the North Country

ALTHOUGH street railway development in Canada closely paralleled that in the United States, there were nonetheless a number of distinguishing features to Dominion traction.

Some of the most intriguing differences were in matters of rolling stock. Early Toronto cars, for instance, were constructed with a removable right-hand side. When balmy summer weather arrived, side paneling was removed from the one side, open car running boards were fitted, and the longitudinal seating used during winter operation was replaced with transverse benches. In order to provide a wider car than would ordinarily have been possible with the narrow 3-foot 6-inch "devil strip" that was the standard clearance between Toronto tracks, the cars were mounted 2½ inches off center on their trucks and a 2-inch rake was introduced in the devil strip side to ensure adequate clearance in the event of sidesway.

The stepped open-air sight-seeing car, developed in the shops of the Montreal Street Railway in 1905 and subsequently adopted by the car lines of Quebec, Vancouver, and Calgary as well, was a uniquely Canadian institution. Calgary's "Scenic Car," as it was called, was particularly unorthodox in decoration. Plate glass mirrors made up the side paneling.

Montreal's special prison trolleys were well known, and the Edmonton (Alta.) Radial Railway provided what was probably the only trolley library in North America. An old streetcar, fitted out with shelves, wandered about the city dispensing library books in a manner similar to that of the present-day "bookmobile." During the summer months Toronto ran special "free bathing" cars. Chartered by the city, the cars operated over principal routes in the city to transport children free of charge to Sunnyside Beach on Lake Ontario.

A few Canadian systems, among them those of Saint John, N. B., and Vancouver and Victoria, B. C., originally were compelled to run according to the British left-hand rule then in force in their respective cities. When the change was finally made to right-hand operation, the trolley companies were obliged to spend substantial sums in rebuilding the door arrangement of their cars.

The severity of winter weather in the north country introduced a number of difficult operating conditions for the Canadian traction systems. The most general problem, of course, was that of snow removal, which proved to be no easy task in cities where annual snowfalls of 100 inches or more were common and as much as 20 inches sometimes fell in a single night. Extreme low temperatures created still other winter operating problems. To maintain some degree of passenger comfort, Canadian trolleys tended to be somewhat heavier in construction and were usually better insulated. Coal-fired hot water heating systems were often employed in older trolleys operated in some of the prairie cities. In Edmonton, for example, a heating stove and coal pile were carried on the front platform.

In Winnipeg, where temperatures of 35 degrees below zero or even colder were not uncommon, contraction of the running rails sometimes left gaps of an inch or more at the rail joints. Track crews then hurried out to place small filler pieces of rail, called "flying Dutchmen," in the open joints. If a sudden rise in temperature caught the track men unprepared and the fillers were not removed, humping or spreading of the rails was the usual result.

Perhaps because of the severe winter operating conditions, which made conversion to motorbus service less attractive, as well as the somewhat slower trend to private automobile ownership in Canada, Canadian traction systems survived considerably longer than most of their U. S. counterparts, and extensive abandonment of street railways did not begin until after the end of World War II.

St. Catherine Street, shown here in the late 1930's with a steady parade of trolley and automobile traffic, was one of downtown Montreal's principal trolley thoroughfares. Fashionable shops and restaurants lined the street. — *Canadian Pacific Railway*.

Two Montreal trolleys, painted in the red and cream livery reserved for front-entrance cars, rolled past Canadian Pacific Railway's 1888-1889 Windsor Station in the summer of 1956. — *Jim Shaughnessy.*

In a setting more Continental than North American, Montreal trolley car 1974 rolled through Rue St. Jacques on the Rosemont line in 1957. Indirect dash lighting was a distinctive Montreal feature. — *Theodore M. Meyers.*

THE greatest street railway system in Canada was that of the Montreal Tramways Company, which at its peak comprised nearly 300 miles of track and more than 1000 cars. Even as late as 1944 the Montreal system was transporting nearly 300 million trolley passengers a year. In matters of equipment the Montreal system was at once one of the most individualistic and the most advanced properties in North America. In the early years of electric traction, Montrealers were treated to car types such as the "Klondyke," so nicknamed in reference to its large size, the inference being that the streetcar company was trying to "strike it rich" with cars that could pack in more revenue passengers. At about the same time, another new type of car became popularly known as the "Scotch Cars," since they were an adaptation of a design used in Glasgow, Scotland. Soon afterward still another new model was dubbed the "Windsor Airs," evidently in reference to their operation on Windsor Street.

In 1905 two Montreal Street Railway officials, Messrs. Ross and McDonald, developed the "Pay As You Enter" car design, which greatly improved

fare collection and safety, and speeded boarding and alighting. The first P.A.Y.E. car was built in the company's own shops the same year, and a short time later the design was widely adopted by street railway companies throughout North America. In 1907-1908 the company became the first street railway to operate all-steel equipment when it received 10 new steel cars from the Pressed Steel Car Company of Pittsburgh.

The Montreal street railway system operated under some of the most severe conditions found in North America. The hilly terrain characteristic of parts of the city required grades as steep as 11 per cent. Few cities of comparable size were subjected to winter weather equal to that of Montreal, which had an average annual snowfall of 115 inches. Only a limited number of main thoroughfares were available for street railway tracks in the downtown area, resulting in exceptionally intensive trolley traffic. On some, streetcars ran on headways as short as 24 seconds, and over 400 cars an hour passed through such key intersections as St. Catherine and Bleury streets during rush-hour periods.

293

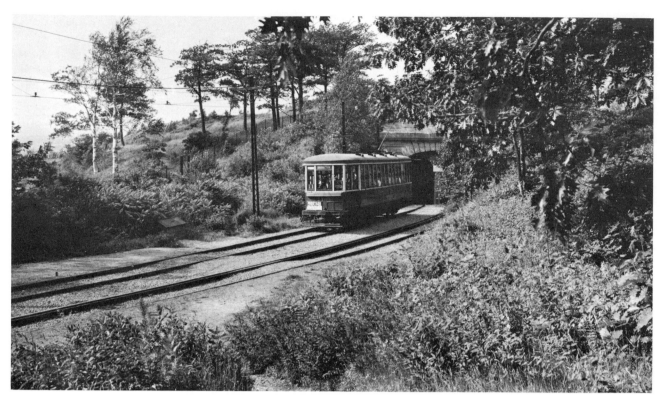

In 1956 a trolley emerges from the 338-foot tunnel that pierced a ridge near the top of Mount Royal on Montreal's Mountain line. Gradients as steep as 10 per cent necessitated dynamic braking. — *Herbert H. Harwood Jr.*

Canadian Car & Foundry built two 90-seat "duplex" articulated cars for Montreal Tramways in 1928. The design, not very successful, was not repeated and plans for a "triplex" car were shelved. — *Collection of Frank E. Butts.*

294

Bound for Lachine, a Montreal car raced under Canadian Pacific tracks near Ville La Salle. — *Jim Shaughnessy.*

Ottawa was the second city in the Dominion to receive year-round electric car service when the Ottawa Electric Street Railway opened in June 1891. The inaugural run along Albert Street was attended by more than 100 Otta-wa dignitaries. Upon arrival at the Exhibition Grounds the party was served a luncheon laid on a 95-foot table. Car No. 7 and a trailer are shown on the South Ottawa line in the 1890's. — *Collection of Charles C. Robinson.*

Surely no trolley ever surpassed Ottawa's magnificent *Duchess of Cornwall and York*, which was specially constructed by the Ottawa Car Manufacturing Company for a 1901 visit to the Dominion by the Prince of Wales and the Duchess — the future King George V and Queen Mary. Interior appointments included upholstered armchairs and potted palms. The car is shown at the corner of Bank and Wellington streets. — *Both photos, Ottawa Transportation Commission.*

A pleasant Ottawa diversion was the trolley ride over private right of way on the Britannia line to company-operated Britannia Park. No. 830 was westbound on the line in 1956. — *Herbert H. Harwood Jr.*

Streetcars remained the principal means of public transportation in Ottawa until well into the 1950's, and trolleys still passed through Confederation Plaza on close headways at the time of this 1951 photo. Street railway operation ended in 1959. — *John Stern.*

The last "standard" streetcars constructed in North America were four cars built for the Ottawa Transportation Commission by the Ottawa Car Company in 1948.

"Noiseless" trucks were applied under the cars. No. 1001 passed through Confederation Plaza on the Bronson line soon after delivery by the builder. — *J. William Vigrass.*

Until 1950 the Sudbury-Copper Cliff Street Railway operated several suburban lines from Sudbury, Ont., to neighboring mining communities north of Georgian Bay. Trolley No. 30, running on the refinery shuttle, transferred passengers to Sudbury-bound No. 31 at Copper Cliff Junction. Both were ex-Schuylkill (Pa.) Railway cars built by Brill in 1918. — *Frank E. Butts.*

Typical of Canadian small city systems was Quebec's Sherbrooke Railway & Power Company, operated throughout its existence exclusively with single-truck equipment. No. 19 was one of four single-truck cars built in 1911 by the Ottawa Car Company. A few years later the railway built some cars of advanced design in its own shops, then soon afterward converted to all-Birney operation. Buses took over in Sherbrooke in 1931. — *Collection of Gerard Auray.*

Gaily decorated in celebration of Queen Victoria's Diamond Jubilee, a Toronto Railway open trolley and trailer traveled along Sherbourne Street in 1897. — *Toronto Transit Commission.*

SECOND in size only to the great Montreal system was the street railway network of Toronto, which operated a system of well over 250 track-miles and more than 1000 cars. Initial electric traction development in the city was carried out by the privately owned Toronto Railway Company. The company's operations were confined to the city's 1891 city limits; and in order to provide service to the growing Toronto suburbs, the municipal Toronto Civic Railway was organized in 1911 to construct car lines which extended beyond the end of Toronto Railway lines into the newer suburban districts. The privately owned system was purchased by the city in 1921 and merged with the Civic Railway under the new Toronto Transportation Commission.

Under TTC management the Toronto street railway system was developed into what was unquestionably the finest property in the Dominion. Under a massive rehabilitation program during the first

5 years of Commission operation, some 90 miles of track extensions were constructed and nearly 60 miles of track rebuilt. At the height of the work a track force of some 3500 men was employed. Between 1921 and 1923 TTC purchased 575 new steel cars and trailers and sent nearly 500 old trolleys to scrap.

A second equipment modernization program was begun in 1938 when TTC placed an order for the first of a fleet of PCC streamliners which grew to a total of 540 cars by 1951. During the next 6 years another 205 cars were acquired on the secondhand market from street railways in Cincinnati, Cleveland, Birmingham, and Kansas City to assemble the greatest trolley streamliner fleet in all of North America. Except for car lines and equipment rendered surplus by Toronto's expanding rapid transit system in the last decade, virtually the entire Toronto trolley network remains in service today.

During the first few years of TTC operation, nearly 500 obsolete trolleys were sold for junk as a new fleet of steel cars entered service. In 1923 Eglinton Yard was jammed with surplus cars. — *Toronto Transit Commission.*

On a 1952 excursion, Peter Witt car No. 2666 paused on the loop at historic old Queen's Wharf Lighthouse, which once guided mariners into Toronto Harbor. — *Paul Ziegler, from Railroad Magazine.*

An order for 100 all-electric PCC's from Canadian Car was added to the TTC fleet in 1949. They came equipped with multiple-unit controls for operation on heavily traveled routes. — *Toronto Transit Commission.*

An unusual feature of TTC operations was a ferry service across Toronto Harbor to Centre Island, where picnic grounds, beaches, an amusement park, and summer cottages were located. (Right) TTC steamers *John Hanlan* and *Clark Brothers* prepare to leave for the island in the spring of 1928. (Below) Bathers enjoy the beach on the north shore of Centre Island. — *Both photos, Toronto Transit Commission.*

From almost the beginning of Toronto Transportation Commission operation in 1921 until after World War II, Peter Witt cars were the backbone of the Toronto trolley fleet. Peter Witt No. 3014, one of 60 received from Canadian Car & Foundry in 1923, worked the heavily traveled Yonge Street line in 1932. — *Toronto Transit Commission.*

Winnipeg Electric Company trolley No. 808, rolling down the broad expanse of the Manitoba city's Portage Avenue, bore the characteristic lines of a product of the Twin City (Minn.) Rapid Transit Company shops. Twenty cars built by TCRT's Nicollet shops in 1900 were bought by the Winnipeg system in 1920. — *National Film Board.*

Winnipeg Electric's old wooden trolley No. 374 was a cheery sight as it waited for passengers at Broadway and Osborne. — *Stan F. Styles.*

A quiet moment at the carbarn of the Brantford (Ont.) Municipal Railways. This 18-mile system ended trolley operation in 1940. — *Van-Zillmer Collection.*

Trolleys of the Edmonton Radial Railway shared the High Level Bridge over the North Saskatchewan River with vehicular traffic and steam trains of the Canadian Pacific Railway. The single-end cars operated left-handed over the structure so that doors would open onto the structure instead of empty space in case of an emergency. — *Both photos, Foster M. Palmer, courtesy of Sprague Library, Electric Railroaders' Association.*

A wooden trolley of the British Columbia Electric Railway laid over at Cambie and Hastings streets in downtown Vancouver at the end of the Oak Street line. BCE oper-ated trolley service in Vancouver, North Vancouver, and Victoria, as well as the largest interurban railway system in the Dominion. — *Stan F. Styles.*

Nelson, B. C., claimed to be the smallest city in the British Empire to operate a trolley line. The municipally owned Nelson Street Railway Company ran three trolleys over a little more than 3 miles of track in Kootenay Can-yon, high in the Selkirk Mountains. No. 22, an aged product of the Ottawa Car Company, looped around a floral centerpiece at the eastern end of the line. — *Richard L. Neuberger, courtesy of Sen. Maurine B. Neuberger.*

304

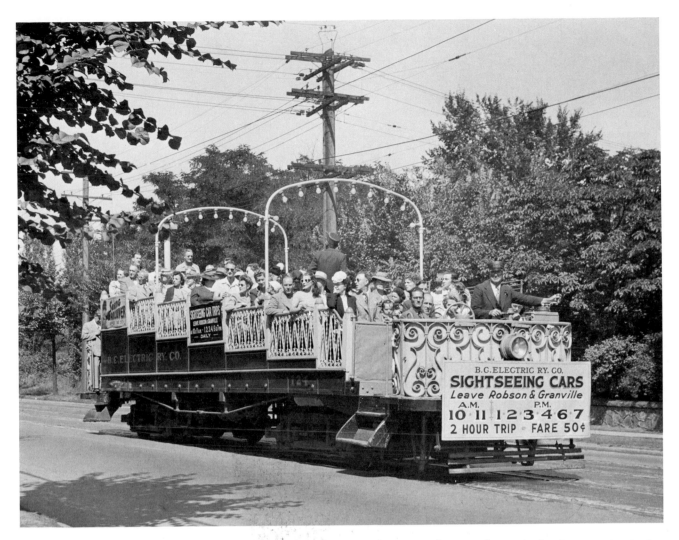

Observation car No. 124, one of two built by BCE shops in 1911 and patterned closely after the original Montreal design, rolled through Vancouver streets in 1946. For many years the 50-cent "Seeing Vancouver" tours were in the charge of BCE conductor Teddy Lyons, who gained a reputation as a showman by arranging impromptu singing and dancing by children along his route for the entertainment of his sight-seeing passengers. Declining street railway mileage brought an end to Vancouver trolley sight-seeing in 1950. — *Van-Zillmer Collection.*

Red-and-cream dashes of three British Columbia Electric PCC cars protrude from the 13th and Main streets carbarn in Vancouver. When BCE put its first PCC in service in 1938, the operator was promptly arrested for speeding. BCE bought 36 of the streamliners between 1938 and 1945. — *Stan F. Styles.*

An international trolley line operated by El Paso City Lines crosses the Rio Grande from El Paso, Tex.; loops through Ciudad Juarez, Mex.; and then returns to El Paso. Since 1950 a fleet of 20 former San Diego PCC's has provided the service. One of them squealed around a tight curve in Ciudad Juarez in 1959. — *F. W. Schneider III.*

The Trolley Goes South of the Border

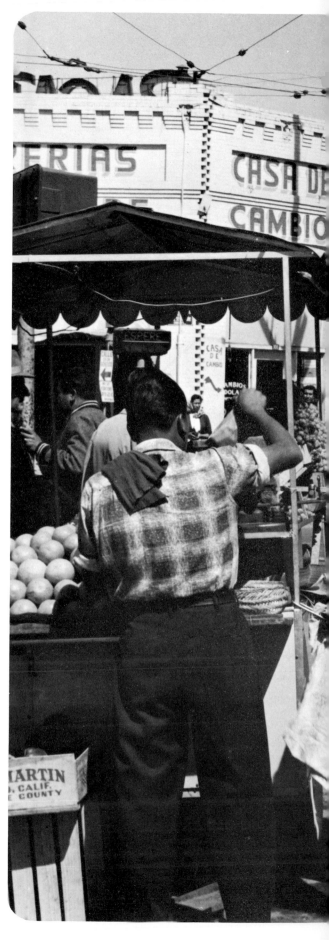

IN the cities of Latin America the trolley flourished in the same manner as it did north of the Rio Grande. Most often the necessary capital for construction of the Central and South American street railway systems was supplied by foreign investors. British, Canadian, and European capital was well represented, but American investment was probably greater than any other.

Although rolling stock and operating practices sometimes conformed to those of the owners' home country, and German, Belgian, Italian, and British equipment and methods occasionally were found, the Latin American traction systems were predominately American in equipment and practice. From the earliest days of electric operation, and sometimes even as far back as horsecar days, American builders supplied these lines with a large share of their original and replacement equipment. Even in those few cases of systems which constructed equipment in their own shops, American practice was generally followed. During the 1930's and 1940's, as abandonment of U. S. trolley systems became increasingly frequent, large numbers of still-service-

Peter Witt No. 613 was one of 30 cars built for Mexico Tramways by Brill in 1924. — *Collection of Alfred E. Barker.*

Mexico Tramways No. 00 provided extra-fare charter service in the early years. As pay car No. 0 it survived until the 1950's. — *Collection of Alfred E. Barker.*

able trolleys were sold for further service in Central and South America.

What was presumably the last major movement of American equipment south of the border came during the 1950's, when hundreds of PCC streamliners rendered surplus by U. S. abandonments were sold to a few of the more prosperous Latin American systems. Mexico City completely re-equipped its street railway system with used PCC cars from U. S. lines, and Tampico acquired a modest fleet of former Kansas City and St. Louis streamliners. The Pacific Electric Railway's entire fleet of 30 PCC cars was sold to the Ferrocarril Nacional General Urquiza at Buenos Aires in 1959. One ex-Baltimore PCC streamliner even turned up in Costa Rica re-

built into a narrow-gauge diesel-powered rail car.

The lack of private automobile ownership south of the border prevented the decline in street railway traffic that was general throughout the U. S. and Canada. As a consequence, the traction systems of Central and South America survived largely intact into recent years. Because of insufficient capital for either replacements or improvements, however, the majority of the systems became increasingly dilapidated. Often, abandonment became the only recourse, and the decline of electric traction during the 1950's and 1960's was abrupt. Today only a handful of systems remain in operation in the entire Central American-Caribbean area, and the trolley is fast vanishing from the South American continent.

One of the busiest Mexico City lines is the run to Xochimilco, site of the "Floating Gardens." Headed by former Detroit PCC 2214, a line of trolleys loaded Sunday afternoon crowds at Lake Xochimilco. — *Jim Shaughnessy*.

PCC 2232 swings around Huipulco loop at the junction of Tlalpan and Xochimilco routes. — *Jim Shaughnessy*.

THE greatest traction system in all of Central America was the vast electric network of Mexico City. As early as 1886 Mexico City had a 1500-mule, 200-car street railway system that operated nearly 100 miles of track and carried 10 million passengers a year. Electrification began shortly before the turn of the century, and the city's first electric cars operated on January 15, 1900. By 1907 the American-owned Mexico Tramways was operating some 500 cars over a network of 133 miles of electrified track. At the peak of its growth as an electric railway, the company operated in excess of 200 miles of track and as recently as 1948 was transporting more than 230 million passengers a year.

During the system's earlier years, nearly 4 per cent of its total revenues were derived from funeral car operations. All of Mexico City's cemeteries were at locations remote from the city, and the street railway handled all city funerals, providing a "trolley hearse" and an appropriate number of special cars for the mourners. Another unusual business carried on by the company was an extensive traffic in general freight, household effects, and even domestic animals, which were conveyed over the system in special freight trolleys.

Operation of the system passed from American to Belgian hands and finally into government ownership in 1945. The rolling stock operated by the company into the 1950's included a tremendous variety of cars built new for the system by U. S. builders as far back as the first few years of electric operation, U. S.-style cars constructed in the company's own shops, and secondhand cars from a variety of U. S. properties. A single PCC streamliner purchased in 1947 provided an extra-fare service to the famous

Mixcoac-Portales and La Villa route PCC cars gather at the loop in front of the Cathedral of Guadalupe on the north side of Mexico City. — *Jim Shaughnessy*.

Floating Gardens at Xochimilco, Mex., until the 1950's when 274 used PCC cars were purchased from the Twin Cities and Detroit. By the late 1950's all trolley operation in the city was with PCC cars, a new 4½-mile rapid-transit-type line had been constructed to accommodate four of the busiest routes, and several track extensions had been built into new suburban areas.

309

A fleet of secondhand Kansas City and St. Louis PCC cars, which had reached a total of 29 by the end of 1964, operates over Tampico's 7-mile suburban line to the Gulf Coast beaches at Miramar. A former Kansas City PCC, No. 798, rumbled over a wooden trestle on the way to downtown Tampico in 1958. — *Richard F. Glaze.*

Inbound from Miramar, an aged trolley of Tampico's Sociedad Cooperativa de Transportes Electricos de Pasaje y Cargo Tampico-Miramar approached the Prison stop in the summer of 1958. — *Richard F. Glaze.*

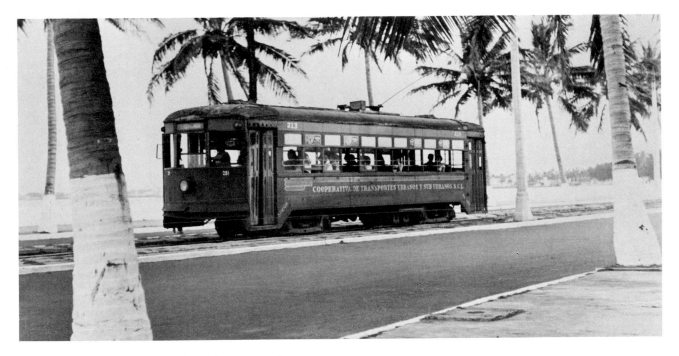

Still in the red and orange colors of its original owner, Pacific Electric Railway, a Veracruz trolley rolls down a palm-lined avenue beside the Gulf of Mexico. Fifteen of the cars, built by St. Louis Car Company in 1930, came to Veracruz in 1950. — *Jim Shaughnessy.*

One of the four surviving street railways in Mexico, Cooperativa de Transportes Urbanos y Sub Urbanos de Veracruz is a remarkable property which operates a museumlike collection of old trolleys of widely varied types and origins. In 1956 a former El Paso (Tex.) Birney negotiated a sharp curve at the Veracruz lighthouse on the way downtown. — *Allan H. Berner.*

311

A single-truck car eased through a narrow street in the old quarter of Havana, Cuba, on the Santos Suarez-Muelle de Luz route. A double trolley pole arrangement was an unusual characteristic shared by the Havana and Cincinnati systems. — *A. J. Kozla, courtesy of Sprague Library, Electric Railroaders' Association.*

Equipment of the Havana Electric Railway remained virtually unchanged throughout the more than half century of the company's existence. Brill-built car No. 237 worked the Cerro-Parque Central line in April 1921. — *Collection of Howard E. Johnston.*

On a hot summer afternoon in 1947 an elderly single-truck trolley discharged passengers at Queens Park in Port-of-Spain, Trinidad. — *William D. Middleton.*

Until recent years trolleys continued to provide the principal public transportation in São Paulo, Brazil, with an annual traffic of over 300 million passengers. The almost unlimited carrying capacity of the open trolley, illustrated here by São Paulo car No. 1035 in 1957, was just the answer for such traffic conditions. — *Allan H. Berner.*

Open cars were popular in the balmy climate of Rio de Janeiro, and the Canadian-owned Brazilian Traction Company operated them exclusively in the city. No. 188 worked the Voluntarios line in 1957. — *Allan H. Berner.*

314

Variety was the keynote for the National Tramways Company of Lima, Peru. Rolling stock ranged from Italian-built single-truck cars to secondhand U. S. interurbans. No. 247, a St. Louis Car Company Robertson semi-convertible car of uncertain origin, loaded passengers for the Chorrillos suburban line in downtown Lima on a sunny day in March 1956. — *Allan H. Berner.*

A flourishing trolley system operated into recent years in the Andean city of Arequipa, Peru, with rolling stock purchased new or used from the U. S. Exceedingly narrow streets posed some problems for the line. Two cars acquired from a defunct Elmira (N. Y.) system in 1939 had to be cut short by company shops before they could make the system's curves without scraping buildings. In 1956 two cars of probable Brill origin met on the Antiquilla line. — *Allan H. Berner.*

During the 1950's, Buenos Aires' Ferrocarril Nacional General Urquiza acquired a variety of former United States interurban and suburban rolling stock. Former Pacific Electric No. 1754, one of 28 PE "Hollywood" cars bought in 1951, worked the Federico Lacroze line in 1952. – *Collection of William D. Middleton.*

Argentina's extraordinary Tramway Rural, which extended some 90 miles from Buenos Aires, was probably the world's only animal railway to offer sleeping-car service. Shown here is an inspection car built for the line by J. G. Brill of Philadelphia. It was claimed to have the most effective lifeguard ever invented. If an object or person was thrown on the track, a small wheel, on striking the obstruction, was thrown backward against a car wheel, acquiring a reverse motion which lifted and threw clear the obstruction. – *Courtesy of Railroad Magazine.*

The Jackson & Sharp Company of Wilmington, Del., delivered this capacious double-deck trolley to the Buenos Aires street railway system in the late 1890's. Trolley operation in the Argentine capital ended abruptly in December 1962. — *Smithsonian Institution.*

Just as it was in North America, in South America the Birney Safety Car was popular with many street railway systems. Birney No. 2, one of 14 delivered to the Paraná (Argentina) system by J. G. Brill during the 1920's, differed from its North American counterparts in its arrangement for left-hand operation, then standard in Argentina. Paraná's durable Birneys continued to run until mid-1962. — *Duke-Middleton Collection.*

The Trolley
International

Greatest of all British tramways was London County Council Tramways, which at the time it was succeeded by London Passenger Transport Board in 1933 ran 2360 cars over 328 miles of track. A month before abandonment of the last London lines in 1952, an outbound double-decker on the Woolwich line passed the statue of Queen Boadicea as the car turned onto Westminster Bridge from Victoria Embankment. — *William D. Middleton.*

WITHIN little more than a decade of its first important practical application in the United States in 1888, the electric trolley had become a worldwide institution. Most of the early traction development outside the Western Hemisphere took place in Europe, but by 1896 lines had also been constructed in Africa, Asia, and Australia, and by the turn of the century the cars were running almost everywhere in the world.

Much of the equipment and technology required for world street railway development came from such industrially advanced European nations as Germany and Great Britain, where electric car experimentation and development had largely paralleled that in the United States. The American influence on world trolley development was surprisingly strong, though, mainly as a result of the technical superiority of much of the early equipment developed by American manufacturers. American-made motors, controllers, generating equipment, and trucks captured a large share of the world market, and the standard U. S. trolley voltage of 500 volts became virtually a worldwide standard. It has been estimated, for example, that until 1914 approximately 50 per cent of European trolley cars employed U. S. motors and controls and were mounted on U. S.-built or U. S.-pattern trucks. Materials for track and overhead systems, however, were generally supplied from local sources, and complete cars were only infrequently exported because of the high costs of shipping.

Initially, the export market was supplied from the U. S. plants of the principal traction manufacturers, but around 1900 there was a general move to either construct overseas plants or develop license arrangements with foreign manufacturers. The influx of American firms into Britain was so great that in 1900 an editorial in the British trade journal *Tramway & Railway World* discussing a proposed British plant for the St. Louis Car Company was headlined "The American Invasion." General Electric, operating under the Thomson-Houston name, developed a strong position in European traction. A British branch contracted for construction of a number of complete street railway installations, and in 1901 set up a British factory which, together with exports from the parent Schenectady plant, supplied electrical equipment for thousands of British trams.

The first European street railway
opened at Birkenhead, England, on
August 30, 1860. The line's American promoter, George Francis Train,
seen here with outstretched arm on
the upper deck, imported Philadel-
phia-style horsecars for the 1¼-mile
line. Similar American-type cars
turned out at a "tramcar manufac-
tory" by Train associate George
Starbuck introduced streetcar service to many European cities. — *Collection of J. H. Price.*

The most common type of British
tram was a single-truck car provided with an open upper deck for
the accommodation of smokers.
No. 5 of the Burton & Ashby Light
Railway, shown on rural track between Burton-on-Trent and Ashby-
de-la-Zouch in the Midlands of
England, was typical. — *London
Midland Region, British Railways.*

For British tramway systems on
which clearances precluded the
usual upper deck, there was a demand for a car with a closed section
for nonsmokers and an open section
for smokers. In 1901 G. F. Milnes &
Co. secured a license from the Laconia Car Company for production
of this "California-type" car, which
was subsequently produced for systems in Middlesborough and Manchester. — *Tramway Museum Society, from J. H. Price.*

A notable British trolley oddity was Magnus Volk's celebrated "Daddy-Long-Legs" seagoing electric railway at Brighton. Designed to avoid the costly construction required for a conventional line along the Channel chalk cliffs, Volk's 3-mile Brighton & Rottingdean Seashore Electric Tramroad ran on rails laid on the ocean bed. The remarkable *Pioneer* built for the railway resembled a hybrid of a trolley car, an ocean vessel, and a seaside pier. Twin trolley poles drew current from wires set on poles along the track, and two motors connected to the underwater trucks by shafting drove *Pioneer* at an 8 mph speed. The lavishly furnished saloon and decks accommodated 150 passengers, and the craft was fully equipped with life rings, flag, ship's bell, and a lifeboat. A few days after its November 1896 opening, the line was lashed by a severe storm and the *Pioneer* broke loose and capsized. Volk rebuilt the vehicle and operation of the line continued until 1901. — *Both photos, British Railways Board.*

The A.E.G. company, GE's German subsidiary, captured about a quarter of the market in that country, and a French Thomson-Houston subsidiary equipped a number of lines in France. Westinghouse was equally powerful in the European market and built large plants in Great Britain and France to supply it. The British plant at Manchester was a huge affair modeled after the parent firm's East Pittsburgh plant. It managed to supply the electrical needs for 25 per cent of Britain's tramways.

Ireland's last trolley line was the Hill of Howth Tramway, which operated through a picturesque rural setting near Dublin until 1959. The line's double-deck tram No. 7 emerged from a private right of way at Stella Maris in 1956. The stone wall shielded a convent garden from the eyes of upper-deck passengers. — *J. H. Price.*

Philadelphia carbuilder J. G. Brill was easily the most successful of all U. S. firms in the export market. In addition to carrying on a substantial business in complete cars exported to countries where there was no local carbuilding industry, Brill did a tremendous worldwide business with its well-designed car trucks. After carving out a large share of the British market, Brill licensed several local firms to build its trucks, and by mid-1901 Brill trucks were in use on more than 50 British tramways. An overseas Brill plant was set up at Paris in 1912 which supplied both cars and trucks to systems all the way from the Scandinavian countries to Africa.

St. Louis Car Company, the second largest U. S. builder, was less successful in the foreign market. The proposed British plant never materialized, but the firm still managed to do a sizable business in Europe, much of it in the form of trucks built under license in Germany. Other U. S. manufacturers, among them McGuire and Peckham, participated less extensively in the foreign traction market. The McGuire snow sweeper was a popular item on dozens of European tramway systems.

Along with sending material and equipment, the

This large single-truck car served the Swedish seaport of Malmo, across the sound from Copenhagen. The pantograph was a common means of current collection on European street railways. — *Collection of William D. Middleton.*

This 19th century German drawing depicts fare collection on a Berlin horsecar line. — *New York Public Library*.

U. S. occasionally exported its experience in electric railway construction, operation, and management. In 1900 a New York electric railway construction firm, J. G. White & Co., set up a British subsidiary which built dozens of electric railway properties throughout the world. United States operating men and managers sometimes turned up on overseas systems. When the British carbuilding industry was expanding rapidly around the turn of the century, a number of experienced American managers, among them traction pioneer Prof. Sidney H. Short, were hired to help set up mass production of cars and their electrical components.

In more recent years the U. S. exports have been

A Stuttgart tram delivered travelers to the terminal of a mountain funicular railway at Bad Cannstatt, a popular mineral springs spa, during the 1920's. — *Courtesy of Sprague Library, Electric Railroaders' Association*.

A modern single-truck tram and trailer glided along in suburban Stuttgart early in 1961. — *Vitaly V. Uzoff, courtesy of Headlights, Electric Railroaders' Association.*

Anticipating the postwar "sun roof" Volkswagen was the "roller ceiling" trailer car introduced on the Leipzig (Saxony) tramway system during the early 1930's. In 1962 the East German city introduced the "Glasserner Leipziger," a glass-roofed trolley car for sight-seeing. — *Courtesy of Railroad Magazine.*

324

Because of restrictive clearances and curvature, the use of secondhand American trolleys was seldom possible on European systems. One exception was in Vienna, Austria, where ample clearances existed on four former steam tram routes. During 1949-1950 the Vienna system installed a fleet of 42 former Third Avenue (New York) Railway lightweight cars of 1938-1939 vintage. One is seen in 1956 at Friedrich Engelsplatz. — *J. H. Price.*

largely in the form of ideas. Steel carbody construction was taken up by European manufacturers after U. S. firms originated the practice. The Peter Witt car arrangement developed in Cleveland was later copied by several Italian systems. Most recently, the PCC car has enjoyed a modest European success. Following World War II a few complete PCC cars were shipped to Belgium and Holland in either assembled or knockdown form. A few more were constructed overseas utilizing trucks and electrical

The American PCC streamliner even penetrated the Iron Curtain in the form of cars built under license in Czechoslovakia. In addition to nearly 150 Prague cars, two of which are shown here, Czech-built PCC's operate in more than a dozen other cities in Czechoslovakia, Poland, and the Soviet Union. Including more recent designs evolved from the PCC-type car, over 1400 Czech-built streamliners were in service by 1964. — *Collection of J. H. Price.*

In 1952 a boxy little single-truck trolley of the Versailles Tramways turned a corner in the one-time royal town of Louis XVI and Marie Antoinette. Versailles streetcar operation ended in 1957. — *William D. Middleton.*

At the turn of the century there was considerable interest in the use of three-phase alternating current for street railway systems instead of the usual direct current. The A.C. system, however, never achieved even a modest degree of success for trolley lines. This car ran on a rare three-phase line installed at Evian-les-Bains, France, in the late 1890's by Messrs. Ganz & Co. of Budapest. — *Collection of Edward T. Francis.*

Even into recent years the street railway remained an almost inevitable fixture of Spanish cities. A single-truck trolley of North American pattern rattled through the principal square of Malaga in 1952. Streetcar operation in the Mediterranean resort came to an end on New Year's Eve 1961. — *William D. Middleton.*

A dilapidated wooden trolley paused on the Maracena line at Granada, Spain, in 1952. Although of local manufacture, the car was mounted on the ubiquitous J. G. Brill maximum traction truck. — *William D. Middleton.*

equipment furnished from the U. S., and during the late 1950's 75 Belgian-built PCC's were equipped with secondhand trucks and electrical equipment from retired Kansas City cars. However, the preponderance of overseas PCC cars — well over 600 in number — is represented by cars constructed abroad in their entirety under licenses to use the PCC car patents.

Principally because of the limited clearances and narrow track gauges common on overseas systems, the export market for surplus U. S. equipment was never large outside of Central and South America. Surplus U. S. cars went to Austria, India, and Korea shortly after World War II, and more recently former Washington (D. C.) PCC cars have gone to Yugoslavia and Spain, while the bulk of Los Angeles' PCC fleet was sold to Cairo, Egypt, in 1965. Still more PCC's went to Egypt in 1966 when the Toronto Transit Commission sold some 211 surplus cars to the Alexandria Transport Company.

A PCC car glided past an elegant fountain along Madrid's Paseo del Prado in 1952. Fiat of Italy built 125 of the streamliners for the Spanish capital during the late 1940's and early 1950's. — *William D. Middleton.*

U. S.-built PCC's came to Spain in 1961 when Barcelona Tramways bought the first of a fleet of secondhand Washington (D. C.) streamliners that reached 100 cars by 1965. The cars were completely rebuilt in the Barcelona system's shops. No. 1601, first of the PCC's to enter service, is shown at Plaza Universidad in 1963. — *J. H. Price.*

An exception to the general rule that few complete cars were sold by American builders to European traction systems was to be found in Portugal. J. G. Brill filled numerous car orders for Portuguese tramways. This single-truck Brill semi-convertible circled the Praca de Goncalves Zarco on the waterfront at Porto in 1962. — *Frank E. Butts.*

Milan was one of several Italian cities that built cars to the U. S.-originated Peter Witt arrangement during the 1930's. A Milanese Peter Witt passed beneath the Gothic walls of the Duomo in 1962. — *Herbert H. Harwood Jr.*

The "two-rooms-and-a-bath" articulated arrangement adopted by Boston in 1912 also proved popular with several European systems, which had similar problems of narrow streets, sharp curves, and restricted clearances. A Milan version snakes through the plaza at the city's railway station in 1957. — *Herbert H. Harwood Jr.*

330

In the early days of Italian traction, a Sorrentine Tramways single-truck car headed out across a massive stone viaduct on a run between Castellamare and Sorrento along the shoreline of the Gulf of Naples. — *Collection of William D. Middleton.*

A double-truck trolley that would not have seemed out of place in North America rolled through Jedinstva Square in front of Belgrade's central railway station in 1960. The extensive street railway system serving Tito's capital includes among its equipment 29 Belgian-built PCC streamliners. — *William D. Middleton.*

One would hardly expect to find a less likely scene in the ancient capital of Yugoslavia's Bosnia-Hercegovina than this one of an American PCC trolley, still painted in the colors of the Washington (D. C.) system, racing along suburban right of way beneath catenary and a big pantograph. Sarajevo bought 74 of the surplus D. C. Transit streamliners between 1958 and 1961 and constructed a completely new standard-gauge trolley system on which to operate them. — *John H. Meredith, from J. H. Price.*

Street railway service came to the Ottoman Empire capital of Constantinople in 1869, when a Belgian firm opened a horsecar line. The open-air upper deck of this early two-horse model was ideal for a quiet smoke or a leisurely view of the passing scene. Constantinople horsecars were preceded by a man who ran through the city's narrow streets blowing a brass bugle to warn of the approaching car. — *New York Public Library.*

332

Construction of electric tramways in Constantinople was delayed by Sultan Abdul-Hamid II, who feared electricity and refused to permit installation of trolleys. The Sultan was deposed in 1909, and 5 years later the first electric car made its inaugural run between Sishane and Harbiye in the Beyoglu district. One of the single-truck cars that served the Ottoman capital passed through Sultan Ahmet Square in 1960. Istanbul trolley operation ended in 1961. — *William D. Middleton.*

Until electric car operation ended in Istanbul proper, on the European shore of the Bosporus, the Istanbul Electric Tramway & Tunnel System (IETT) enjoyed the distinction of being the world's only street railway system running on two continents. In the summer of 1961 a single-truck trolley waited with an open trailer at the outer end of the pleasant Kadiköy-Fenerbahce (Lighthouse Garden) line, one of several IETT routes which continued to operate on the Asian shore of the Bosporus into the mid-1960's. — *William D. Middleton.*

Trolleys continued to operate in the Lebanese capital city of Beirut into the 1960's. (Left) This gathering of Beirut trams took place in Rue President Dodge at the western terminus of the Damas-Phare (Damascus-Lighthouse) line in 1962. Disgruntled with the service of the French-owned tramway company, a Beirut citizen once took revenge by placing a chair in the middle of the car tracks and calmly smoking while the trams piled up to the cheers of hundreds of onlookers. Service was restored when police carried the gentleman, chair and all, away. (Right) A single-truck Beirut tram and trailer whipped through narrow streets on the loop at the south end of Route No. 1, at the intersection of Rue Marchand and Rue de Ouzai. – *Both photos, William D. Middleton.*

Except for the reversed door arrangement necessitated by Australia's left-hand operation, St. Louis Car Company-built Birney No. 218 of the Melbourne & Metropolitan Tramways was identical to the thousands of Birney trolley cars constructed for North American street railway systems in the 1920's. – *Van-Zillmer Collection.*

Two center-entrance trams of the Brisbane Municipal Tramways traveled down Queen Street, the Australian city's principal thoroughfare. Trolleys still run in the State of Queensland capital. — *Courtesy of Railroad Magazine.*

Until the abandonment of street railway service in 1961, the steel arch Harbor Bridge at Sydney, Australia, carried trolleys as well as electric M.U. trains and highway traffic. At its peak the Sydney system was one of the greatest in the entire Southern Hemisphere, operating some 200 miles of track and over 2000 cars. Center-entrance car 1922 is shown leaving the bridge. — *Collection of Gilbert Hayman, courtesy of Railroad Magazine.*

335

Single-truck trolley No. 12 of the Rangoon Electric Tramways & Supply Company Ltd., was lavishly decorated in 1937 on the occasion of a visit to Burma by the Viceroy of India. The car was equipped with a Brill truck. — *Collection of Robert P. Sechler Jr., courtesy of Headlights, Electric Railroaders' Assn.*

Although it was largely financed by British capital, the street railway system at Manila, Philippines, was built by a U. S. engineering firm in conformance with American practice. Even though much of the Manila rolling stock was constructed in company shops, trucks and other equipment were obtained from U. S. suppliers and the cars were in the American style. Two Manila Electric Railway & Lighting Company open cars negotiated a narrow Escolta street around 1918. — *Library of Congress.*

On the eve of Pearl Harbor, a Manila trolley rolled past the Bureau of Posts building. Although operation continued during the Japanese occupation, the system deteriorated rapidly during the war years. Much of what remained was destroyed during the battle for the city in 1945. — *Gordon Zahorik, courtesy of Railroad Magazine.*

Probably the most widely celebrated of Japanese electric railways in recent years was the modest 4-mile No. 10 route of the Kyoto Municipal Transportation Bureau. The No. 10's claim to fame comprised both its status as Japan's first streetcar line (it opened in 1895) and the fact that it continued to operate into 1961 with a fleet of trim single-truck cars turned out by J. G. Brill of Philadelphia in 1905. — *Collection of Stephen D. Maguire.*

During the late 1940's a fleet of retired Atlanta trolleys journeyed across the Pacific for further service at Seoul, Korea. A decade later they were joined by 40 secondhand cars from Los Angeles, whose 3-foot 6-inch gauge handily coincided with that of the Korean system. Cincinnati-built ex-Georgia Power Company trolley No. 405, one of the last deck-roof cars built in the United States, took on passengers in the Korean capital in 1954. — *Allan H. Berner.*

Boston's first subway/elevated rapid-transit line began operation between Sullivan Square and Dudley Street on June 10, 1901. The Dudley Street station, shown shortly after its opening, was designed to facilitate transfer between El trains and surface trolleys. Elevateds looped through the upper level of the terminal, which was flanked by two elevated loops for surface cars terminating at the station. Other platforms for through surface cars were installed at ground level. – *Collection of Stephen D. Maguire.*

Riding the Rapid

LONG BEFORE the end of the 19th century, even the rapid growth of street railways was to prove inadequate to meet the public transportation requirements of America's principal urban centers. Far from being a product of the automotive age as many now regard it, street traffic congestion was a fact of urban life many decades earlier. New York City, long since established as the nation's largest metropolitan center, began to feel the effects of severe congestion as early as 1850.

New York's problems were compounded by the long, narrow shape of Manhattan Island. The city's limited north-south thoroughfares were jammed with inordinate numbers of drays, cabs, omnibuses, and horsecars. An 1850 traffic check revealed that omnibuses made up nearly 40 per cent of Broadway traffic, and a rush-hour count found them moving on average headways of only 13 seconds. Travel by horse-drawn vehicle between downtown business areas and the uptown residential districts had already become so time-consuming that increasing numbers of New Yorkers were fleeing across the Hudson and East rivers to the New Jersey suburbs and Brooklyn, which could be reached more quickly by ferry services.

Matters rapidly worsened during the next two

Among the earliest New York rapid transit schemes was an 1870 proposal for an "arcade railway" under Broadway, depicted here in an early lithograph. Several decades were to elapse before electric traction was to reach the practical stage, and steam locomotives were proposed as the line's motive power. Arcade Railway promoter Melville C. Smith managed to get a series of bills authorizing the construction through the New York State legislature between 1870 and 1885, but all were vetoed by the incumbent governors.—*Library of Congress*.

decades. By 1860 New York's population had passed the 800,000 mark, and annual traffic on the city's omnibuses and street railways exceeded 36 million passengers. This figure more than doubled during the next 5 years, but the omnibus and horsecar services were becoming ever more inadequate for the demands of New York traffic, if an 1864 editorial in the New York *Herald* is taken as a fair evaluation of the service. Raged the *Herald*:

> Something more than streetcars and omnibuses is needed to supply the popular demand for city conveyance. Modern martyrdom may be succinctly defined as riding in a New York omnibus. The discomforts, inconvenience, and annoyances of a trip in one of these vehicles are almost intolerable. . . . It is in vain that those who are obliged to ride seek relief in a city railway car. The cars are quieter

than the omnibuses, but much more crowded. People are packed into them like sardines in a box, with perspiration for oil. The seats being more than filled, the passengers are placed in rows down the middle where they hang on by straps, like smoked hams in a corner grocery. To enter or exit is exceedingly difficult. Silks and broadcloth are ruined in the attempt. . . . It must be evident to everybody that neither the cars nor the omnibuses supply accommodations enough for the public, and such accommodations as they do supply are not of the right sort.

What seemed to be needed was some form of transportation that could handle New York's enormous traffic volume quickly, free from the restrictions imposed by the city's clogged streets. There soon proved to be no shortage of promoters who

340

Alfred Ely Beach's experimental pneumatic subway was the talk of New York City after Beach unveiled it to an incredulous public following nearly 2 years of secret construction carried out beneath Broadway in the dead of night. The "richly upholstered" car that was wafted back and forth through the 312-foot tunnel by a giant fan afforded comforts that exceeded anything the city's subway riders have seen since. Beach, with a shrewd sense of

salesmanship, lavished particular attention on the subway's waiting room. The walls were decorated with frescoes and elegant paintings, and Beach installed a grand piano, fountain, and goldfish tanks. As a final touch, the spacious room was illuminated with zircon lights. The Beach Pneumatic Subway and its construction are shown here in a series of woodcuts from an 1870 issue of *Frank Leslie's Illustrated Newspaper.* — *Library of Congress.*

thought they had the solution to the problem.

One of the first to appear was a Michigan railroad-man named Hugh B. Willson, who returned from a visit to London in 1863 much impressed by that city's new Metropolitan Railway Company, a 4-mile subway operated with coal-burning steam locomotives. Willson promptly rounded up New York backers and incorporated his own Metropolitan

Railway Company to build a similar line in New York City. Willson's chief engineer, A. P. Robinson, came up with plans for a double-track brick-arch tunnel to be constructed under Broadway from the Battery to 34th Street and thence under Sixth Avenue to 59th Street. Motive power, as on the London system, was to be steam. A bill to grant the subway enterprise a charter failed to make it through the

After several years of unsuccessful trials with cable propulsion, New York's pioneer New York Elevated Railroad began operation with steam dummies in 1871 and the city finally had its first regular rapid transit service. The early train shown in this contemporary woodcut included two of the line's original drop-center "shad belly" passenger cars. The low center of gravity arrangement was provided in order to overcome passengers' fears of tipping over. After a few years the cars were rebuilt into a more conventional pattern. — New York Public Library.

Success of the New York El inspired this 1875 musical effort. — Smithsonian Institution.

New York State legislature in 1864, more than likely as a result of the intense opposition of the city's existing transportation companies. A second try the following year got past the legislature only to be vetoed by Gov. Reuben Fenton. And that was as far as Mr. Willson's subway went.

Another subway enterprise a few years later actually reached the prototype stage. Its promoter was Alfred Ely Beach, an inventor, publisher, and patent lawyer who had probably been the first man to advance the subway concept when as early as 1849 he wrote of his ideas for a Broadway subway in the pages of his *Scientific American*.

Originally Beach had contemplated horsepower for his subway, but around 1866 his interest shifted to pneumatic power. Under Beach's new concept, subway cars would fit into an underground tube like bullets in a rifle barrel, and would be driven under the streets at fantastic speeds by air pressure from giant fans. The first Beach experiment was a small 10-seat car that was operated in a 6-foot-diameter wooden tube at the 1867 American Institute Fair at New York's 14th Street Armory. A helix fan 10 feet in diameter sent the little car racing from 14th to 15th streets, then was reversed to draw it back. The venture was a great success.

Rivaling the New York Elevated Railroad was a second El company organized by Dr. Rufus H. Gilbert. The first train on the Gilbert Road's Sixth Avenue line is shown near the Jefferson Market Police Court in a view from the pages of *Frank Leslie's Illustrated Newspaper*. The line's cars were painted in light green with pea green and gold trim; they rolled on wheels made of highly compressed paper with steel rims. Interiors were finished in oak and mahogany, and floors were laid with Axminster carpeting. — *Library of Congress*.

Beach's next step was to devise a special shield for driving a tunnel beneath the streets without interfering with traffic above. In 1868 Beach obtained a state charter for construction of a pneumatic postal dispatch system; and soon afterward, from the rented basement of Devlin's Clothing Store on Mur-

ray Street, Beach forces quietly began digging an experimental section of tunnel under Broadway. Although the 312-foot tunnel itself was driven in only 58 days, almost 2 years were spent in completing the elaborate pneumatic subway that Beach finally unveiled to the public early in 1870.

The little 22-seat car that traveled through the 9-foot tube was a veritable jewelbox on wheels. The giant steam-driven fan that powered the subway — called the "Roots Patent Force Blast Blower" — sent the car racing through the tube at speeds up to 10 mph. At the far end of the tube, a trip wire rang a bell in the engineroom, the operator reversed the giant fan, and the car was "inhaled" back to its starting point. In its first year of operation the Beach tube transported some 400,000 curious sight-seers and became a sensational public success. Unfortunately, Beach needed a charter to construct the 5-mile mile-a-minute subway system he planned for New York, and New York's notorious Boss Tweed had other ideas. Tweed was backing something called the Viaduct Plan, a rapid-transit proposal that called for construction of a massive masonry elevated structure. Both Tweed's Viaduct Plan and the Beach Transit Bill passed the state legislature in 1871 and landed on the desk of Gov. John T. Hoff-

Employees of the elevated were less than courteous if this depiction by a 19th century cartoonist is to be accepted. Then, as now, crowded cars were an inescapable rush-hour feature. — *New York Public Library*.

343

Appreciative male commuters eye a demure traveler on the New York Elevated in a drawing by Charles Dana Gibson, the incomparable delineator of American womanhood who created the "Gibson girl." — *New York Public Library*.

Judging from this cartoon in a July 1878 issue of *Puck*, the coming of the elevated railway was not happily received everywhere. The opening of the Sixth Avenue line was the occasion for the weekly's displeasure. — *New-York Historical Society*.

man. Hoffman, a Tweed lackey, signed the Tweed plan and vetoed the Beach bill.

The persistent Beach kept his experimental line going and tried again. Once more in 1872 the Beach bill made it past the legislature but fell victim to Hoffman's veto. By 1873 Tweed was in jail and Hoffman had discreetly refrained from running for re-election. This time the Beach Transit Bill sailed through the legislature and won an enthusiastic signature from Gov. John A. Dix. But alas, Beach had expended his fortune in the effort to promote his subway. No one seemed interested in risking the 10 million dollars needed to construct the Beach subway, and shortly afterward the state charter was withdrawn. So much for the Beach subway.

Even as Beach was perfecting the details of his pneumatic subway, still another inventor appeared on the rapid-transit scene. In 1866 Charles T. Harvey, a canal engineer who had devised a scheme for a cable-powered elevated railway, managed to obtain an amendment to the state's railway law of 1850 that permitted him to build his rail line. Harvey promptly organized the ambitious West Side & Yonkers Patent Railway Company, and in 1867 set to work on an experimental half-mile section extending northward in Greenwich Street from Battery Place. A trial run in 1868 was a modest success, and work was started on extending the elevated toward its ultimate Yonkers destination. The panic of 1869, however, brought bankruptcy and a temporary halt

There was no dearth of ideas for elevated railway systems. This strange proposal by James H. Swett for a Broadway elevated was presented in an 1883 *New York Illustrated News.* — *New-York Historical Society.*

Still another elevated railway scheme was this "prismoidal railway" developed by a General Stone of Phoenixville, Pa., about 1875. The line's "saddle-bag" car was draped over a prismoidal girder supported by a single row of iron columns. The car seated passengers on two levels. Motive power was to consist of a locomotive with two boilers, one on each side of the girder, supplying steam to a rotary engine. — *New York Public Library.*

345

A three-car train of the New York Elevated Railroad rumbled along the company's new Third Avenue line near Ninth Street in 1878, the year of its opening. One of Mat-thias N. Forney's double-end tank locomotives, specially designed for elevated service, provided the motive power. — *New-York Historical Society.*

The Hardie compressed-air locomotive, depicted in a drawing from an 1882 issue of *Scientific American,* was an early effort to find a more satisfactory means of elevated railway motive power. A single charge of air proved sufficient to power a three-car train on a 9-mile trip over the Third Avenue El in 1881. — *New-York Historical Society.*

This aerial curve, 100 feet above the street at 110th Street and Eighth Avenue, was known as "Suicide Curve" after it became popular for death leaps. A Forney tanker led a Ninth Avenue line train around the curve in 1894. — *New-York Historical Society.*

Typical of the versatile little Forney locomotives which werc virtually the standard means of elevated railway motive power until the advent of electric traction was this compound 0-4-4T built for Chicago's South Side Elevated Railroad by the Baldwin Locomotive Works in 1893. The sturdy 28-ton locomotives were capable of reaching their maximum speed of 25 to 35 mph with a heavily loaded five-car train in a distance of only 350 to 400 feet. — *Collection of H. L. Broadbelt.*

The Manhattan skyline was hidden in heavy snow as a six-car cable-drawn train descended the Brooklyn end of the Brooklyn Bridge in a memorable photograph taken in a 19th century blizzard. — *Library of Congress.*

Soon after the 1883 opening of the Brooklyn Bridge, cable-powered rapid transit trains began operating over it utilizing a system of cable propulsion. A *Scientific American* drawing illustrated the massive steam-powered cable plant. — *Library of Congress.*

to the work. Finally the line, reorganized as the New York Elevated Railroad, made it as far as 30th Street. Cable operation proved to be unsatisfactory, and the company soon obtained permission to convert to steam operation. Steam dummy engines began pulling the El trains in 1871, and at last the project was on the way to success.

Boss Tweed's Viaduct Plan briefly threatened the new enterprise, but the Tweed downfall in 1872 removed this rival before it got beyond the paper stage. More serious competition arrived on the scene in 1872 when Dr. Rufus H. Gilbert and his associates managed to obtain a charter for a patent elevated railroad of his invention. The Gilbert system called for tubular iron roadways suspended above the street from Gothic arches, with cars pro-

pelled through by atmospheric or other means. No lines were ever built utilizing the Gilbert system; but in 1878 the company, reorganized as the Metropolitan Elevated Railway, opened the steam-powered Sixth Avenue El. By 1877 the New York Elevated was operating a line that extended along Ninth Avenue all the way from South Ferry to 59th Street, and a year later a second line was operating from South Ferry via Third Avenue to 125th Street. Both systems were taken over by the Manhattan Railway in 1878; and within 2 years another elevated was running on Second Avenue to 67th Street, and the Ninth Avenue line went all the way to Harlem. By 1880 the New York elevateds were transporting over 60 million passengers a year.

Within little more than a decade, two other cities

Advances in the development of electric traction were so rapid that Chicago's Metropolitan West Side Elevated Railroad, which was organized in 1892 as a steam line, canceled its orders for steam equipment and opened in 1895 as America's first electrically powered rapid transit system. The line was operated with powerful locomotive cars capable of drawing as many as 14 trailers. No. 2724 was one of 54 original motor cars delivered from the Barney & Smith Car Company in 1895. It is shown some years later after modification for multiple-unit train operation. — *Collection of H. L. Broadbelt.*

An order of 20 Forneys for Chicago's South Side Elevated was shipped all in a row from the Philadelphia plant of the Baldwin Locomotive Works in 1892 and arrived in time to help accommodate the heavy traffic that rode the "L" to the 1893 World's Columbian Exposition in Jackson Park. — *Courtesy of Railroad Magazine.*

349

Chicago's elevated lines joined during the late 1890's to form the Union Elevated Railroad, which built the "Union Loop" that became the symbol and distinguishing characteristic of downtown Chicago. Opened in 1897, the Loop connected the independent "L" companies and provided them a common entrance into the city's center. A train is shown on the Wabash Avenue leg of the Loop around the turn of the century. — *Library of Congress*.

The festive opening of Brooklyn's first elevated railway on May 13, 1885, was depicted for *Harper's Weekly* by artist W. P. Snyder. — *New-York Historical Society*.

had followed New York's lead. Shortly after the opening of John Roebling's magnificent Brooklyn Bridge in 1883, cable-powered trains were shuttling back and forth across the bridge between Manhattan and Brooklyn, and by 1885 Brooklyn had opened its first elevated line. Chicago's first elevated, the South Side Elevated Railroad, was opened from downtown Chicago to 39th Street in 1891. It was extended as far south as the fairgrounds in Jackson Park in sufficient time to help accommodate the huge crowds that attended the 1893 World's Columbian Exposition. Unlike the previous New York and Brooklyn elevateds, which were built above streets, the South Side line was constructed above the alley between State Street and Wabash Avenue, thus earning the title of the "Alley L."

In an effort to appear a little less frightening to horses and the general public, the earliest Manhattan elevated lines used four-wheel steam dummy locomotives; but the little engines proved woefully inadequate for the task. About this time a Pennsylvania-born inventor and locomotive designer named Matthias N. Forney came up with a design for a small double-end tank engine that was just what the elevateds were looking for. Forney's locomotive, a four-coupled design with a swivel truck under the

350

Typical of early rapid transit cars were these steel multiple-unit cars built for Philadelphia's Market Street Elevated Passenger Railway Company. Two hundred and fifteen cars of this type were delivered by Pressed Steel Car and J. G. Brill between 1906 and 1913. Known as the "Easy Access Car," the units were provided with three air-operated doors on each side to speed loading and unloading. — *Collection of LeRoy O. King.*

Following the successful testing of a Sprague system multiple-unit train on the Second Avenue El in 1900, the New York elevated roads decided to electrify. Two years and 18 million dollars later, electrification was complete. Here multiple-unit trains of the Third Avenue line rumbled along above Bowery trolley traffic. — *Library of Congress.*

351

A dim rumble far down the dark tunnel gradually increases in volume. Headlight beams probing the darkness grow in intensity. Suddenly in a burst of sound and air the subway train lunges out of the darkness. Dozens of brake shoes claw at spinning wheels as the long string of dingy cars grinds to a halt. Pneumatic doors hiss open and the city's hordes rush in and out. The drama of the subway was captured in this scene from New York's Seventh Avenue line. — *Lead Industries Association, Inc.*

tank, was capable of maintaining a 12 mph schedule, including stops, with as many as six or seven cars; and it proved to have such superior hauling capacity, tracking ability, and reduced cost of maintenance that it quickly became standard on the New York lines. Brooklyn and Chicago later adopted the Forneys, and by the early 1890's there were more than 500 in elevated railway service.

But if the early elevated railway proprietors learned anything, it was that steam was far from an ideal form of motive power. Residents and businesses along the elevated lines objected violently to the steady rain of smoke and cinders from the trains, and hot coals and sparks had a habit of dropping

The new Interborough subway was one of New York's showpieces in the early years of the century, and both the elite and the masses made use of the underground trains. For a 1909 periodical, artist G. W. Peters drew this view of an elegant theater party waiting for a train at Grand Central Station. — *New York Public Library*.

into the streets below to the discomfiture of pedestrians. Moreover, steam power was manifestly uneconomical and inherently limited in its performance characteristics.

One of the earliest efforts to come up with a better form of El motive power was the Hardie air locomotive, tried on New York's Third Avenue Elevated in 1881. Looking much like a conventional steam locomotive, the air locomotive had four big air reservoirs with a total capacity of 460 cubic feet. Before the locomotive set out on its run, its reservoirs were charged to a pressure of 600 pounds per square inch. Air was released through an expansion valve and, after passing through a small boiler where it was heated and moistened, drove the locomotive by means of conventional reciprocating machinery. A novel feature of the locomotive was an arrangement whereby the cylinders could be used as air pumps, thus providing a means of braking. Nothing, however, came of these or similar tests conducted on several other occasions.

At times the complexity of big city rapid transit almost defies comprehension. This maze at Queens Plaza funneled subway and elevated traffic between Manhattan and the Borough of Queens. An inbound Astoria line train raced through the junction toward Manhattan. — *Courtesy of Headlights, Electric Railroaders' Association.*

One of the earliest major electric subways was London's 6-mile Central London Railway, which opened between Shepherds Bush and the Bank in 1900. The 40-ton electric locomotives that powered trains on the "Twopenny Tube," as the line was popularly known, were soon replaced by M.U. equipment.— *London Transport Board.*

On a wintry day in Brooklyn two rapid transit trains of the BMT Division met at an elevated station on the Brighton Beach line. — *Henry Raudenbush, courtesy of Electric Railroaders' Association.*

During the 1880's interest began to grow in the possibilities of electric power for the elevateds. For several weeks in 1885 electrical inventor Leo Daft operated his experimental 9-ton electric locomotive *Benjamin Franklin* between 14th and 53rd streets on the Ninth Avenue line of the Manhattan Elevated Railroad, reaching speeds as high as 30 mph with trains of as many as four cars. The same locomotive was later rebuilt and for about eight months in 1888 operated over the Ninth Avenue line, pulling trains of up to eight cars. Some of Frank J. Sprague's earliest electric traction experiments were carried out on the New York Elevated in 1886, and a year later electrical pioneer Stephen D. Field carried out tests of an electric car on the 34th Street El in New York.

The first full-scale application of electric power to elevated railway operation didn't come until 1895, however — well after electric traction had proven to be a practical means of propulsion for street railways. The first elevated to operate entirely with electric power was a new Chicago line, the Metropolitan West Side Elevated Railway. Although steam power had originally been contemplated for the Metropolitan at the time of its formation in 1892, the success of the electrically powered Intramural Railway at the 1893 World's Columbian Exposition prompted the line's builders to adopt electric power instead. When the first 5-mile stretch of the Metropolitan was opened on May 17, 1895, it was operated wholly from a third-rail electric power system. Another new Chicago "L," the Lake Street Elevated Railroad, converted its 6½-mile system to electric power a year later.

Both of the early Chicago "L" electrifications retained the locomotive-drawn train concept. Acting as a locomotive, a single heavy motorized passenger car powered a train of several trailer cars. This method was patently superior to steam operation, but it still retained the limitations inherent in locomotive operation. Train size was restricted to the hauling capacity of the motor cars, and the modest acceleration characteristics imposed by the limited power and adhesion available from a single motorized car in turn limited the over-all schedule speeds possible in stop-and-go elevated service.

At this point the opportunity arose for a re-entry into active electric traction development by trolley car pioneer Frank J. Sprague. Soon after the suc-

The Lake and Wells streets tower on Chicago's elevated, which guards the junction of the North Side and Lake Street divisions with the downtown Loop, has been called the "world's busiest railroad crossing." Before subway construction somewhat diminished "L" activity, the tower commonly passed 200 rush-hour trains, made up of 900 to 1000 cars, in a single hour. When a memorable snowstorm in March 1930 disrupted surface traffic, 21,270 elevated cars passed the tower during a 24-hour period. — *H. A. Atwell Studio, courtesy of Railroad Magazine.*

Now in its 70th year of operation, Chicago's elevated Loop still serves the city well. A Lake Street train made a Loop passenger stop at the Randolph and Wabash station in April 1963. — *John Gruber.*

cessful street railway electrification in Richmond, the Sprague firm was absorbed by the growing General Electric empire, and Sprague resigned to take up the development of the electric elevator. In one of his first major elevator installations — for New York's Postal Telegraph Building in 1893-1894 — Sprague had evolved a system of control whereby a single master switch in the basement could be used to regulate the movement of any elevator in the building, or the simultaneous movement of all of them.

Pondering the problem of elevated railroad train operation, Sprague conceived the idea of applying the same control principle to train operation. Why, he reasoned, couldn't a train be made up of any number of electric cars, with provision made for working all of their controllers at the same time through a train line from a master switch on any car, thus giving a train of any length the performance characteristics of a single car? Details for the necessary equipment were speedily developed, and Sprague's "multiple unit system," as he called it, was shortly to prove one of the most fundamental developments in the history of electric traction.

There remained the problem of exhibiting the practicality of the new Sprague control system. Two efforts to gain the privilege of demonstrating the system on the Manhattan Railway elevated system, at Sprague's own risk and expense, were rebuffed. But in 1897 came unexpected opportunity. Chicago's South Side Elevated, then in the process of electrifying its line, retained Sprague as a consulting engineer. An inspection of the property convinced Sprague that the line would be an ideal showcase for his multiple unit system, and his report recommending its adoption in place of the contemplated locomotive cars was accompanied by an offer to personally undertake the installation.

Sprague won a contract to provide the entire equipment for 120 South Side cars, but only under conditions that were no less onerous than those imposed on him for his epochal Richmond street railway electrification a decade earlier. Under terms of the contract, Sprague had but two months to prepare a group of six cars for testing. Should the tests prove unsatisfactory or the time limit not be met, the contract was subject to cancellation. Rigid requirements were established for delivery of the remainder of the cars, and a further stipulation was imposed for the testing of 20 cars under service conditions for a period of not less than 10 days once the powerhouse and power installation were complete. If this final test proved unsuccessful, the elevated company had the right to cancel the contract and to require waiver of all claims. Moreover, Sprague must post a $100,000 performance bond.

The contract was executed while Sprague was in London in connection with an elevator proposal, and most of his initial instructions for preparation of the trial equipment were transmitted by cable. When Sprague returned to New York on June 24, only 21 days remained before a July 15 deadline for test operation of the six-car train. On July 16 two cars were put into operation on the test track of the General Electric Company at Schenectady, N. Y., and on July 26 the entire six-car train was successfully operated in the presence of South Side Elevated officials by Sprague's 10-year-old son.

By November 1897 a test train of five cars was running in Chicago. By the following April 20 the stipulated 20 cars were in operation, although no fewer than 17 of them (one in flames) were taken

Chicago's first subway, a 5-mile line connecting the North Side and South Side elevated divisions, opened in 1943 after 5 years of construction. This is a train of PCC-type cars at State and Randolph station. — *John Gruber.*

out of service before the end of the day because of defective rheostats. Sprague took some satisfaction from the occasion in seeing the remaining three-car train push a stalled steam train around a curve. The defects were soon remedied, and within three months the entire 120 cars were operating satisfactorily. By the end of July 1898 steam operation on the South Side Elevated had been discontinued, and by the end of the year the elevated railway's monthly net earnings had more than trebled. Electric rapid transit was a success.

The accomplishments of the Sprague multiple-unit control system on the South Side Elevated quickly prompted similar installations elsewhere. Both of the Chicago elevateds which had already commenced electric operation with locomotive cars soon converted to multiple-unit operation, and the city's new Northwestern Elevated Railroad, which had been planned for electric operation from its inception, opened in 1900 with multiple-unit equipment. In 1898 Brooklyn's steam-operated elevated system began a conversion to electric power, utilizing multiple-unit equipment, and by 1903 the entire New York City elevated system ran electrically.

Even more important than the elimination of steam operation on the elevated railways was the fact that electric traction provided the first really practical form of motive power for subway service. The world's first electrically powered subway, London's City & South London Railway, opened in 1890 using locomotive-drawn trains. North America's first subway was the West End Street Railway's trolley subway, which began running under Tremont Street in Boston in 1897. The first true rapid-transit subway operation in America was that of the new Boston Elevated Railway, which inaugurated the first of its multiple-unit-equipped subway-elevated lines through the same Tremont Street subway in 1901.

After more than 30 years of New York City subway talk, construction finally began in 1900 on what was to become one of the world's greatest underground railway systems. When New York finally did get started, it began with a giant first step. The city's initial subway, operated by the Interborough Rapid Transit Company, comprised nearly 13 miles of underground line — made up of as many as four tracks — and more than 3 miles of elevated railway extensions between Manhattan and the Bronx

357

The opening of the first section of the new IRT subway on October 27, 1904, was the occasion for one of the greatest civic blowouts in New York history. The festivities began after lunch when Mayor George B. McClellan led a party of dignitaries from the Aldermanic Chamber of the City Hall to the ornate City Hall station of what was already being described as "the greatest underground railroad in the world." There orations suitable to the occasion were delivered by the Mayor; Frank Hedley, the head of the IRT company; contractor John B. McDonald, whose firm constructed the line; and subway financier August Belmont.

Promptly at 2:30 p.m. the dignitaries boarded the ceremonial first train for the 9-mile run from City Hall to the then terminus of the line at 145th Street and Broadway. Mayor McClellan himself took the controls of the train, utilizing a silver controller handle thoughtfully provided for the occasion by August Belmont.

Throughout the afternoon the Mayor and his party, together with some 27,000 invited near-celebrities, enjoyed free rides on the newly completed subway. Finally, at 7:00 p.m. the IRT was opened to the public, and the crush that followed was regarded with astonishment even by those accustomed to life in the crowded metropolis. The city's newspapers of the following day, in reporting the fact that some 150,000 fare-paying passengers had been transported by the IRT subway between 7 p.m. and midnight on opening day, felt compelled to observe that this phenomenal traffic had been carried "without a single casualty."

All along the line men had fought, kicked, and shoved for the honor of riding the first trains. The jam was greatest at the 145th Street terminal, where passengers from the first northbound trains struggled with residents of Washington Heights for places on the first downtown trains. In their eagerness to board, many prospective passengers pushed dollar bills into the ticket windows and ran gleefully for the train with a five-cent ticket without bothering to wait for their change.

Before the subway opened, gloomy predictions had been made that the general public would be afraid to ride the subterranean trains. Taking note of rumors that "the fluttering sensation of the eye experienced when a passenger looks out of the car window at the rows of pillars flitting past caused pain," the New York *Tribune* reassured its readers that there was no truth to the report that riding in the subway caused a new disease of the eye.

Any doubts about public acceptance of subway travel, whatever the reasons, were quickly dispelled by the success of the IRT line, which before the end of its first year of operation was carrying over 400,000 passengers a day. The subway, along with the recently electrified elevated railways, released New Yorkers from the tedium of lengthy surface travel in the city's congested streets, and it seemed that New York's rapid transit system could never grow fast enough to satisfy the demand. For nearly 40 years after the start of work on the initial IRT system, subway construction continued almost without interruption.

By 1908 the IRT system, together with its elevated extensions in outlying areas, had grown to a total route length of some 25 miles, and had assumed operation of the lines of the Manhattan Elevated Railway. A second round of subway construction began

A perennial rapid transit concept that has yet to achieve significant success is the suspended monorail. One of the earliest experiments was this electrically operated line at South Park, Minn., in 1883 (above). The only suspended monorail installation to achieve commercial success is Germany's now famous Wuppertal Schwebebahn, or "suspended railway" (left), which has operated since 1901. A more recent monorail installation was this mile-long line built on the grounds of the Los Angeles County Fair at Pomona, Calif., in 1962 (right). — *Collection of Stephen D. Maguire (above); Collection of William D. Middleton (left); William D. Middleton (right).*

about 1911, when new lines were built for the Brooklyn-Manhattan Transit Company, and further extensions were completed for the IRT system. By 1920 another 100 miles of subway and elevated rapid transit were in service. Still another period of massive subway construction started in the late 1920's, when work began on the city owned and operated Independent Subway. Between 1932 and 1937 more than 50 additional miles of subway were opened.

Long since combined under the operation of the New York City Transit Authority, the New York rapid transit system represents the greatest passenger transportation system in America and one of the greatest in the world. Operating some 236 miles of subway and elevated lines, more than 200 of which have been built since 1900 at a cost of well over a billion dollars, the New York system transports some 4.5 million passengers and operates 9000 trains every weekday. Its annual passenger traffic of 1.37 billion is equal to more than 3 times the combined passenger total for all U. S. railroads.

In other American urban centers, too, the new century brought a speedy growth of electric rapid transit. A few months after Boston's pioneer subway-elevated line began service between Sullivan Square and Dudley Street in 1901, the Boston Elevated opened its new Atlantic Avenue El. A rapid transit tunnel under the harbor to East Boston was opened in 1904, and the Cambridge-Dorchester elevated-subway began operation in 1912. During the next decade rapid transit service was extended to Everett and Forest Hills, and by the early 1920's Boston was operating 37 miles of rapid transit line.

Philadelphia's first rapid transit line, the Market Street subway-elevated, opened the first section of its line from the Delaware River to the 69th Street terminal in Upper Darby in 1905. An elevated extension to Frankford opened in 1920, and the first section of a new north-south Broad Street subway began operation in 1928. Rapid transit service between New York City and Hoboken, Jersey City, and Newark began in 1908 with completion of the Hudson & Manhattan Railroad organized by William Gibbs McAdoo, later President Wilson's Secretary of the Treasury.

Chicago, which had completed its comprehensive 91-mile elevated railway system in 1900, was the only one among the several largest American urban centers to undertake no additional rapid transit construction during the first few decades of the new century. Work did not begin on the city's first subway — a 5-mile line under State Street — until 1938, and the line was opened to traffic early in 1943. A second Chicago subway, the 4-mile Milwaukee-Dearborn-Congress route, was started in 1939. Construction was interrupted by World War II, and the line did not open until 1951.

Recoiling in mock fright, these Brooklynites look aghast at the trolley window that has just been shattered by a rock thrown by a boy. The windows of passing transit vehicles have historically proven irresistible to a boy with a rock or snowball. This scene was posed for a safety campaign of the Brooklyn Rapid Transit Company. — *Library of Congress*.

Life on the Cars

TO a casual observer in the trolley's declining years, when streetcars were generally aged, docile vehicles operated by employees who themselves more often than not were getting on in years, employment on the cars must have seemed a tranquil occupation indeed. That this is far from the case is amply documented by the historical record.

In the early years, when traction was a vigorous, growing industry, the job of running the cars was a much more demanding one than it was to become later. It was a job for a young man with a sturdy constitution. Until enclosed vestibules came into common use after the turn of the century, conductors and motormen alike were exposed to the rigors of the weather in all seasons, frequently for the length of a workday that lasted 12 hours or more. As long as the open cars remained in service, conscientious fare collection required of conductors the utmost agility in order to negotiate the exposed running boards. Before air brakes came into general use a sturdy physique was essential to a motorman, who was expected to bring a heavy car to a halt with only hand brakes at his disposal. In a time when public behavior tended to be more boisterous than it is today, facility with a controller handle or a switch iron was a prerequisite if a trolley crew

Employment on the street railway was a highly respected occupation in the early years of electric traction. This young Duluth (Minn.) trolley man was fairly bursting with pride in his brass-buttoned uniform when he posed for a studio photographer in 1910. — *Collection of Wayne C. Olsen.*

hoped to maintain order in a car loaded with Saturday night revelers.

A job in the street railway service was a highly prized one. A handsome blue uniform with brass buttons gave a man an air of authority, and the work was considered vastly superior to occupations that required manual labor. Understandably, the trolley companies demanded the highest standards of appearance and deportment from their operating employees. A typical early rulebook prohibited any kind of profane or vulgar language, smoking, gambling, or reading of newspapers and magazines while on duty or on company premises. Rules regarding drinking were especially severe. Drinking to excess at any time, constant frequenting of drinking places, and even appearing in a saloon while in uniform were considered grounds for dismissal.

The employment of women as conductors or motormen was not infrequent, particularly in periods of wartime manpower shortages. One of the earliest reported uses of women in street railway service was in Chile in the early 1880's, when young women were employed as horsecar conductors to replace men drafted into the army during the war with Bolivia and Peru. The lady conductors wore an outfit consisting of a Panama hat, a blue flannel uniform, and a many-pocketed white pinafore reaching from breast to ankles and trimmed in dainty frills.

In the United States, women were widely employed in streetcar operation during both World Wars, and in some cases continued to work as conductors and motormen long after the war was over. There was at least one instance of a husband and wife trolley crew. During World War II, Reuben Lindquist, a Twin City Rapid Transit motorman,

Early motorists were wary of the Washington Railway & Electric Company's special instruction car, which rolled through the streets of the national capital training prospective motormen in the intricacies of streetcar operation. Most larger street railway systems had some such instruction car. — *Collection of LeRoy O. King.*

These three veteran female trolley motormen, originally hired during the manpower shortage of World War I, were still running Baltimore trolleys when the first PCC cars came along in the late 1930's. — *Courtesy of Railroad Magazine.*

In the earlier years, company-sponsored recreational activities were common. This was the Duluth Street Railway band of the 1920's. — *Collection of Wayne C. Olsen.*

363

persuaded his wife to apply for a position when the company began hiring women. After landing a job as a conductor, Mrs. Lindquist managed to get assigned to her husband's car.

On one occasion women were employed as trolley car hostesses in the manner popularized by airlines and the new steam railroad streamliners during the 1930's. In 1941 the Birmingham Electric Company hired several girls to ride the company's trolleys wearing band uniforms and caps and "hostess" armbands. Startled streetcar riders were offered hot coffee and magazines. The device was only a publicity stunt intended to promote trolley riding, and the girls soon vanished from the cars.

The rise of the street railway more or less coincided with the growth of organized labor, and street railway systems were involved in some of the bitter strikes that characterized the union drive for recognition and strength. Strikebreaking was a recognized tactic on the part of street railway companies. A regular advertiser in the pages of *Street Railway Journal* early in the century was the detective and strikebreaking firm of Waddell & Mahon that proudly claimed "we have never lost a strike," and "call on us if you anticipate a labor disagreement." The Waddell & Mahon operatives were especially proud of their handling of a 1907 Birmingham strike, modestly pointing out in their advertising copy the noteworthy "efficiency and dispatch with which this strike was handled and broken up."

An example of a particularly violent strike is that which occurred on the Denver Tramways in 1920. After granting the newly organized platform men a 10-cent raise, the company found that it was suffering heavy losses and proceeded to cut wages back to their original level. The union men promptly began a bloody strike. On the first day, strikers killed two men and wrecked five cars in citywide fighting. Five days later union mobs stopped 12 cars, beat their crews, and demolished the cars, after which they wrecked one of the city's newspaper offices. Federal troops were finally called out after strikers stormed the carbarns with bricks and guns, and bombed cars stored in the yards. Thereafter two armed soldiers rode each of the company's cars until a sufficient number of old employees returned to work or until strikebreakers were hired to restore service to a normal level and the strike was broken.

A more recent labor dispute in New Delhi, India, was handled in a much more peaceable, though whimsical manner. On the appointed day over a thousand of the city's trolley motormen and conductors showed up for work dressed only in their underwear. Attached to each man's shorts was a notice informing the public that he wanted more pay and a free uniform from the company. The temperature was 110 degrees, so there was little risk to health owing to exposure. Reportedly, the company's women conductors did not participate.

Although the era of the train robber had long since ended, a surprising number of instances were recorded of attempts to hold up the electric cars in imitation of the Jesse James style. Needless to say, such attempts usually took place on a stretch of deserted suburban track rather than in crowded downtown districts. At Richmond in 1900, for instance, holdup men blocked a suburban line with a pile of stones in order to stop a trolley at a deserted spot. The motorman and conductor were quickly taken by surprise when they left the car to remove the obstruction. Another method employed to halt a car was for one or more of the holdup men to ride the car and simply pull down the trolley pole at the desired location. One attempt of this kind at Lima, O., in 1900 was thwarted by an intrepid motorman who providently had a revolver in his possession. When two holdup men halted the car at a deserted location, the motorman drew his revolver and sent the bandits scrambling for a nearby wood pursued by a hail of lead.

In still another holdup attempt, on New Jersey's Bridgeton & Millville Traction Company, four bandits were set upon by passengers and thrown from the car, which continued on its way in a shower of stones hurled by the chagrined thugs.

At Seattle in 1910 a trolley was successfully held up in the heart of town. Four young men stopped a Seattle Electric Company car at First Avenue South and Spokane Avenue at 1 a.m. and relieved the passengers of $1500 in money and jewels. All four were later apprehended and sentenced to the state penitentiary.

A Cleveland Electric Railway conductor was separated from his cash in more subtle fashion in 1900. On two consecutive mornings the conductor was confronted by a passenger who boarded at the same spot and tendered a $20 bill in payment of his fare. Unable to change the bill, the conductor allowed the man to ride free. Anticipating a repetition on the third morning, the conductor secured $20 in nickels and gleefully waited for his man. The passenger boarded at his usual corner and again proffered the $20 bill. This time the conductor promptly accepted it and presented $19.95 change in nickels to the amusement of passengers on the car who thought it a first-rate joke. The conductor's enjoyment quickly vanished when he turned in the bill at the office and was told it was counterfeit.

Operating as it did almost entirely in public streets, the trolley was particularly vulnerable to traffic mishaps. Although the streetcar's inability to deviate from its fixed path and its relatively sluggish braking action often made avoiding accidents difficult for trolley men, the electric car's greater

A dramatic rescue by an alert policeman saved a boy from the consequences of careless playing in the street.

A narrow squeak for another negligent youngster, who has been scooped up in this trolley's "life guard" fender. The life guard, normally carried in a raised position, was dropped to rail level by a mechanical linkage whenever the guard at the front struck an obstruction.

Although the trolley car's superior size and weight normally provided ample protection for its passengers in the event of street accidents, such mishaps were still the source of numerous and costly claims and no little amount of bad publicity. This set of photographs, posed on the Brooklyn Rapid Transit Company as part of a safety campaign around 1915, depicts some of the street accident hazards faced by trolley men.

This scene illustrated the tragic result of carelessly riding a scooter in a busy street.

Hitching rides on the back end of trolleys, a favorite pastime for boys everywhere, was something to be discouraged. As we are shown so graphically here, the practice could have unfortunate consequences. — *All photos, Library of Congress.*

Crossing collisions with steam railroad trains represented some of the most serious accidents in street railway history. In this early New Jersey scene, a Public Service Railway work car has arrived to help pick up what little remains of Raritan Line trolley No. 524 after the car unsuccessfully contested the Chimney Rock spur crossing with a Central Railroad of New Jersey locomotive. — *Collection of Howard E. Johnston.*

"Accidents That Happen Daily" was the title of this lurid drawing from a National Railroad Trolley Guard Company advertisement in a 1911 issue of *Electric Railway Journal.* The firm specialized in the manufacture of a "trolley guard" designed to prevent dewirements at hazardous points. — *Collection of William D. Middleton.*

Left unattended while its crew enjoyed a smoke at the end of the line, Manchester (N.H.) Street Railway trolley No. 82 rolled off down Derryfield Hill, narrowly missed another trolley, and finally crashed into the front of a furniture store after failing to negotiate the curve at Bridge and Elm streets. Here the battered trolley is extricated from the wreckage of the 1912 mishap. — *Collection of O. R. Cummings.*

Thirteen died and a score were injured in this smashup at the end of a wild runaway on the Mountain Lake Electric Railroad at Gloversville, N. Y., in 1902. Running at an excessive rate of speed with a load of Fourth of July excursionists, closed car No. 5 (right) overtook and collided with open car No. 1. Both cars then ran out of control at an estimated speed of 60 mph on the 11.5 per cent grade between the Mountain Lake resort and Gloversville before derailing on a curve at the bottom. Damage claims bankrupted the line. — *Collection of William D. Middleton.*

A runaway trolley of the Carbon Transit Company almost made it into the lobby of a Lehighton (Pa.) hotel. This kind of mishap was a constant and dangerous threat in the anthracite country of eastern Pennsylvania. The hilly terrain was a frequent cause of many such accidents. — *Collection of Howard E. Johnston.*

367

Excitement ran high in Superior, Wis., in 1914 when the Billings Park trolley derailed on the Great Northern viaduct, crashed through the guard rail, and dropped to the ground. — *Collection of Wayne C. Olsen.*

This Duluth Street Railway trolley tied up Duluth-Superior traffic after a 1913 derailment on the approaches to the Interstate Bridge. — *Collection of Wayne C. Olsen.*

size and weight in comparison with almost anything else on the street at least minimized the chances of injury to its passengers. Even in the most violent collisions with other vehicular traffic, the trolley usually came away with little more than some scratched paint and a damaged fender.

In the earlier years of electric traction, of course, horse-drawn vehicles were the principal hazard. Until the horses became accustomed to the electric cars, the animals tended to be skittish, and often a startled horse would overturn his carriage or wagon without ever being touched by the offending car.

In one early accident recorded at Minneapolis in 1893, a trolley en route downtown from Fort Snelling was charged by a runaway team of horses. One of the horses plunged over the front dash of the car, through the door, and fell dead on the floor, evidently of fright. The startled motorman narrowly escaped instant death by jumping out of the path of the crazed beast. "It was one of the liveliest and

most unusual accidents on record," concluded a news account.

Although the electric cars customarily came out best in street collisions, in a few instances the trolley was at a decided disadvantage. A relatively recent accident of this kind, and one of the most tragic, occurred in Chicago in 1950. A PCC streamliner packed with rush-hour passengers split a switch and collided with a gasoline truck near 63rd and State streets. In the ensuing explosion and conflagration the trolley was destroyed, nearby residences were set afire, and 33 passengers lost their lives.

One type of collision to which the trolley cars seemed particularly prone was the grade-crossing crash with steam railroad trains. These often resulted from the inadequacy of warning signals; another frequent cause was an untimely dewirement of the trolley pole, which left a car stranded without power in the path of an approaching train. So serious was this latter hazard regarded by street rail-

Nothing tied up rush-hour traffic quite like a strategically located derailment. Seven trolleys waited while emergency crews rerailed this Albany (N. Y.) car on North Pearl Street in 1944. — *Collection of Jim Shaughnessy.*

369

Passengers on this Rhode Island Company trolley had a narrow escape in 1921 when the Providence-Attleboro car derailed and plunged off Lebanon Bridge into Ten Mile River. Underbody equipment caught on the bridge structure and kept the car from going all the way into the river. Motorman Percy Titus escaped through a broken window, waded ashore, and joined the conductor in aiding passengers. — *Collection of Richard L. Wonson.*

One of the worst accidents in New England traction history was this 1903 head-on collision not far from Pelham Center, N. H., between two open cars of the Hudson, Pelham & Salem Electric Railway. The two cars, traveling between Nashua and Canobie Lake Park, met on a blind curve with lethal effect. The cars collided with such force that both roofs collapsed onto the terrified passengers, adding materially to the casualty toll and greatly hampering rescue efforts. Six persons were killed and 72 injured. — *Collection of O. R. Cummings.*

Accidents in which the elevated railway cars left the rails and plunged into the street below have been infrequent.

A Ninth Avenue (New York) El train took a plunge at Albany Street in 1921. — *Collection of Jeffrey Winslow.*

This New York Railways trolley landed with a devastating jolt in 1915 when the temporary shoring and planking supporting the street gave way during construction of the Broadway subway. — *Collection of Jeffrey Winslow.*

371

Considering the density of traffic, collisions between rapid transit trains have been rare. This savage telescoping took place on an El line of New York's Interborough Rapid Transit in 1922. — *Collection of Jeffrey Winslow.*

Among the most serious accidents in American railway history was the Malbone Street subway wreck on the Brooklyn Rapid Transit Company's Brighton Beach line in 1918, which took 97 lives. Following a derailment due to excessive speed, the train smashed against a tunnel abutment. Three of the train's five wooden cars were severely damaged, and the third car in the train, shown here, was almost entirely reduced to kindling. — *Collection of Jeffrey Winslow.*

waymen that a special protective mesh, mounted above the trolley wire to keep the pole in contact in case of dewirement, was frequently installed at steam-railroad crossings.

Typical of grade-crossing accidents was a 1927 collision at Superior, Wis., between a Billings Park streetcar and the Great Northern Railway's crack *Gopher*. Accounts differed concerning the cause of the accident, the most likely being that the crossing watchman lowered the gates after the streetcar was on the crossing, knocking the trolley pole from the wire and stalling the car in the path of the train. The passenger train, traveling at a speed of over 25 mph, demolished the wooden streetcar. Seven persons were killed and another 16 seriously injured. Among the dead was the locomotive fireman, who was fatally injured when he jumped from his locomotive in an effort to escape the collision. The crossing watchman narrowly escaped death when his watchtower was toppled by flying wreckage and burst into flames, ignited by coals from a heating stove.

Perhaps the most common cause of serious street railway accidents was the runaway car, and traction history is filled with harrowing tales of cars hurtling downhill out of control after brake failure or some similar mishap, almost invariably derailing and wreaking havoc before finally coming to rest. One of the most serious accidents in the early years of electric traction occurred at Tacoma, Wash., in 1900 when a crowded car inbound from South Tacoma and Spanaway Lake with a Fourth of July crowd lost its brakes on the Delin Street hill. After derailing at a sharp curve at the bottom of the grade, the trolley hurtled into space over a deep gully and landed on its roof after a fall of 75 feet. The heavy car trucks and motors crashed through the floor of the car, crushing many of the occupants. Forty-one passengers lost their lives, and more than 50 were injured.

A runaway trolley on Cleveland's Scranton Road line in 1916 set in motion a chain of mishaps. After derailing on a sharp curve at the foot of a long, steep grade, the runaway car crashed into the end posts of a 105-foot iron truss bridge, causing its collapse onto the tracks of the Baltimore & Ohio Railroad 23 feet below. A second trolley entered the span just as it failed and, together with the wreckage of the bridge, crashed onto the steam railroad tracks. Miraculously, only two persons lost their lives.

The worst accident in street railway history took place at Mexico City in 1953 as the result of a runaway on a single-track suburban line. After failing to wait for an outbound car in the siding at the top of a steep grade, an inbound car lost its air brakes and plunged head-on into the approaching car with brutal force. Both cars left the rails and rolled down a mountainside. Of some 200 passengers aboard the two cars, 66 were killed and close to 100 received serious injury.

One spectacular runaway that ended without serious property damage or any casualties was an incident described as "the great tram chase," which took place at Southampton, England, in 1942. A 15-year-old boy managed to set in motion two trolley cars left unattended in a storage track. Observing the two cars rolling downhill on The Avenue, a truck driver named Jesse Clark gave chase with his 5-ton lorry loaded with 6 tons of sand. By the time Clark caught up to the runaways they were traveling at better than 40 mph. Blowing his horn and frantically waving oncoming traffic out of the way, the truck driver finally managed to pass the speeding cars, pulled in front of them, allowed the leading car to overtake him, and then carefully braked all three vehicles to a halt. A bit of scraped paintwork was the only mark Clark's lorry had to show as a result of the spectacular chase and rescue.

Several street railway lines with particularly perilous grades equipped their cars with such devices as dynamic braking or magnetic track brakes to supplement ordinary braking equipment. Another safety measure was the installation of periodic derails that could be released only if a car was moving at a safe speed. The Lake Burien line of the Seattle Municipal Railway had a particularly dangerous 4.5 per cent grade with a sharp curve at the bottom, so the railway installed a safety siding which had a 15 per cent reverse grade to stop runaway cars. Shortly after installation of the safety siding, a descending car ran out of control; it reached an estimated speed of 60 mph before being diverted into the siding and safely brought to a halt. The motorman and eight passengers, who crouched on the floor during the wild ride, escaped injury. Only the conductor, who lost his nerve and jumped, was hurt.

A scattering of miscellaneous causes account for several of the more serious accidents recorded in street railway history. Second only to the Mexico City disaster of 1953 among North American street railway wrecks was an 1896 crash at Victoria, B. C. An overloaded iron bridge collapsed under the weight of a heavily loaded trolley carrying part of the crowd en route to a Queen's birthday celebration. The car plunged 75 feet to the bottom of a gorge, killing 54 of the 80 passengers aboard.

What was probably the worst trolley disaster in the United States took place in 1916, when the motorman of a heavily loaded Boston car failed to stop at the gate guarding the open Summer Street drawbridge. The car crashed through the gate and toppled into the Fort Point Channel, turning end over end before coming to rest in 30 feet of water. Forty-five passengers were drowned.

Because of the difficulty in reaching a trouble scene with rail work equipment, most street railways preferred off-rail emergency equipment. (Above) This horse-drawn tower wagon of the San Diego Electric Railway was all set to gallop off to the scene of trouble. (Right) A truck-mounted model was used by the Toronto Transportation Commission in 1931. — *Collection of Frederick W. Reif, from Eric Sanders (above); Toronto Transit Commission (right).*

What must be regarded as one of the most unusual accidents in trolley history occurred at Brooklyn in 1900. As a result of heavy rains, settlement took place in some new earth fill under a double-track car line, lowering the inner rail of each track by several inches. Two cars traveling in opposite directions leaned inward simultaneously as they met on the uneven track. The corner of the roof of one car caught under the roof of the other and ripped out every roof support on one side before the cars could be stopped. Terrified passengers crawled under their seats for safety as the car roof crashed down on them. Somehow, all aboard the car escaped injury.

Considering the billions of passengers carried, the heavy density of traffic, and the relatively high operating speeds customary in rapid transit service, the safety record of America's rapid transit railways over nearly a century of operation has been little less than phenomenal. Surely this safety record must rank as one of the finest in transportation history.

Despite wide fears of just such mishaps when the first elevated railway began regular operation at New York in 1871, only three instances are recorded of accidents in which the El cars actually left the rails and plunged into the streets below. All three of these occurred on the New York system and involved derailments at curves or switches. The total death toll for all three accidents was only 23 passengers. There are more frequent instances of ordinary

collisions and derailments on the elevated, but even these are remarkably few in number. The most serious accident of this nature, a 1936 rear-end collision between an interurban train and a Chicago elevated train, resulted in the death of 11 persons, all of them passengers in the wooden rear car of the "L" train, which was almost completely telescoped by a heavy steel interurban car.

The safety record for subway systems has been equally good. The New York subway system, for example, has not had a fatal passenger accident on its trains since 1928, during which time it has transported well in excess of 60 billion passengers. In the entire period since 1910 the New York rapid transit system, including both elevated and subway lines, has had but 141 passenger fatalities, almost all of them concentrated in two tragic subway crashes.

The first of these took place in wartime 1918 on the Brooklyn Rapid Transit Company's Brighton Beach line. Following a wildcat motormen's strike on the morning of November 1, the company pressed into service every available nonunion motorman and any other employees with experience at operating trains. One of these, a crew dispatcher named Luciano, was assigned to a rush-hour run on the Brighton Beach line. Unfamiliar with the line, Luciano failed to make the necessary speed reduction to 6 mph on a sharp curve where the line made a transition from surface level to subway trackage at Malbone Street. The train entered the curve at a speed later esti-

374

The carbarn fire was a distressingly frequent occurrence in street railway history. This was the wreckage of a 1923 blaze that destroyed the Columbia Street carhouse of the Chicago, South Bend & Northern Indiana Railway at South Bend with a loss of eight cars. Full service was restored three days later with nine cars hastily purchased from Cleveland. Only 4 years earlier the same carbarn had burned down with similar results. On that occasion replacement cars were bought from Akron. — *Van-Zillmer Collection*.

A Cleveland flood during the 1950's stranded this two-car Shaker Heights Rapid Transit train. City firemen in a boat rescued the helpless passengers and crew. — *Cleveland Plain Dealer, from Railroad Magazine*.

Virtually hidden in a cloud of snow, a rotary sweeper of the Regina (Sask.) Municipal Railway cleared a car line of a light snowfall in 1947. — *Collection of Allan H. Berner.*

The Berkshire (Mass.) Street Railway had to call out its snowplow to clear the line between Glendale and Housatonic after the Housatonic River overflowed and left the railway track covered with ice. — *Collection of Howard E. Johnston.*

The severe winter of 1919-1920 proved too much for Massachusetts' financially shaky Blue Hill Street Railway. Matters came to a head during the severe blizzard of February 5, 1920. As crews struggled to rescue snowbound trolleys, the powerhouse coal supply ran out and the trolley wire went dead. This car and a snowplow were stuck fast in drifts on Ponkapoag Hill for more than a month. The railway never resumed operation. — *Collection of Carl L. Smith.*

A little Taunton snowplow of the Georgetown, Rowley & Ipswich Street Railway led two single-truck trolleys through deep drifts near Byfield, Mass., as the crew looked on. – *Collection of LeRoy O. King.*

mated to be as high as 30 mph, the second car derailed at the entrance to the tunnel, and it was followed off the rails by three more cars. Thrown against the tunnel abutment, in which heavy iron uprights had been imbedded, three of the wooden cars were torn open and one was demolished. Some 97 passengers lost their lives.

New York's second major subway crash occurred just short of 10 years later when the ninth car of a 10-car southbound express derailed at a defective switch south of the Times Square station on the IRT subway. The car swung diagonally across the track; and while the rear end was torn open against a concrete wall at one side of the track, the front end was smashed against a row of steel columns on the other side. At the same time, the tenth car of the train crashed into the wreckage. Seventeen passengers lost their lives in this unfortunate mishap.

In addition to experiencing the perils of accidents, the street railways were exposed to the year-round hazards of fire, flood, and storm. Fire in particular posed a continuing threat to the traction companies. On those lines which employed some type of coal-burning heaters on their cars, fire aboard the cars was a frequent occurrence. The folklore of the street railway is filled with accounts, some of them more than likely true, in which a cool-headed trolley

crew ran their blazing car to the nearest firehouse, where the flames were extinguished by quick-acting firemen. Far more serious in its consequences was the carbarn fire, which appears as a recurring theme in street railway history. According to the *National Fire Prevention Quarterly*, there were 240 serious fires at North American street railway carbarns or workshops between 1897 and 1940.

The classic carbarn fire was a nighttime happening, breaking out perhaps as the result of a discarded cigarette or an electrical fault. The cars themselves were a highly combustible mixture of wood, grease, paint, and varnish, and the carbarn structures were often no better. Even if the fire was promptly discovered, damage to the trolley wire or power failure frequently made it impossible to run the cars out in time. With this eventuality in mind, a Massachusetts trolley company, the Athol & Orange Street Railway, when reconstructing its carhouse in 1896 placed the storage tracks on a slope from rear to front in order that cars could be run out without power in the event of fire.

Typical of the consequences of a major carhouse fire was the experience of the Georgetown, Rowley & Ipswich Street Railway of Massachusetts in 1901. On the night of February 20 fire broke out in a car stored in the company's Byfield carbarn and swiftly

Snow removal in the wake of a severe blizzard required a major effort on the part of the street railway companies. From 75 to 100 of these horse-drawn snow removal boxes were in operation at Ottawa, Canada, after each snowstorm. A V-bottom and hinged sides facilitated unloading at the snow dumps, which were conveniently located close to trolley lines. Teamsters who provided the service were paid in the form of a disk for each load. These were later exchanged for cash at the company's general office. — *Ottawa Transportation Commission.*

After experiencing increasing difficulty in hiring sufficient horse teams for snow removal, the Ottawa Electric Railway bought a fleet of Model T Ford trucks, equipped with oversize boxes, which bore the brunt of snow removal requirements for some 25 years after their purchase in 1918. — *Ottawa Transportation Commission.*

spread to the other cars stored in the building, as well as the building itself. By dawn only three walls of the carbarn remained standing, and 16 trolleys and three snowplows had been reduced to smoldering embers and twisted metal. So quickly had the flames spread that workmen had been able to push only a single car to safety, and even that was badly scorched. Until new cars could be purchased the company was able to maintain service only by means of equipment borrowed from two neighboring street railway companies. In the declining years of electric traction such a disastrous event was sufficient to bring a permanent end to streetcar operation on more than one hard-pressed system.

Weather conditions frequently raised havoc with street railway operations. Wind and thunder storms often damaged the overhead trolley wire, and sometimes tracks were inundated by floods. Probably no weather condition gave more trouble — at least in northern locations — than snow. Most street railway companies took seriously their obligation to provide dependable public transportation, and maintained fleets of snowplows, sweepers, scrapers, and other snow-fighting equipment which was hurled against the elements in an effort to keep the car lines open.

Usually the battle against a blizzard began with the dispatching of extra cars to run up and down the tracks just to keep them open. Track men were sent out to keep switches clear. As the snow became heavier, the big rattan-broomed rotary sweepers went into action, followed by snowplows if the going got really rough. In the aftermath of exception-ally heavy snowfalls the trolley companies had to organize a massive snow removal effort to remove drifts and the windrows thrown up by the plows in streets on which the cars ran. Even when the trolley lines were successful in keeping their tracks open, maintaining satisfactory service was sometimes difficult during and after a heavy snow. Often the car tracks represented the only cleared path in principal thoroughfares, and the trolleys were forced to contest their right of way with all manner of street traffic.

During the late 1920's the Duluth (Minn.) Street Railway, which contended with extremely severe winter weather conditions, designed and built an unusual piece of equipment for removing the heavy accumulations of ice and snow that built up in the company's tracks during the long Minnesota winter. Nicknamed *Goliath* by company employees, Duluth's ice-breaker was a heavy four-wheel vehicle that could be pushed or pulled through the streets by another piece of equipment. A large cast-iron roller, 2 feet in diameter and weighing 6 tons, was suspended between the unit's axles. Mounted on the roller were diagonal cutters, similar to the cleats mounted on the wheels of an old-fashioned steam tractor; these helped to break up troublesome accumulations of ice. *Goliath* was reported to be extremely noisy, and residents complained that windows rattled and the ground shook as it passed through the streets.

Life on the cars, it would seem, provided plenty of excitement.

One of the greatest snowfalls in Seattle history paralyzed street traffic throughout the city in January 1916. A line of Seattle, Renton & Southern trolleys was stalled in deep snow on Fourth Avenue. — *Collection of Robert S. Wilson.*

A parade of battered old trolleys, handsomely decorated in flags and bunting, marked the end of 57 years of streetcar service at Knoxville, Tenn., in 1947. — *Collection of Allan H. Berner.*

The Trolley Vanishes

DIRECTLY, at least, the trolley car was usually displaced by the motorbus, or on occasion that hybrid vehicle, the trolley bus. In a larger sense, however, the trolley was a victim of the automobile. As America made a swift transition from a mass-transportation- to a private-transportation-oriented way of life in the years after World War I, the street railway became increasingly superfluous. As a growing number of families took to the streets in their own automobiles, the demand became less and less for the kind of high-capacity mass transportation the streetcar provided, and the operating companies quickly learned that the newly developed motorbus provided a more economical way of transporting whatever traffic remained.

Made mobile by their automobiles, Americans no longer were tied to a trolley line; and the new suburbia, almost totally dependent upon private transportation, began to spring up in the outer reaches of the American city. Even if the street railways had been financially able to build new extensions — which they weren't — they would have found it impossible to economically serve the scattered population char-

acteristic of the new automobile-oriented suburbs.

The potential competitive threat of the automobile was being weighed and considered as early as the turn of the century. Said a 1900 Louisville *Courier-Journal* editorial of the vehicle: ". . . It has never been put to practical use, though it has become to some extent a fashionable fad. How large a use can be made of it for carrying passengers and freight cannot be foretold with certainty, but it is reason-

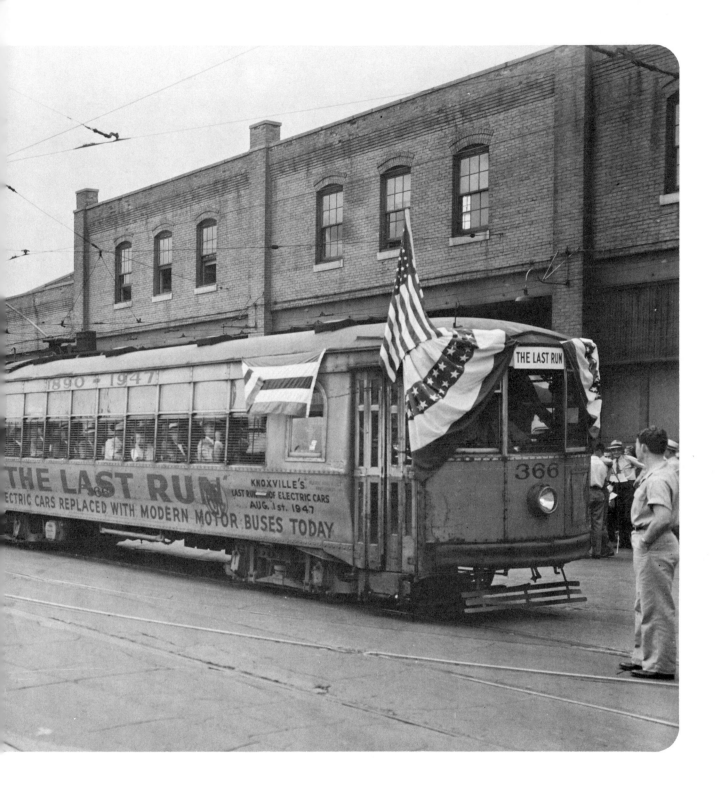

ably sure it can never compete with streetcars."

During the same year, the *Street Railway Journal*, taking note of a new automobile stage line that was providing a regularly scheduled service at Cleveland, commented, "It is not thought, however, that automobiles can ever practically compete with electric cars in Cleveland."

For well over another decade the automobile remained little more than a curiosity or, upon occa-

sion, a traffic nuisance. Street railway traffic continued to grow at an encouraging rate, and the only cause for alarm among the trolley men was an unhealthy upward trend in operating costs.

Oddly enough, an economic depression shortly before World War I brought the first real competition from the automobile. Beginning in Los Angeles about mid-1914, unemployed motorists began to solicit passengers along streetcar routes for a five-

Downtown Peoria was nearly deserted on an October evening in 1946 as an Illinois Power Company Birney waited for a traffic light at Adams and Main streets on a trip over the Knoxville route. It was the last night of trolley operation in Peoria. — *Paul Stringham.*

Except for the electric car itself, no other development in street railway history met with public enthusiasm comparable to that afforded the PCC cars. A crowd jammed downtown St. Louis streets in 1940 for the debut of 50 new PCC's. — *Collection of William J. Clouser.*

cent fare. The "jitney" craze, as it was called, spread rapidly. By the end of the year nearly 800 jitneys were operating in Los Angeles alone, and at the height of the fad in 1915 an estimated 6000 to 10,000 jitneys were running in U. S. cities.

For a time the jitneys posed a serious threat to the earnings of street railway systems. Operating only when and where there was traffic, the jitney drivers made no effort to provide the scheduled, all-day service that was required of the traction companies, but simply skimmed off the "cream" of the peak-hour traffic. The experience of the Los Angeles Railway was typical of that of the harder hit large city systems. By the end of 1914 LARy was losing an estimated $600 a day in revenues to the jitneys, and the company was forced to cancel an ambitious car rebuilding program and lay off a hundred men in its shops. During 1915 jitney losses totaled an estimated half million dollars. The company halted all track extensions and canceled its new carbuilding program.

The trolley companies fought back against the jitneys as best they could. The Richmond (Va.) street railway company put on its own jitney fleet in an effort to drive the private owners off the streets. The public seemed to resent this strategem; and the trolley company's "one-eyed jitneys," as the distinctive single-headlight Briscoe automobiles used were called, never proved popular. The San Diego Electric Railway simply suspended service on several routes hard hit by jitney competition. The Eastern Massachusetts Street Railway, announcing "war to the finish" against unregulated jitney competition, threatened to discontinue service in cities where jitneys were allowed to "run wild." The most frequent anti-jitney tactic, however, was simply a vigorous campaign carried on by the streetcar companies

World War II brought unaccustomed activity to U. S. trolley systems. Los Angeles Railway's South Park shops were the scene of intense activity in 1942 as cars were readied for wartime service.—*Collection of Donald Duke.*

for some licensing and regulation for the jitneys.

After 1915 the craze began to subside. Finding that jitney driving was not a very profitable occupation, many of the drivers dropped out, although for a time it seemed there was always a new one ready

Trolleys got their first real automotive competition in the jitney craze around World War I. Two open cars and an early jitney roll through an intersection in Washington, D.C. — *Collection of LeRoy O. King.*

to go into business when another quit. Improving business conditions helped too, as many drivers went back to more remunerative jobs. Most important, more and more regulatory bodies began to see the wisdom of the trolley companies' argument that permitting unregulated competition to weaken a city's mass-transportation system was not in the long-term public good. As soon as the jitneys were required to obtain licenses, post bonds, and maintain some degree of regular service, most of them vanished from the streets. Before the end of 1916 the situation was

encouraging enough for street railway executive Dr. Thomas Conway Jr. to remark that "the plague has run its course." By 1921 only an estimated 2000 to 3000 jitneys remained in operation in the United States.

In a few areas, though, the jitneys hung on tenaciously. As late as 1925 private jitney buses still accounted for fully 25 per cent of the mass transport traffic at Norfolk, Va., before they were finally driven out of business. In Honolulu, jitney competition did not succumb to regulatory control until 1940,

In its declining years, trolley No. 3 of Mount Mansfield Electric Railway reposed forlornly in a ramshackle carbarn at Stowe, Vt. The line's cars made their final runs through the Green Mountain countryside in 1932. — *Collection of Howard E. Johnston.*

A cheery sight on a wintry day was Elmira (N. Y.) Birney No. 117 as the little trolley bravely fought her way through a January 1939 blizzard. Abandonment of the system was barely two months away. — *Collection of Allan H. Berner.*

Southbound to Drake, a Pittsburgh Railways interurban PCC car raced along under the thunderhead of an approaching storm in 1959. Trolleys remained the principal mode of Pittsburgh public transportation into the 1960's, but declined rapidly after the new Port Authority of Allegheny County took over in 1964. By early 1967 only 58 track-miles and little more than 100 active cars remained. — *F. W. Schneider III.*

less than a year before the trolleys themselves vanished from the streets.

On a few occasions jitney service was used as a weapon against the street railway companies during strikes. In a 1916 strike at Wilkes-Barre, Pa., striking trolley men organized both a streetcar boycott and a competing jitney service. When the Denver Tramways attempted to maintain service with nonstrikers and strikebreakers during a bitter 1920 strike, the union retaliated with a free jitney service operated by automobile-owning strikers. After Portsmouth (Va.) trolley men organized a jitney service during a 1922 strike, they found the business so profitable that they kept right on operating it even after the strike was settled. Eventually the trolley company was forced to close three lines.

Even though the jitneys had no lasting effect on the traction companies, the World War I period found the industry facing grave problems. Although street railway mileage and passenger traffic were still growing, profits had begun to drop. Often extensions of service into new territory at the same

Two old trolleys of the Northern Indiana Railway met on the Notre Dame line at South Bend in the summer of 1940. Streetcar operation in the Indiana city ended shortly afterward. — *Van-Zillmer Collection.*

uniform fare contributed to the decline in net earnings. Most street railways were confronted with an increasingly heavy tax burden. Labor and material costs were rising rapidly; during the World War I period they almost doubled. To make matters worse, many companies were obliged by their franchises to operate at a fixed five-cent fare that had been in effect for many years, and regulatory bodies showed little inclination to change it. There was a growing number of street railway receiverships, and the situation became so serious that President Wilson appointed a Federal Electric Railway Commission to investigate conditions in the industry. In due time the commission reported that the industry was indeed in serious financial difficulty, and submitted a number of recommendations that helped somewhat, at least where they were heeded.

Meanwhile, there were some other encouraging developments in the industry's search for ways to get

costs in line. The Birney Safety Car, developed in 1915, was a huge success at cutting costs and increasing earnings on lightly traveled lines. Even more important, the thousands of Birney cars demonstrated that one-man operation was entirely practical. Soon street railways were ordering large numbers of new cars or rebuilding older equipment for one-man operation.

Throughout the 1920's unaccustomed activity on the part of both the carbuilders and the larger street railways was directed toward the development of improved equipment. More interest than ever before was shown in providing greater passenger comfort, imaginative new color schemes were applied to equipment, and merchandising and traffic promotion assumed new importance. The Electric Railway Presidents' Conference Committee, organized in 1929, put 5 years and a million dollars into a research effort aimed at development of a radically new trol-

Although its regular services had long since been operated exclusively with PCC cars, Washington (D. C.) Transit Company retained a few older cars for occasions such as this 1957 outing of the Washington Electric Railway Historical Society. All trolley operation in the nation's capital ended early in 1962. — *John J. Bowman Jr.*

Iowa's last trolley line was a suburban route operated between Waterloo and Cedar Falls by the Waterloo, Cedar Falls & Northern Railroad. During its last decade of operation the line was served by three former Knoxville (Tenn.) lightweights built in 1930 by Perley A. Thomas. One is shown near Cedar Falls in the spring of 1954. — *William D. Middleton.*

ley car. From this emerged the technical triumph of the PCC car, which was produced by the thousands over a period of 15 years.

Even as the trolley was enjoying its years of greatest triumph, its eventual successor, the motorbus, was already making a name for itself. The first big success for the bus was on New York's Fifth Avenue, where in 1908 a fleet of French-built double-deckers was installed in place of the Avenue's old horse-drawn omnibuses. Trolley cars had never been permitted on the exclusive thoroughfare.

The jitney craze led to the development of better-designed buses, and by the early 1920's a few street railway companies had timidly tried out the bus for service on lightly traveled outlying lines. As late as 1922 only some 370 buses were being operated by street railway companies. But in 1924 alone streetcar companies bought 1200 new buses and tripled their annual bus mileage. Another 1800 were bought in 1925, and annual bus traffic was doubled over that of the preceding year. Bus transportation was solidly on the path to success. By 1932 some 15,000 buses were in service, transporting more than a billion passengers annually. Only 5 years later the number had almost doubled, and annual bus traffic was running

Refurbished in its original colors, San Francisco Municipal Railway's first trolley reappeared in 1962 to celebrate the city-owned system's 50th anniversary. By this time regular service was being provided with a fleet of 105 postwar PCC streamliners. — *James C. Wren.*

A Dallas trolley rattled across the Tenth Street bridge on the last day of operation on the Trinity Heights route in August 1949. Streetcar operation continued elsewhere in Dallas for 10 more years. — *George A. Roush.*

By 1967 the sole surviving American example of conventional streetcar operation was the St. Charles line of the New Orleans Public Service Company. Trolley No. 948, a two-man standard car built by Perley A. Thomas in 1924, rolls past Tulane University and an elaborate fountain in Audubon Park. — *F. W. Schneider III.*

Operating a fleet of 165 narrow-gauge streamliners, Los Angeles was among the major users of PCC's until all trolley operation ended in 1963. This PCC lineup waited for "P" line service in 1951. — *Donald Sims.*

Threatening the supremacy of the streetcar as well as the motorbus was the hybrid vehicle known as the "trolley bus" or the "trackless trolley," whose proponents argued that it combined the best features of both. These early trackless trolleys, introduced on Staten Island in the 1920's, resembled diminutive streetcars mounted on rubber tires. — *Library of Congress.*

Aged trolleys rumbled through downtown streets on Denver's last day of streetcar operation on July 1, 1950. — *Courtesy of Electric Railroaders' Association.*

A decorous ceremony at the Vassar College terminal of Poughkeepsie's Main Street line in 1935 marked the last run of the Poughkeepsie & Wappingers Falls Railway Company. — *Collection of Allan H. Berner.*

Their long years of service over, Los Angeles trolleys were stacked three deep in a Terminal Island junkyard in 1960 awaiting conversion to scrap metal. — *Gary G. Allen*.

A usual part of the scrapping process for old trolleys was burning to remove unwanted materials. After the remains cooled, the junkman carried away the usable scrap metal that was left. These surplus Third Avenue Railway cars were put to the torch at the company's Garden Avenue yard in 1940. — *Jeffrey Winslow*.

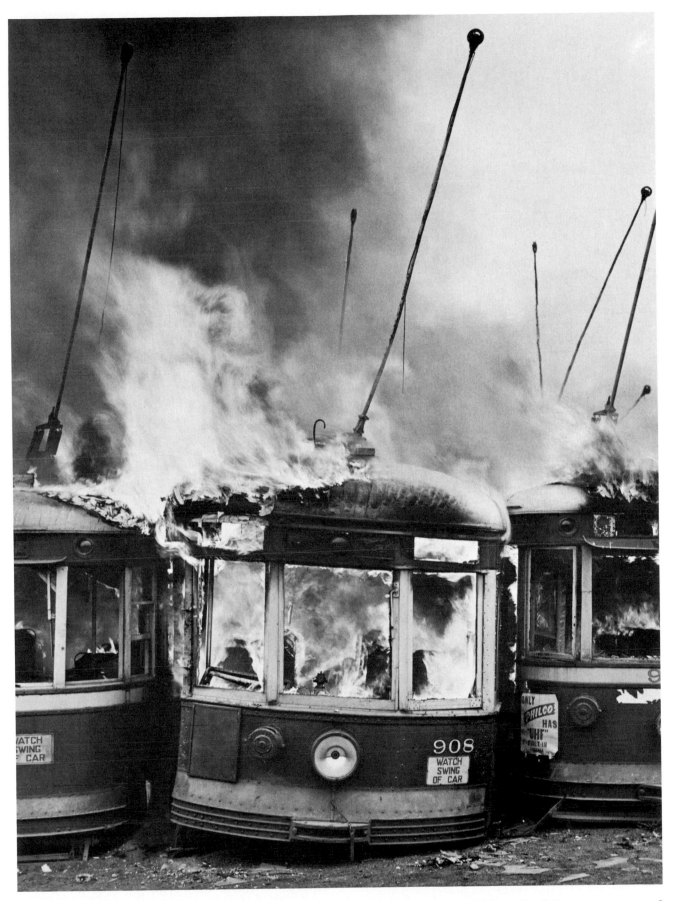

With their trolley poles reaching vainly upward, a group of Lehigh Valley Transit streetcars were consumed by roaring flames at a Bethlehem Steel Company scrapyard in 1953. — *Collection of Allan H. Berner.*

Ready to begin its Sunday afternoon schedule, a former Connecticut Company trolley emerged from the carhouse at the Connecticut Electric Railway Association's Warehouse Point Trolley Museum. — *William D. Middleton.*

well in excess of 3 billion passengers a year. The rise of the motorbus seemed relentless.

The reasons for the success of the bus were many. Its operating costs were low, and no costly maintenance of track and overhead systems was required. The ability of the bus to swoop into the curb to pick up passengers was a safety asset, and its independence of fixed routings was regarded by many as a decided advantage over the trolley car. In an automobile age the lumbering trolley car seemed very much out of date, and motorists everywhere complained about rough trolley tracks and the hindrance to free traffic flow represented by safety islands for car riders.

By the early 1930's the trolley car had for the most part vanished from the smaller American cities, and even in the larger cities the bus was playing an increasingly important role on lightly traveled routes.

A major victory for the bus came in 1933 when San Antonio, Tex., with a population of over 200,000, became America's first large all-bus city.

The trolley car's greatest advantage was on routes of heaviest traffic, and it was here that it survived longest. The roomy cars were capable of packing in passenger loads far exceeding anything with which a motorbus could cope, and the high fixed costs of maintaining track and overhead were spread over a greater number of passengers. Indeed, many proponents of the "balanced" transit system maintained that each type of vehicle had its own area of best application and that the trolley car remained superior to all others for heavily traveled routes. The thousands of PCC cars placed in service beginning in 1936 were largely applied to this kind of service, and on many big city systems the trolley car seemed to have retained a permanent place.

In a dramatic example of after-dark photography, three retired New England trolleys met on the Connecticut Electric Railway's operating museum trackage in the Connecticut woods at Warehouse Point. — *Jim Shaughnessy.*

World War II halted for a few years the decline of the street railway, and elderly trolley cars of every description that had somehow escaped earlier scrapping were pressed into service to accommodate a tremendous wartime traffic. Once the war was over, however, traction's decline resumed. Despite record PCC car production in the years immediately after the war, the number of active cars and total track-miles were rapidly reduced. By 1951, when domestic streetcar production ended with a 25-car PCC order for San Francisco, it had become evident that the street railway, in its customary form at least, was on the way to extinction in North America.

Despite the superior qualities of the PCC car, the remaining street railway operations were becoming increasingly uneconomical. Even though the American urban population was growing at a rapid rate, the volume of public transportation traffic continued to decline, and fewer and fewer lines enjoyed sufficient patronage to warrant streetcar operation.

The cost of new trolleys was substantially higher than that for mass-produced motorbuses, and many cities found that growing traffic congestion made it almost impossible for the more expensive PCC cars to realize their superior earning potential. Chicago was a notable example. By 1953, when the newest of its 683 PCC cars was barely 5 years old, the Chicago Transit Authority came to the conclusion that traffic congestion had so hampered its surface lines that continued trolley operation was hopelessly uneconomical. During the next 5 years some 570 of CTA's newest PCC's were sold to the St. Louis Car Company for scrapping and reincarnation as PCC-type rapid-transit cars, and all Chicago trolley operation was ended by the summer of 1958.

By the early 1950's trolleys were even disappear-

Loaded with Sunday visitors, a single-truck open car rattled through the Connecticut woods on the Branford Trolley Museum at East Haven, Conn. The Branford group has preserved more than 50 items of electric rolling stock, one of the largest such projects operated by a museum. — *Jim Shaughnessy.*

The oldest and largest operating trolley museum is that of the Seashore Electric Railway at Kennebunkport, Me. Former Blackpool (England) double-decker No. 144 is one of a fleet of some 75 cars acquired from points throughout the U. S. and cities as distant as Rome, Nagasaki, and Sydney. — *Jim Shaughnessy.*

ing from many of the major cities that had adopted the PCC car in large numbers. San Diego, one of the earliest cities to acquire PCC's, ended streetcar operation in 1949. Cincinnati gave up trolleys in 1951, and Birmingham and Cleveland followed a year later. Notwithstanding the purchase of a large fleet of postwar PCC's, Minneapolis and St. Paul trolleys were gone by 1954. The Detroit, Brooklyn, and Vancouver systems folded up in 1956. Kansas City cars made their last runs in 1957, and 2 years later the Dallas system was also gone.

By mid-1967 trolleys remained in only a handful of North American cities. Large fleets of PCC cars continued to operate in Toronto, Boston, Philadelphia, Pittsburgh, and San Francisco. At Newark and Cleveland, PCC cars provided service on lines of semi-rapid-transit character. In New Orleans, standard two-man cars continued to operate over a single route that afforded the only surviving Amer-

ican example of conventional trolley operation. At El Paso an aging fleet of PCC cars still rattled across the Mexican border to Ciudad Juarez in an international operation with a tenuous future, and in Mexico itself the cars still ran only at Mexico City, Tampico, and Veracruz.

The departure of the streetcar from the streets of the American city almost invariably was an occasion for some form of municipal celebration and often a good deal of public nostalgia. On a few occasions the departure of the trolleys was made the excuse for uninhibited hooliganism by local riffraff. The most notable example was the "last run" celebration on the Norfolk (Va.) system of the Virginia Transit Company in July 1948.

The company's last regular run left downtown Norfolk for Ocean View at 12:40 a.m. on July 11 crowded with drunks attracted to the affair. Soon after the trip got under way the celebrants ripped down the advertising placards in the car, and then proceeded to wrench down the standee straps. Next someone pulled out the rear roller sign and began tearing it to pieces. Then a seat handle was used to smash out the car's rear window, and soon afterward the car's seats were torn loose one by one and hurled through broken windows. The car limped into Ocean View at 1:30 a.m. with every light broken, including its headlight, and with but a single window unsmashed. By the time police arrived in response to a riot call, all but two of the hoodlums had escaped into the darkness. An hour later a second trolley arrived to tow the battered "last car" back to the carbarn.

There were several occasions, too, when the trolleys faded from the scene in the midst of acrimonious conflict between the streetcar company and local authorities. One early case in 1920 involved the Eighth Street local line operated at Goshen, Ind., by the Northern Indiana Railway. The line was a consistent money loser, but the city council regularly refused the company permission to abandon it. Finally, after learning that the local judge would be out of town for a weekend and things would be pretty quiet in Goshen, the company decided to act. A crew of men hastily brought in on Friday evening worked through the night and into the next day tearing up the rails and pulling down the overhead. By the time local authorities realized what was happening and halted the work, the destruction was a *fait accompli* and the line never resumed operation.

A somewhat different incident occurred at Council Bluffs, Ia., in 1948. After the Omaha & Council Bluffs Street Railway had rejected a proffered new franchise, the city awarded one to a new bus company instead. Protected by a court injunction, the streetcar company continued to operate its cars on the interstate line to Omaha in competition with the new bus service. Just to be on the safe side, the trolley company ran its own bus service as well, giving Omaha-Council Bluffs travelers a surfeit of service while the dispute lasted. When the injunction protecting the trolley operation ended at noon on September 25, Council Bluffs police forced the cars into the barn one by one; and on this note the trolley era ended in Council Bluffs.

In a majority of cases, however, the trolley car made its departure in a suitably dignified manner. Frequently a Sunday rotogravure spread, depicting transportation progress from horsecar to bus, would appear to underscore the occasion with appropriate nostalgia. The last days of operation were usually marked by a noticeable increase in riding as sentimental old-timers journeyed for the last time, or parents hurried to give their children their first and only trolley ride. Typically, the last cars were decorously draped in bunting or black hangings, although occasionally there were lapses in taste in the form of lugubrious faces or similar decorations painted on the cars. Quite often the old cars were paraded, generally followed by a string of the shiny new buses that were taking over. In more recent years, as trolley enthusiasts multiplied, at least one chartered car was usually on hand to transport the faithful over the system for the last time; and on the occasion of any major abandonment, a good deal of more or less good-natured jockeying took place among rival fan groups for the privilege of operating the very last car.

An unusual variation in the customary "last day" celebration marked the end of trolley operation at Atlantic City, N. J., on December 28, 1955. The trolley company decided to contribute the entire day's revenues to the Atlantic City hospital, which stationed its most attractive nurses aboard the cars to hand out suitable "last day" certificates to every rider.

The decline of trolley operation in North America was characterized by a growth of organized interest in the preservation of the history of the street railway era. Three national railway enthusiast organizations formed during the 1930's devoted their activities to electric railways, and dozens of local organizations occupied themselves with similar interests. The pursuits of the traction enthusiasts included the operation of excursions over remaining electric railway properties, the compilation of exhaustively detailed historical publications, and the collection of maps, timetables, and other traction memorabilia.

The ultimate achievement of the fans was the preservation of the trolley car itself. The first group formed for this purpose was the Seashore Electric Railway, organized at Kennebunkport, Me., in 1939. By 1967 more than 40 similar organizations had been established in the U. S. and Canada — almost all of them volunteer in character — which had preserved over 400 items of electric railway equipment of every description. A dozen or more of the museum groups were operating traction equipment over their own trackage or were at the point of doing so. Indeed, by the beginning of 1967 there were as many operating trolley museums as there were surviving trolley systems in North America.

A two-car PCC train inbound on the Shaker Heights Rapid Transit meets a four-car train on Cleveland's postwar rapid transit east of Kinsman Road. — *Herbert H. Harwood Jr.*

The Return of Electric Traction

EVEN AS the trolley car in its conventional form was rapidly vanishing from the streets of the American city, the electric railway was beginning a modest resurgence. The trend toward urbanization of America, which had continued ever since the formation of the republic, had, if anything, accelerated in modern times. The requirement for urban transportation was a constantly growing one, then, and if the trolley car had become unable to satisfy it, the motorbus and the private automobile weren't doing much better at the job.

From the time automobile ownership had become almost universal in the years after World War I, America had been committed to a massive road construction program that sought to provide for the relentless flow of motor vehicles pouring forth from the Detroit production lines. Somehow the millennium never arrived; and no matter how vast the expenditures for highways and parking facilities, only rarely were America's urban centers able to do much more than stave off total traffic strangulation. Disenchanted with the notion that the expressway provided the total answer to the urban transportation requirement, America's cities began showing renewed interest in electric traction.

One form in which the trolley itself seemed occasionally destined to survive was in the "limited tramline" concept, a mode of private right-of-way trolley operation that represented a compromise

Four cars packed with Shaker Heights commuters burst forth from the subterranean depths of Cleveland Union Terminal aboard a rush-hour Van Aken Express with ex-Twin Cities PCC 68 leading. — *Herbert H. Harwood Jr.*

Outbound from Cleveland Union Terminal, a Van Aken Local of Shaker Heights Rapid Transit and an Erie Railroad passenger train race eastward through the Cuyahoga River Valley in 1954. — *Herbert H. Harwood Jr.*

A three-car train of former Cleveland trolleys leans into a curve west of Lee Road on the Van Aken Division of Shaker Heights' trolley/rapid-transit system. PCC's now provide all SHRT service. — *Herbert H. Harwood Jr.*

between the extremes of conventional streetcar operation in public thoroughfares and a full-fledged rapid transit system.

What is probably the best North American example extant of the limited tramline concept is a remarkable electric railway completed at Cleveland in 1920. Conceived by Cleveland's renowned real estate and railroad tycoons, the brothers Oris P. and Mantis J. Van Sweringen, the Cleveland Interurban Railroad, or Shaker Heights Rapid Transit as it is presently known, was constructed to provide rapid transportation between downtown Cleveland and the exclusive new residential community the Van Sweringens were promoting at suburban Shaker Heights. The inner portion of the 15-mile line, which terminated at the expansive Cleveland Union Terminal, was constructed to high standards characteristic of a heavy-duty rapid transit system. Two outer branches of the system, however, were laid in the broad center malls of Shaker and Van Aken boulevards, much as conventional trolley trackage in a similar circumstance. Initially, a fleet of leased Cleveland Railway trolleys, equipped for multiple-unit operation, were employed on the line. More recently, PCC cars have been acquired to operate all services.

In 1935 the Public Service Corporation of New Jersey opened its Newark Subway, a subway-surface trolley line installed in part in the bed of the abandoned Morris & Essex Canal which provided a fast run downtown for several suburban routes. Although trolley operation ended on the last of the connecting lines in 1952, a fleet of PCC cars continue to run on the 4-mile subway route, offering a connecting service with the company's bus routes.

A more recent example of the limited tramline is Boston's Riverside line, opened in 1959. Constructed to a great extent on the right of way of the abandoned Highland Branch of the Boston & Albany Railroad, the 12-mile line reaches downtown Boston via the venerable Tremont Street trolley subway. As is the Shaker Heights Rapid Transit, the Riverside line is operated with multiple-unit PCC trolleys.

Indeed, in nearly every American city in which the trolley car continued to operate in 1967, the cars had survived largely as a result of operating conditions which provided, at least in part, the freedom from general street traffic contemplated in the limited tramline concept.

At Boston a network of PCC-equipped trolley lines ran almost entirely over either private right of way or in a downtown trolley subway system. Similarly, the principal surviving trolley lines of the Philadelphia Transportation Company comprised routes which reached City Hall from West Philadelphia via a long trolley subway. The most recent extension to the city's trolley subway dated to only 1955.

In Pittsburgh, until recent years one of America's most trolley-oriented cities, all of the city's surviv-

A two-car PCC train inbound from Riverside to Park Street in downtown Boston pauses at Longwood on the Massachusetts Bay Transportation Authority's 12-mile Highland Branch. The trolley/rapid-transit route, opened in 1959 over the former Newton Highlands Branch of the Boston & Albany Railroad, is Boston's newest line. — *Jim Shaughnessy.*

On the opening day of service over Boston's new trolley/rapid-transit Highland Branch in July 1959, picture-windowed PCC No. 3280 raced past the Newton Reservoir outbound to Riverside. — *F. W. Schneider III.*

A single car sufficed for late evening traffic as a Boston-bound PCC car made a passenger stop at the Chestnut Hill station on the new MBTA's Highland Branch to Riverside. — *Jim Shaughnessy.*

ing car lines enjoyed extensive reserved right-of-way operation. The seven remaining Pittsburgh lines were those running to the city's South Hills suburbs by means of the long Mt. Washington trolley tunnel and beyond the tunnel on private right of way.

San Francisco's remaining trolley lines benefited similarly from long tunnels and extensive private right of way which permitted a standard of service that could not be approached by motorbuses. Construction plans of the new Bay Area Rapid Transit District, which included a Market Street subway for the trolley lines, assured their future.

In Texas there was even new construction along the lines of the limited tramline concept. Early in 1963, Leonards, a Fort Worth department store that refused to join the rush to the suburbs, completed a ¾-mile-long trolley line, part of it in subway, to provide a free rapid transit service between the downtown store and a company-owned parking lot on the banks of the Trinity River. Former Washington (D. C.) PCC cars, air-conditioned and rebuilt for high-level platform operation, provided the service.

Among the larger American cities there was also

Boston PCC car No. 3078, operating inbound on the Arborway-Park Street surface-subway line, enters the Huntington Avenue trolley subway at Northeastern University in July 1959. — *F. W. Schneider III.*

PCC car No. 19 of the Public Service Coordinated Transport plunges into the company's Newark subway in 1958.

Thirty former Twin Cities PCC's have operated all service on the 4-mile subway since 1954. — F. W. Schneider III.

A Pittsburgh Railways interurban PCC car laid over on the Library loop at the Shannon-Library suburban line in 1958. Limited tramline characteristics have made this and other South Hills lines Pittsburgh's longest-lived trolley routes. — F. W. Schneider III.

PCC 1031 is outbound from downtown San Francisco on the "J" line in 1959. By 1970 a contemplated Market Street trolley subway will give San Francisco PCC's a fast route downtown. — *Bart Gregg*.

Almost totally transformed former Washington (D. C.) PCC cars — air-conditioned, sheathed in stainless steel, and rebuilt for double-end, high-platform operation — serve Leonards' M&O subway in Fort Worth, Tex. The mile-long route, opened in 1963, connects the company's department store with a parking lot. — *George A. Roush*.

A bi-level Chicago & North Western commuter train overtakes a Chicago Transit Authority Lake Street "L" train approaching the Central Avenue station. Relocation of the Lake Street line to North Western right of way in 1962 permitted abandonment of 2½ miles of surface-level operation. — *John Gruber*.

Operating in the median strip of Chicago's Eisenhower Expressway to the western suburbs, the Chicago Transit Authority's new West Side rapid transit line represents a notable example of co-ordinated rail-highway development to meet modern urban transportation needs. A train of PCC-type rapid transit cars operates westbound on the line. — *John Gruber*.

This is rush hour at the Dempster Street terminal of CTA's "Skokie Swift" high-speed shuttle on Chicago's North Side. Traffic so exceeded expectations that within a half hour of the line's opening on April 20, 1964, the initial timetable was discarded in favor of more frequent service. — *Chicago Transit Authority*.

A fleet of 180 of these technologically advanced rapid transit cars entered service on Chicago's Lake Street and Douglas Park routes during 1964. Among the features of the Pullman-Standard cars are an exceptionally light carbody constructed of high-tensile steel, welded aluminum, and molded fibreglass; high-speed trucks; and air conditioning. A two-car train is shown on the CTA Lake Street "L" near the Chicago River. — *Chicago Transit Authority*.

A westbound train on Cleveland Transit's new rapid transit system rolled into the East 55th Street station in 1959. Trackage is shared at this point with trains of the Shaker Heights Rapid Transit, which uses the low-level center platforms while CTS trains use the high-level platforms on either side. — *F. W. Schneider III.*

Toronto's Yonge Street subway, opened in 1954, was North America's first new rapid transit system in several decades. Headed by one of 36 aluminum cars built in 1962, an Eglinton train loads in the Bloor Street station. The 75-foot, 84-seat cars, constructed by Montreal Locomotive Works, are the longest subway cars used anywhere in the world. — *Toronto Transit Commission.*

Specially equipped ex-Washington (D. C.) PCC No. 1304 was employed by the General Electric Company in a series of automated operation tests conducted late in 1961 on GE's Erie (Pa.) test track. A continuous trackside communication system fed information to equipment aboard the car that automatically started and stopped the car, and opened and closed its doors.— *General Electric Company.*

a renewed interest in the creation of rapid transit systems as a means of combating the problems of motor vehicle traffic congestion. Except in New York, where subway construction has been almost continuous for more than a half century, and Chicago, which finally began long-delayed subway drilling during the 1930's, building of rapid transit lines had virtually ended in North America during the 1920's. The depression economy of the 1930's and the wartime restrictions of the 1940's discouraged the development of plans for either new systems or extensions to existing lines.

With the end of World War II, however, several cities were able to undertake the long-contemplated rapid transit systems. Toronto, Canada's second largest city, was the first North American municipality to begin construction. Work started in 1949, and by early 1954 Toronto's 4½-mile Yonge Street subway was transporting a traffic approaching 39,000 passengers an hour. A second section of Toronto's subway, the 2-mile University line, opened in 1963; and the 10-mile east-west Bloor-Danforth subway opened early in 1966. Another 6½ miles in extensions were scheduled for opening by early 1968. Still other extensions of rapid transit lines and development of limited tramline routes were under consideration.

Early in 1952 Cleveland finally began work on a rapid transit system that initially had been proposed more than 30 years earlier by the Van Sweringen brothers. The first section, more than 8 miles in length, was placed in service between Cleveland

An outbound Orient Heights train of postwar PCC-type cars rolls into a station on Boston's 6-mile Revere Beach rapid transit line, constructed between 1952 and 1954 on right of way of the abandoned Boston, Revere Beach & Lynn Railroad. — *Jim Shaughnessy.*

409

Montreal's new Métro, opened late in 1966, represents a radical departure from previous North American rapid transit practice. A fleet of 369 of these handsome blue and white Canadian Vickers cars, running on pneumatic-tired trucks and capable of a 50 mph top speed, operates over the 16-mile system. — *Canadian Vickers Industries, Ltd.*

Union Terminal and Windermere, on the city's East Side, in 1955. By 1959 another 7 miles of "rapid" service had been extended to Cleveland's West Side, and in 1966 construction started on a 4-mile extension to the city's Hopkins Airport. A 1968 summer opening is planned. Other extensions were being considered.

A major extension to Boston's rapid transit system was completed between 1952 and 1954 with the building of a 6-mile route to Revere Beach over the right of way of the narrow-gauge Boston, Revere Beach & Lynn Railroad, abandoned in 1940. In 1966 the Massachusetts Bay Transportation Authority, which succeeded the old Boston MTA in 1964, approved a 340-million-dollar regional transit program that provided for both modernization of the system's existing rail lines and major extensions of rapid transit and limited tramline service into new areas by 1973. By the end of the year construction was under way on new rapid transit extensions to South Weymouth and Everett totaling over 21 miles.

In Chicago during the 1950's, construction of a new high-speed rapid transit route in the median of the Eisenhower (formerly Congress Street) Expressway, extending from the Loop to the western suburbs, afforded an excellent example of co-ordinated highway and rapid transit development. Completed between 1958 and 1960, the 10-mile line replaced the former Garfield Park elevated route.

In April 1964 the Chicago Transit Authority opened its "Skokie Swift," a high-speed shuttle service between Dempster Street, Skokie, and CTA's North Side "L" line at Howard Street operating over 5 miles of track purchased from the defunct Chicago North Shore & Milwaukee Railroad. So successful was the project that in less than six months CTA had gone through seven schedule revisions, each increasing the frequency of service, and by late 1965 the line was transporting more than 7000 passengers daily.

Under discussion in Chicago were plans for a 300-million-dollar rapid transit improvement program that included replacement of the famed "L" Loop with a new downtown subway and new rapid transit lines in the medians of the Kennedy and Dan Ryan expressways to northwest Chicago and the far South

410

Side, as well as modernization of existing CTA lines.

In October 1966 Montreal became the latest North American city to operate a rapid transit system when the first lines of the city's new "Métro" were placed in operation. By April 1967 a system of three lines totaling over 16 miles was in service. Designed with technical assistance from the Paris Métro, the 214-million-dollar system incorporated such French-originated features as rubber-tired rolling stock, automatic fare collection, and automatic platform gates. A further addition to the Montreal rapid transit system, in the form of the conversion of 17 miles of electrified Canadian National Mount Royal tunnel suburban line to rapid transit standards, was under consideration.

Also at Montreal, the "Expo Express," a 3-mile automated rapid transit line, opened in the spring of 1967 to transport visitors to the city's Expo 67 site on Notre Dame and St. Helen islands in the St. Lawrence River.

Elsewhere, several other major rapid transit installations were moving ahead.

In 1962 residents of three San Francisco Bay area counties voted approval of a bond issue that would provide a 75-mile, 1.2-billion-dollar regional rapid transit system serving over 30 cities and communities. By 1965 exhaustive testing programs of highly sophisticated train control systems and equipment components were being carried out on the Bay Area Rapid Transit District's 4½-mile Diablo Test Track, and by 1966 construction was under way on more than 16 miles of line, including a new 4-mile transbay tube. The first trains were scheduled to begin operation on portions of the fully automated 70 mph system by late 1969.

In southern New Jersey work started in 1964 on a 12-mile, 77-million-dollar extension to the Delaware River Port Authority's Philadelphia-Camden rapid transit line that would provide 75 mph electric train service to suburban Lindenwold by mid-1968. In Philadelphia itself, plans were in hand for extensions to the city's Broad Street subway totaling 8 miles and costing 90 million dollars. Completion was forecast for 1970.

In other cities comprehensive rapid transit plans were undergoing detailed study and public scrutiny. Late in 1965 President Johnson signed into law a bill authorizing a 25-mile, 431-million-dollar rapid transit system for Washington, D. C. Opening of the first routes was planned for 1970. Also in 1965, voters of the Atlanta (Ga.) metropolitan area approved formation of a rapid transit authority to build a rail system that could ultimately total 66 miles. At Baltimore, consulting engineers presented the Metropolitan Transit Authority of Maryland with a report recommending a 65-mile, 697-million-dollar rapid transit system. Design work was under way in Seattle for a proposed 20-mile, 111-million-dollar "rapid." At Los Angeles preliminary planning and engineering were in progress for a proposed 64-mile, 800-million-dollar rail system, with the Southern California Rapid Transit District scheduled to present a plan to the voters in 1968. Similar plans had reached varying stages of development in other major North American metropolitan centers. Increasing Federal support of urban mass transportation projects, beginning with the Urban Mass Transportation Act of 1964, promised to provide substantial help to these and other rapid transit projects in American cities.

Abroad, the electric railway was making a similar comeback. The limited tramline concept was getting attention in such diverse locations as Holland, Germany, Switzerland, Denmark, Italy, and Japan. Major extensions to subway systems were under way in London, Paris, Berlin, Hamburg, Stockholm, Oslo, Moscow, Tokyo, and elsewhere. Entirely new subway systems were under construction or planned in Rotterdam, Milan, and Mexico City.

A highly sophisticated technology was swiftly emerging for the new electric railways. In New York an automated subway train was actually running in regular service on the Grand Central-Times Square shuttle, and both General Electric and Westinghouse Air Brake Company were conducting advanced experiments in the automatic operation of electric railway equipment. Computer technology was being applied to systems controlling the operation of an entire system. Other experiments were being carried out in such areas as noise reduction and fare-collection systems. Rapid transit rolling stock itself was rapidly changing. Air conditioning was becoming increasingly common in new equipment orders. Lightweight metals and plastics were being used to produce cars that were both lightweight and low in maintenance cost. Montreal's new rubber-tired trains were proving exceptionally quiet in operation. Equipment designers were finally paying some attention to the appearance of rapid transit equipment, and the utilitarian dingy olive green rolling stock of earlier years was being displaced by handsome and colorful cars whose appearance was more in keeping with the America of the 1960's.

But if the new electric railway of the 1960's bore little outward resemblance to its predecessors of a half century and more before, the fundamental principles of electric traction so painstakingly developed by Frank Sprague, Leo Daft, Charles Van Depoele, and many others before the end of the 19th century remained unchanged.

Frank Sprague, were he alive in 1967, would not be surprised at what has become of the infant he started on its way at Richmond 80 years ago.

411

The technology of the trolley

PRINCIPAL CAR TYPES

CLOSED CAR: Throughout the history of electric traction the ordinary closed car, either single- or double-truck, was by far the most common type of trolley car. Although the most frequent arrangement for the closed car was with full front and rear platforms, this car was constructed in almost every conceivable entrance and exit arrangement, depending upon the method of fare collection employed and whether the car was built for single- or double-end operation.

OPEN CAR: Designed for summer trolley riding, the open car was enormously popular in the early years of electric traction. The usual pattern provided transverse benches extending the full width of the car, and longitudinal steps running the full length of the car to permit boarding and alighting at any point. On some lines, open cars were arranged with end platforms and center aisles, and were equipped with some sort of wire mesh along the lower section of the sides for a safer boarding and alighting arrangement.

SEMI-OPEN CAR: The semi-open car, an attempt to compromise between the closed and open car arrangements, was usually divided equally between open and closed sections. This type was most popular on the West Coast, where the climate was relatively mild and weather changes were frequent.

CALIFORNIA CAR: The original variety of semi-open car, the California car, was developed for the California Street Cable Railroad Company at San Francisco. This design placed the closed section in the center with an open section at either end.

CONVERTIBLE CAR: In order to obviate the high cost of duplicate sets of closed and open cars for winter and summer operation, the convertible car was developed during the 1890's. Side panels and windows which could be removed for storage, or slid into various types of roof pockets, were employed to enable conversion to an open car.

CLOSED CAR

OPEN CAR

SEMI-OPEN CAR

CALIFORNIA CAR

CONVERTIBLE CAR

SEMI-CONVERTIBLE CAR

CENTER-ENTRANCE CAR

DOUBLE-DECK CAR

ARTICULATED CAR

SEMI-CONVERTIBLE CAR: A far more practical and popular arrangement than the "full convertible" was the semi-convertible. It employed various types of window sash which could either be removed or slid into roof or wall pockets during mild weather. Side panels below the windows remained fixed in place.

CENTER-ENTRANCE CAR: Arranged for entrance and exit at the center of the body, rather than at the ends, the center-entrance car was most commonly used in a variety of "low floor" designs intended to speed boarding and alighting by reducing the number of steps.

PAY-AS-YOU-ENTER CAR

NEAR-SIDE CAR

PETER WITT CAR

DOUBLE-DECK CAR: Although the double-deck car was never a popular car type in North America, it was the subject of frequent experimentation by traction companies looking for equipment with a greater passenger capacity. A variety of configurations were tried; some of the most nearly successful placed a second story on what was essentially a "low floor" center-entrance car.

ARTICULATED CAR: Articulation, with either two carbodies resting on a common center truck or two independent carbodies permanently connected by an intermediate suspended conductor's platform, was employed by a number of systems to provide a car with a tremendous seating capacity that still was able to negotiate the restrictive curves common to street railways.

PAY-AS-YOU-ENTER CAR: The P.A.Y.E. car, a patented arrangement intended to improve fare collection, enjoyed wide application. Passengers boarded at the rear and paid their fare to a conductor stationed on the rear platform before passing into the car. Exit was normally at the front only, but sometimes was permitted at the rear as well by means of an arrangement that separated boarding from alighting passengers. In order to provide ample room for passengers waiting to pay their fares, most P.A.Y.E. cars had an unusually large rear platform.

NEAR-SIDE CAR: Another patented fare-collection design, the "Near-Side" car placed the conductor directly behind the motorman. Passengers boarded at the front and paid their fares as they passed the conductor. Exit was usually through the rearmost of two front doors. Another exit placed at the rear of the car was employed for emergencies or at terminals only.

PETER WITT CAR: Developed by a Cleveland street railway commissioner, the Peter Witt car had a front entrance and center exit, and passengers paid their fare to a conductor stationed at the center of the car as they either passed to the rear half or left the car. The same front-entrance center-exit arrangement was used in most one-man cars in which passengers paid their fares to the operator as they boarded the car at the front.

BIRNEY SAFETY CAR

PCC STREAMLINED CAR

BIRNEY SAFETY CAR: The Birney, the first really successful standard car design, was a lightweight four-wheel car incorporating a number of patented features that permitted safe one-man operation. Minor variations were made in the thousands of Birneys produced by several builders between 1916 and 1930, and a number of double-truck cars incorporating the same safety features were turned out during the 1920's.

PCC STREAMLINED CAR: Developed by the Presidents' Conference Committee during the 1930's, the PCC car was a standardized streamlined streetcar design of radically improved performance. Although numerous improvements and modifications were made, the basic design concept and arrangement remained unchanged during the more than 15 years that PCC cars were in production. The "standard" PCC was a front-entrance center-exit single-end car, but it was also produced in several other arrangements to suit the requirements of individual systems.

CAR CONSTRUCTION

WOOD CONSTRUCTION: Until well into the current century, wood was almost universally employed as the basic construction material for street railway cars. Heavy timber sills beneath the floor were normally the basic structural element. Later, as longer double-truck cars came into use, metal truss rods were added beneath the carbody to help provide sufficient strength and rigidity. Platforms, usually lower than the car floor itself, were supported by wood or metal members suspended from beneath the car floor. Sides and roofs were framed in wood members and covered with wood sheathing or paneling.

SEMI-STEEL CONSTRUCTION: Shortly after the turn of the century, carbuilders began to use greater amounts of steel in carbody construction. Originally steel was used in place of timber for the main sills supporting the carbody, then was progressively adopted for other parts as well. When steel was employed for the main frame, as well as side plating, the construction was often called "semi-steel." Wood was still used for the side posts and roof.

STEEL CONSTRUCTION: Even before 1910 a number of cars had been built for several systems which were essentially all-steel in construction. Frames, side plating, side posts, and the "car lines" that supported the roof were all of steel. Side panels and the structural framing were riveted together to act as a girder which, together with the center sills, helped to support the car's weight. Although metal was sometimes used, wood was still frequently employed for roof sheathing, windows, flooring, and the interior finish.

Initially, steel cars were extremely heavy in construction, but beginning with the Birney car of 1915, increasing attention was given to weight reduction through better design and more extensive use of lighter metals and other materials. A number of cars of the 1920's and 1930's made wide use of aluminum and a few experimental cars were built almost exclusively of aluminum. The development of high-tensile alloy steels during the 1930's, together with the application of welding to carbody construction, permitted the production of lightweight carbodies of exceptional strength and rigidity for such modern cars as the PCC.

ROOF CONSTRUCTION: The most common type of roof construction in the early years of traction was what was generally referred to as the "monitor roof." A raised clerestory, or monitor, was provided in the central portion of the car roof. Operating sash in the sides and ends of the monitor helped to give better light and ventilation within the car. In the true monitor roof, properly called a "monitor deck" roof, or "deck roof," the raised clerestory was stopped off short of the platforms. A modification in which the raised section curved down at each end to join the main roof was widely used on steam railroad equipment and was consequently called a "railroad roof." It was sometimes used on street railway equipment as well. In later years the arch and "turtle-back" roofs became common. Both of these types curved from one side of the car to the other unbroken by a raised clerestory. Ventilators of

some kind were usually installed to supply ventilation in place of that provided by the sash in the sides of a raised monitor.

TRUCKS

SINGLE TRUCK: Although double-truck equipment began to come into use during the early 1890's, the single-truck car remained the most common type until after 1900. On a very few early electric cars the horsecar practice of supporting the wheels directly in pedestals attached to the carbody was followed; but this method proved inadequate, and the separate metal truck on which the carbody rested was quickly adopted. Although a multitude of manufacturers were producing trucks of their own design, most of the more successful types were essentially similar in design. Journal boxes were free to move in the pedestal jaws of the metal truck frame, and were supported by several coil springs. The weight of the carbody was carried to the truck frames by means of coil springs, usually located at either side of the axles, and by elliptic springs mounted on extensions of the truck frame. The latter feature gave a single-truck car a longer "spring base," which was found to improve riding qualities. The single-truck car enjoyed a revival after World War I with the development of the Birney Safety Car. The Birney was mounted on a four-wheel truck that, although of improved design, was similar in its essential features to earlier types of trucks.

The single-truck car had several inherent limitations. As long as the axles remained fixed in a parallel position, the short-radius curves common on street railways limited the maximum practical wheelbase, which in turn restricted the over-all length of the car. Because of the short wheelbase, too, single-truck cars had a tendency to pitch and to "nose" from side to side. As a result, they were never particularly smooth riding, even under the best of conditions, and were entirely unsuited for high-speed operation.

Several attempts were made to develop a longer-wheelbase single truck to overcome these limitations. Almost all of these were some form of two- or three-axle "radial" truck in which the axles could rotate to nonparallel positions to accommodate short-radius curves. None enjoyed significant success in the U. S.

DOUBLE TRUCK: To permit greater carrying capacity than was possible with single-truck equipment, the double-truck car came into use during the early 1890's and by 1900 had become the most commonly built car type.

Trucks for double-truck cars were supplied by dozens of manufacturers in a wide variety of types. Generally the weight of the carbody was carried to each truck through a center bearing mounted on a transverse bolster beam. A king pin, or center pin, about which the truck rotated, connected the carbody and the truck at the center bearing. Usually side bearing plates mounted on the carbody and truck bolster prevented the carbody from rocking on the center bearing. On some types of trucks the entire weight of the carbody was carried by side bearings. From the bolster beam the weight of the car was carried through varying arrangements of coil or elliptic springs to the truck frame and then through coil springs to the journal boxes, which carried the axle bearings. The equalizer bars employed in trucks designed for rapid transit or interurban railway service were seldom found on street railway trucks.

Generally the wheelbase of street railway trucks was considerably shorter—around 4½ to 5 feet—than that of trucks designed for high-speed service. In the most widely used kinds of two-motor streetcar trucks the motors were "outside hung" (carried outside the axles) in contrast with the "inside hung" (suspended between the axles) mounting customary in long-wheelbase, high-speed trucks for interurban or rapid transit service.

Another common truck was the "maximum traction" truck designed for single-motor applications. By means of an off-center bolster, as much as three quarters of the weight was carried to the single-powered axle. Large-diameter wheels were provided on the powered axle, while the unpowered axle was fitted with small-diameter wheels. Several other designs for single-motor trucks obtained maximum traction by means of locomotive-type side rods which connected wheels on the powered axle with those on the unpowered axle. None of the latter were particularly successful, however.

During the late 1920's a number of attempts were made to create an improved type of truck that would

415

offer a smoother ride and quieter operation. These efforts culminated in the radically improved truck used on the PCC car. Among its many innovations were a longer wheel-base (6′ 3″), inside-mounted roller bearings, hydraulic shock absorbers, extensive use of rubber springing and insulation, and rubber-cushioned "resilient" wheels.

MOTORS

Almost without exception, motors for street railway service were designed for direct current operation at 500 to 600 volts, with horse-power ratings ranging from about 25 to 60. The customary method of installation employed the "wheelbarrow" mounting originally developed by Frank Sprague, which permitted the motor to be directly geared to the axle. One side of the motor frame contained bearings mounted on the axle. This permitted the motor to rotate slightly about the axle as a center, thus maintaining perfect alignment between the gearing on the axle and the armature shaft no matter how irregular the track or the motion of the axle. The other side of the motor was hung from the truck frame on a spring mounting.

Radical improvements were made in both motors and gearing during the various experimental efforts of the 1920's and the PCC car development program. The 55 h.p. motors developed for the PCC car weighed only 700 pounds, less than half as much as motors of similar power of a decade and more earlier. One of the principal sources of streetcar noise had been the gearing that connected the motor to the axle, and the PCC car developers came up with a hypoid gearing and worm drive that virtually eliminated noise from this source.

CONTROLS

The earliest type of controller for streetcars was little more than a simple rheostat operated by the motorman. This made use of a series of diminishing resistance steps in series with the motors to gradually bring the motor up to speed. During the 1890's the series-parallel controller was developed which greatly reduced the loss of electric energy involved in the use of a simple rheostatic controller. Initially, two or more motors were placed in series position together with a

SINGLE TRUCK

DOUBLE TRUCK

MAXIMUM TRACTION TRUCK

PCC TRUCK

resistance. The resistance was gradually reduced until "full series" position was reached, when the motors were switched to a parallel position, again with a resistance in the circuit. The resistance was once more gradually reduced until "full parallel," the normal running position, was reached. The resistance was gradually reduced by means of a hand-operated drum-type controller in which fingers on the controller made contact with copper segments of the drum as each position, or "point," of the controller was reached. Arcing between the points as the drum was rotated was a common weakness of this type of controller, and most were equipped with a magnetic "blowout" coil, which created a strong magnetic field that served to quench an arc.

Another weakness of the conventional type of controller was the limited number of positions, or "points," available, preventing smooth acceleration of a car. During the 1920's extensive development work was done on controllers that supplied a greater number of control points and some form of au-

tomatic operation in order to provide a smooth rate of acceleration. In the development program for the PCC car it was found that surprisingly high rates of acceleration were acceptable as long as they were smooth and uniform. As a result, the controller perfected for the PCC car employed automatic motor operation and more than a hundred control points in place of the hand-operated controller with a dozen or so points typical of those applied on older equipment.

BRAKES

The earliest electric cars used only brakes that were hand operated by the motorman. Although such braking had been reasonably adequate for horsecars, it quickly proved insufficient for the faster, heavier electrics. By the late 1890's air brakes were being widely applied to electric cars. The most common type was a simple straight air system in which the brake shoes were applied against the wheels through a linkage operated by a compressed air brake cylinder and piston. The usual source of compressed air for the braking system was a motor-driven compressor, but many cars employed high-pressure storage tanks which had to be recharged at stationary charging stations along the line. Axle-driven compressors were also frequently used.

Maximum braking effectiveness in a streetcar depended upon applying the greatest possible pressure through the brake shoes short of causing the wheels to slide. As a consequence, a braking system that provided the proper amount of pressure to a car that was empty would apply insufficient pressure when the car was heavily loaded, or brake pressure that was adequate for a loaded car would prove too great for an empty car. This problem was sometimes solved by the application of a "variable load valve," a device which employed mechanical measurement of truck spring deflection to vary the brake pressure setting.

Another early type of brake was the magnetic brake. To brake a car equipped with this system, the traction motors were reversed to act as generators; and the current generated was passed through electromagnetic track shoes suspended above the rails. The shoes were drawn against the rails, creating a braking force, and at the same time conventional wheel tread brakes were applied through a leverage attached to the streetcar's magnetic shoes.

A variation of the magnetic brake was the "traction increaser," in which a magnetic device similar to the track brake was mounted on the truck in such a manner that it did not actually touch the rail. The magnetic pull between the electromagnet and the rail had the effect of increasing the weight on the wheels, thus permitting a greater braking force without causing wheel slip.

To provide the greater braking force required for the high-performance PCC car, its designers used a combination of three braking systems working automatically in sequence. Initially, a dynamic braking system came into play, employing the motors as generators. Next, a magnetic track brake was applied; and finally, as the car slowed to a stop, air-operated drum brakes were applied. In later all-electric models of the PCC car, a spring-applied, electrically

released driveshaft brake replaced the air-operated drum brake.

CURRENT COLLECTION

OVERHEAD SYSTEM: Almost universally used for street railway systems, the overhead system employed a trolley pole which was held against an overhead wire by means of spring tension in a swiveling trolley base. Originally a large trolley wheel, held by a trolley "harp," was used for current collection. Later, a sliding shoe was developed which eventually became the preferred means of current collection on almost all trolley lines. To prevent damage to the overhead wire system in the event a trolley left the wire, many companies used a spring-operated retriever which automatically pulled the pole down if a dewirement occurred. Pantographs and bow trolleys, while common on overseas lines, were only rarely employed in North America for overhead current collection on street railway systems. The pantograph, which employed one or two flat collectors that slid along the overhead wire, was widely used, however, on rapid transit systems using overhead current distribution. The pantograph was raised and held against the wire by spring tension and lowered by compressed-air pressure.

UNDERGROUND CONDUIT SYSTEM: Aside from a few short-lived experimental installations, the underground conduit system was used only on the street railway systems of Washington, D. C., and New York City. Sliding shoes on a truck-mounted "plow," which projected through a slot between the rails, collected current from the underground power rails. Two shoes, one each for the positive and return rails, were required. In a few early experimental installations, various types of surface contact systems were tried in which current collection devices mounted beneath the car drew current from an underground power supply by means of surface contacts that were energized only when a car passed over them.

THIRD RAIL: Although third-rail current collection was obviously unsuited for street railway service, it nevertheless was employed by the majority of rapid transit systems in North America. Truck-mounted iron

collection shoes, held against the top of the rail by their own weight, were employed for current collection. In a few protected third-rail installations in which the power rail was inverted, current collection was by means of an "underrunning" shoe held against the bottom side of the rail by spring tension.

FENDERS AND LIFEGUARDS: A variety of devices intended to prevent an unfortunate pedestrian from being run over by the wheels were applied to streetcars. Fenders, usually resembling a bed spring or a wire net, were mounted on the front of a car. Lifeguards were similar pedestrian catchers suspended beneath the carbody just ahead of the front truck. A lifeguard, normally held in a raised position, was dropped to the pavement by means of a linkage attached to a guard at the front of the car, which was actuated by striking an object on the track. Although fenders were eventually discarded by most street railway companies, some form of lifeguard was employed by almost every system throughout the street railway era.

WARNING DEVICES: Whistles or horns were seldom applied to cars designed solely for street railway operation. The most common type of streetcar warning signal was some kind of gong, usually foot-operated and mounted beneath the motorman's platform, but sometimes mounted on the roof and sounded by means of a hanging cord. Occasionally, pneumatically operated gongs were used, and on the PCC car an electrically operated gong was provided.

HEADLIGHTS: The earliest electric cars were equipped with oil-burning headlights, but soon afterward various types of incandescent lights were introduced. In recent years the automotive-type "sealed beam" headlight was applied to the PCC car. In some experimental cars of the 1920's, double headlights, much like those on an automotive vehicle, were used; and in at least one North American city — Montreal — streetcars carried no headlights at all but relied instead on a hooded indirect lighting arrangement on the front dash. Sometimes streetcar headlights were mounted on the roof, but the usual location was a flush mounting in the front dash below the windows.

417

CONDUIT PLOW

TROLLEY SHOE

THIRD-RAIL SHOE

RETRIEVER

TROLLEY BASE

TROLLEY WHEEL AND HARP

HEATING SYSTEMS: The earliest streetcar heating systems employed coal-burning cast-iron stoves installed within the carbody, a method that provided either too much or too little heat, depending upon the distance of a passenger from the heater. Several manufacturers developed improved car heaters which burned coal or oil and employed either forced hot air or circulating hot water to obtain more even heat distribution. Sometimes such heaters were installed beneath the car floor and were tended by employees at car line terminals, but more often they were located on the front or rear platform where they could be tended by the conductor or motorman.

In later years most street railway systems converted to the use of electric resistance heaters located either under the seats or on the floor along the walls. Although electric heaters were somewhat more costly to operate, they provided clean, even heat and needed little attention on the part of the operating crew. An unusual feature of the modern PCC car was the use of current generated during dynamic braking to help heat the car.

FARE REGISTERS AND BOXES: The earliest type of fare register was a large unit usually mounted above the door on the bulkhead at one end of the car, where it could readily be seen. By means of a rod arrangement and a pull cord the conductor could set the register and ring up a fare from anywhere in the car. Later, as new interior arrangements were developed that provided a stationary location for the conductor, various types of registering fare boxes, into which a passenger dropped his fare, were evolved. The same type of fare box was used for one-man car operation.

SANDERS: To avoid wheel slipping on wet, dirty rail, streetcars were equipped with sanders, which applied dry sand from a protected sandbox onto the rails by gravity or pneumatic feed.

DESTINATION SIGNS: In the early years of electric traction, cars were commonly lettered with the name of the route over which they ran. This obviously made it difficult to assign equipment to another route, and the street railways soon changed to some form of wood or metal destination sign which could be quickly replaced with another when the occasion required. These were hung on the side or front dash of the car, or were mounted on the roof at the front and sides. Signs illuminated from behind were frequently placed in the sash of the monitor deck at the front and on each side. Sometimes revolving signs, mounted on the roof above the platforms or on each side, were used. Later, printed fabric roller signs were introduced.

SEATS: Trolley car seats were generally designed with durability, rather than comfort, foremost in mind. Often seats were simply made of wood slats. When upholstery was provided, it was more than likely some durable material such as rattan. In some cars designed for heavy loading, all or part of the car was given over to longitudinal seating along the sides, with the remainder of the space devoted to standing room. Most often, however, most of the seating was of the transverse type. Double-end cars were usually fitted with the "walkover" seat, on which the back could be flipped over when the car's direction of operation was changed. During the 1920's car designers began to take greater interest in passenger comfort, and innovations such as individual leather-upholstered seating were provided. By the time the PCC car was introduced, such features as fabric upholstery, contoured seats, and spring and rubber cushions had become common.

DOORS: Many early cars were without doors to the platforms, or had only folding gates to prevent boarding or alighting when the car was in motion. When doors came into use, the most common was the folding type, manually operated by the conductor or motorman. Sliding doors were also common. Later, air-operated door mechanisms were developed which permitted doors to be operated from a distance. When one-man operation became common, exit doors were frequently provided with a treadle device in the step well, which, when a passenger stepped on it, automatically opened the door. Electric door motors were developed for later models of the PCC car.

SIGNAL SYSTEMS: As long as two-man car operation continued, trolley cars were provided with some type of bell signal, usually operated by a simple pull cord, with which the conductor could signal starts and stops to the motorman. An electric buzzer system, operated either by a pull cord or push buttons, was supplied to permit passengers to signal their desire to alight at the next stop.

TRACK AND CURRENT DISTRIBUTION SYSTEMS

TRACK: The earliest street railways usually employed some form of wrought-iron bars or flat strips attached to wood stringers for rails. Quite often the iron bars were bent or formed in such a way as to provide a path for the wheel flange. Wrought iron or steel T-rail of the sort used by steam railroads was often used for street railway track, although it was usually lighter in weight. Paving close to the rail with standard paving blocks was difficult, however; and the protruding head of the rail presented a danger to vehicular traffic and brought frequent objections by city officials. In 1877 the Cambria Iron Company of Johnstown, Pa., developed the first rolled steel "girder" rail for street railway use, and this type soon became by far the most frequently used. Girder rail was rolled with various types of protruding lips or grooves which acted as a flangeway for the car wheels. Generally a rather deep rail section — usually 7 or 9 inches — was employed. The 9-inch section was preferred for ease in paving adjacent to the rails. Although continuously welded rail sections did not come into general use on steam railroads until recent years, various forms of welded or cast joints were in common use on street railways

before the end of the 19th century. The earliest method of this type was the cast-welded joint introduced in 1894. In this process a mold was placed around the rail ends and molten iron was poured into it. A similar type of joint was produced by the Thermit process. A mold was placed about the rail ends and the thermit, a mixture of powdered aluminum and iron oxide, was ignited. The aluminum burned with sufficient heat to melt the iron, which then flowed into the mold to make the joint. Electrically welded joints were also used in street railway track, although the joint was usually made by welding iron bars on either side of the rail rather than by the butt-welding common in modern practice.

Street railway rails were often supported on conventional wooden ties, but the requirement for great rigidity and the heavy loads imposed by street traffic also led to the extensive use of various types of steel ties or a concrete supporting structure. Street railway companies were customarily required to maintain the pavement between the rails and for a distance of 2 feet or more on either side. Stone paving blocks or bricks were commonly employed for this purpose, although ordinary concrete or asphalt paving was frequently used as well. One early text on street railway construction suggested that track and paving be designed so as not to attract vehicular traffic, thereby reducing wear on the paving and permitting faster schedule speeds by keeping the tracks clear of traffic.

CURRENT DISTRIBUTION: In the early years of electric railway operation, the streetcar companies quite frequently generated their own power. Initially, power was generated at the direct current voltage — usually 500 to 600 volts — required for car operation. Because of the excessive voltage drop and line loss involved in transmitting low-voltage direct current over any distance, high-voltage alternating current generation and distribution came into general use. Substations, which used transformers to reduce the voltage and motor-generators or synchronous converters to convert the alternating current to direct current, were located at intervals along the streetcar lines. The spacing and capacity of substations were governed by the anticipated density of car operation.

OVERHEAD CURRENT COLLECTION: Current collection by trolley pole from a simply suspended overhead trolley wire was almost universally employed by street railway systems. A hard drawn copper wire, supported at intervals of 80 to 125 feet, was normally used. Initially, soldered "ears" were employed to attach the wire to its supports, but later a grooved wire was developed to which a mechanical clamping ear could be attached. The principal types of supporting systems for trolley wires were span wire construction, in which the trolley wire was suspended from transverse wires extending between poles on either side of the track, and bracket construction, in which the wire was suspended from a metal bracket mounted on a pole. When bracket construction was used on double-

FRONT EQUIPMENT

CAB INTERIOR

419

Duplex Car Company, New York, N. Y. (1896-1902)

The Duplex company was not actually a carbuilder, but it developed an unusual type of convertible car that was produced under franchise by several builders, principally Briggs and Jackson & Sharp. The Duplex design incorporated curved windows and side panels constructed much like the top of a roll-top desk which slid upward into the roof on curved tracks. The intricate arrangement proved costly to build and relatively few were ever constructed.

Federal Storage Battery Car Company, Silver Lake, N. J. (1909-1920's)

The firm, known as the Railway Storage Battery Car Company after 1912, was organized by Thomas Edison to exploit his alkaline nickel-iron storage battery and a battery car developed by Ralph U. Beach. Built in both single- and double-truck models, the Edison-Beach storage battery car enjoyed a modest popularity on street railways during the relatively brief period of interest in this type of equipment. Both the Edison-Beach car and the rival lead-acid storage battery type, built principally by Brill, suffered from the great weight of the necessary batteries, docile performance characteristics, and a tendency to frequent battery failure.

General Electric Company, (1892-   )

Organized in 1892 through merger of the Edison General Electric Company and the Thomson-Houston Electric Company, GE was one of the two giants of the North American electrical industry. Although GE was never a carbuilder, from the time of its formation to the present it has been a major supplier of motors, controls, and other electrical equipment, as well as air-brake equipment, to the electric railway industry. During the early part of the century GE developed a line of gas-electric cars for railway service, and built a few experimental gas-electrics for street railway service.

Gilbert Car Manufacturing Company, Troy, N. Y. (1820-1895)

The firm was organized in 1820 by Orasmus Eaton and was initially a builder of stage coaches and other horse-drawn vehicles. It was operated under various names until reorganization under the Gilbert name in 1882. Railway carbuilding began in 1841 and Gilbert production ultimately included horse and electric cars for street railways. Gilbert cars enjoyed wide distribution throughout the U. S., as well as a considerable export market. About 1890 an employee of the firm, John Taylor, developed a highly successful truck design and within a few years manufacture of the Taylor truck dominated the company's production. In 1895 Gilbert was succeeded by the Taylor Electric Truck Company (q.v.).

Hale & Kilburn Manufacturing Company, Philadelphia, Pa.

Hale & Kilburn, a specialist in seating equipment, was one of the largest suppliers of seats of every description for use in street railway equipment.

J. Hammond & Company, San Francisco, Calif. (1883-1907)

Often known as the "California Car Works," Hammond was a leading supplier of horse, cable, and electric cars—many of them mounted on trucks of the company's own design — to street railways in California and elsewhere on the Pacific Coast. The firm claimed to have originated the design for the "California"-type combination open and closed cars, which featured a closed center section and open sections at each end. This car was first built for San Francisco's California Street Cable Railroad Company. Unable to recover from the devastation of the 1906 San Francisco earthquake and fire, the firm ceased operation in 1907.

Harlan & Hollingsworth Corporation, Wilmington, Del. (1836-1944)

Outstanding both as a car manufacturing firm and as a shipbuilder, Harlan & Hollingsworth built a wide variety of rolling stock for steam railroads, street and interurban railways, and elevated lines. Prominent among Harlan & Hollingsworth cars of the 19th century were many of the early passenger cars operated on the New York elevated system. The firm's plant was absorbed by Bethlehem Steel Company in 1905 and continued to produce railway cars until 1944. Notable among the cars produced under Bethlehem management were the all-steel articulateds constructed in 1935 for the Key System transbay lines at San Francisco-Oakland.

Hawker Siddeley Canada, Ltd., Montreal, Que.

An English firm originally established by A. V. Roe Company, Hawker Siddeley acquired the facilities of Canadian Car Company in 1964 and is now active in the construction of all classes of freight and passenger rolling stock. The firm's electric railway production has included 165 aluminum cars built for the Toronto subway in 1965 and 48 similar cars delivered in 1966 for use on the "Expo Express" serving Montreal's Expo 67 fair.

Heywood Brothers & Wakefield Company, Wakefield, Mass.

Another specialist in seating equipment, Heywood-Wakefield was a principal supplier of seats for street railway cars throughout the traction era, and remains active today as a supplier of seating for railway equipment.

Holman Car Company, San Francisco, Calif. (1883-1913)

A general carbuilder, Holman produced a modest number of street and interurban railway cars which saw service in the San Francisco and Central California area, among them a batch of cars for the California Street Cable Railroad Company in 1907-1908. In 1913 the firm undertook construction of the first 20 cars for the new Municipal Railway of San Francisco and went bankrupt in the process.

Jackson & Sharp, Wilmington, Del. (1863-1901)

Eminent as both a shipbuilder and a carbuilder for steam railroads, Jackson & Sharp, popularly known as the "Delaware Car Works," also produced a full range of horse and electric cars for street railway service, many of which were mounted on the firm's own trucks. The Jackson & Sharp plant was purchased by American Car & Foundry in 1901 and continued to produce railway equipment through the Second World War. It is still a part of the ACF organization.

Jewett Car Company, Newark, O. (1894-1918)

Although Jewett was principally noted for the manufacture of exceptionally well built and handsomely proportioned cars for Midwestern interurban railways, the firm's initial production was devoted to horsecars, most of which were built for Pittsburgh, Pa. Shortly after 1900 Jewett built several large orders of elevated cars for New York, Brooklyn, and Chicago, as well as a large volume of streetcars for systems as divergent in locality as Chicago and San Francisco. Jewett went bankrupt and ceased operation in 1918.

Jones' Sons Car Company, Watervliet, N. Y. (1839-1922)

Jones' Sons was originally established as a Schenectady wagon builder under the name of Witbeck & Jones in 1839 and began the manufacture of street railway cars in 1864, producing thousands of cars that were sold throughout the world. An early entrant into electric car production, the firm was active as a carbuilder until about 1912.

G. C. Kuhlman Car Company, Cleveland, O. (1892-1932)

One of the leading streetcar builders, Kuhlman produced street and interurban railway equipment of every description. J. G. Brill absorbed the Kuhlman firm in 1904 as part of a vast expansion program, although production continued under the Kuhlman name. Notable among Kuhlman-built cars were the first "two rooms and a bath" articulated cars produced for Cleveland in 1893, the first "Peter Witt"-type cars, and several lightweight streetcars of advanced design produced during the 1920's. The plant was reorganized as J. G. Brill of Ohio in 1931, but production ceased only a year or so later.

Laclede Car Company, St. Louis, Mo. (1883-1903)

Laclede, a prominent early builder of street railway equipment, built a large volume of both trucks and cars for horse, cable, and electric railways until the firm was purchased by the rival St. Louis Car Company in 1903.

Laconia Car Company, Laconia, N. H. (1881-1928)

Laconia was organized in 1881 from the predecessor Ranlett Manufacturing Company, a carriage and railroad-car building concern established in 1844. The company produced a large volume of horse and electric cars, as well as trucks of its own design, for street railways throughout New England, plus a modest number of cars for more distant systems. After about 1915

the firm also turned out a number of cars for steam railroads. The decline of electric railways, particularly rapid in the New England states, brought an end to Laconia operation in 1928.

Light Weight Noiseless Electric Street Car Company, St. Paul, Minn. (1924-1927)

Organized to exploit a truck designed by W. J. Smith of the Twin City Rapid Transit Company, the Light Weight Noiseless firm manufactured its cars in the Snelling Shops of the Twin City Lines. During the firm's brief period of activity it produced a large order of cars for Chicago, as well as lesser numbers for such cities as Nashville, Chattanooga, and Evansville, Ind. Although the firm's designs were not particularly successful, they were significant efforts toward the development of a modern lightweight car.

McGuire Manufacturing Company, Chicago and Paris, Ill. (1888-1943)

The McGuire Company was later known as McGuire-Cummings Manufacturing Company and finally as Cummings Car & Coach Company. It was initially active as a builder of car trucks, later produced snowplows and sweepers, and finally manufactured a general line of steam and electric railway equipment. McGuire trucks were highly regarded and were widely used, and the company's rugged snow sweeper was popular with traction systems throughout the world. Although its last cars were produced in 1930, the firm remained in business until 1943.

Montreal Locomotive Works, Ltd., Montreal, Que. (1902-   )

Montreal Locomotive Works has been principally a locomotive builder throughout its history, but in recent years it has branched out into railroad carbuilding. In 1962 the firm filled an order for 36 high-capacity aluminum cars for the Toronto subway system which represented both the first subway cars ever built in Canada and, at the time, the largest such cars ever built. Other MLW carbuilding activities have included freight cars for Canadian railroads, and in 1967 the firm constructed the carbodies for five high-speed gas turbine-powered trains for the Canadian National Railways.

National Brake & Electric Company, Milwaukee, Wis.

Although less well known than some of the leaders in the field, National supplied a complete line of air-braking equipment for electric railway service.

Newburyport Car Manufacturing Company, Newburyport, Mass. (1887-1905)

Notable among a proliferation of early New England carbuilders, the Newburyport firm produced a large volume of horse and electric cars for New England street railways. After delivery of a final order to the Boston Elevated in 1903, the company was liquidated in 1905.

Niles Car & Manufacturing Company, Niles, O. (1901-1917)

Despite its short life, the Niles firm achieved a deserved reputation for the quality and handsome proportions of its electric cars. Although the greater part of its production was devoted to the interurban railway equipment from which it derived its reputation, Niles also did a substantial business in street and elevated railway equipment produced for a variety of systems.

Osgood Bradley Car Company, Worcester, Mass. (1820-1930)

Osgood Bradley, originally established as a carriage builder, turned out its first railway cars in 1833. Producing steam railroad and street railway equipment of every description, the Osgood Bradley plant by 1910 was second in size only to the great Pullman works at Chicago. The Osgood Bradley plant was absorbed by Pullman in 1930 and remains in operation as a principal carbuilding facility of the Pullman-Standard organization.

Ottawa Car Manufacturing Company, Ottawa, Canada (1891-1948)

A leading Canadian streetcar builder, Ottawa Car produced a wide variety of street railway equipment that saw service in all parts of Canada. One of the firm's most notable cars was the elegant special car *Duchess of Cornwall and York*, produced for the Ottawa street railway system in 1900 to transport the future King George and Queen Mary during a visit to the Canadian capital. The firm was reorganized as a car and aircraft builder in 1939 and went out of business in 1948 shortly after completing a final order of cars for the Ottawa Transportation Commission.

Pressed Steel Car Company, Pittsburgh, Pa. (1896-1954)

Pressed Steel, originally known as the Schoen Steel Company, initially concentrated on the production of steel freight cars. In 1906 the company began to produce steel passenger cars and soon afterward was outshopping a large number of rapid transit, street, and interurban railway cars. Among these was the first steel trolley cars ever built, which were produced for the Montreal street railway system in 1907. The company continued in the carbuilding business until 1954, when the Pittsburgh plant was closed.

Preston Car & Coach Company, Preston, Ont. (1908-1921)

A carbuilder of modest size, Preston built a distinctive line of street and interurban cars that saw service in many parts of Canada. In order to compete for a Toronto Peter Witt car order, J. G. Brill of Philadelphia bought the Preston plant in 1921 and organized the Canadian Brill Company, Ltd., which subsequently built 50 cars for Toronto. Only 2 years later, however, Brill gave up the operation and the Preston plant passed from the scene.

Pullman Car & Manufacturing Company, Chicago, Ill. (1867-   )

Pullman was organized by sleeping car pioneer George Pullman in 1867 as Pullman's Palace Car Company, and the firm has retained a place among America's greatest builders of railroad cars for nearly a century. In 1899, when it merged with the Wagner Palace Car Company, the firm was reorganized as the Pullman Company. In 1927 Pullman carbuilding activities were consolidated under the Pullman Car & Manufacturing Company which became the Pullman-Standard Car & Manufacturing Company in 1934 a few years after Pullman's acquisition of the Standard Steel and Osgood Bradley car companies. Pullman plunged into the streetcar business in a big way in 1891 with the formation of its Streetcar Department, which produced electric railway equipment of almost every description. Prominent among earlier Pullman streetcars were several experimental double-deck cars of the 1890's and the hundreds of roomy "big red Pullmans" that op-

erated into recent years on the Chicago street railway system. In 1933 Pullman produced the first experimental PCC car, and afterward became one of the principal builders of the streamlined streetcars.

St. Louis Car Company, St. Louis, Mo. (1887-   )

Second only to J. G. Brill in volume, St. Louis Car was one of the great carbuilders of the electric traction era. The thousands of cars constructed by St. Louis included cable and horsecars, electric streetcars of every description, and a substantial volume of rapid transit cars. St. Louis was active as a steam railroad carbuilder as well, and produced carbodies for many of the famous Electro-Motive gas electrics and diesel-electric cars of the 1920's, as well as the bodies for some of the earliest EMD diesel-electric locomotives. St. Louis, like Brill, manufactured a complete line of trucks and trolley car appurtenances of every description. In 1936 St. Louis turned out the first production-model PCC cars and remained the leading PCC carbuilder until the last domestic order was completed for San Francisco in 1951. The firm is presently a division of General Steel Industries and is still active as a principal manufacturer of rapid-transit equipment.

John Stephenson Car Company, New York, N. Y. (1831-1917)

The Stephenson shops were organized as a carriage-building firm in 1831 and only a year later produced the world's first streetcar, the famous *John Mason* for the pioneer New York & Harlem Railroad. Stage coach and omnibus production dominated Stephenson's output for another two decades, however, and not until the great New York street railway boom of the 1850's did the firm come into its own as a carbuilder. Throughout the remainder of the 19th century the company was one of the major builders of horse, cable, and — finally — electric cars. Between 1876 and 1891 alone, Stephenson produced some 25,000 streetcars for companies in the U. S. and abroad. Along with its cars, Stephenson built a full line of single and double trucks for street railway service. J. G. Brill, in its expansion program of the early 1900's, acquired the Stephenson firm in 1904, although production continued under the Stephenson name. The Stephenson plant, lo-

cated at Elizabeth, N. J., after 1898, was never tooled up for the manufacture of steel cars, and Brill discontinued carbuilding at Elizabeth in 1917.

Stockton Combine Harvester & Agricultural Works, Stockton, Calif.

Despite its unlikely title, the Stockton Works produced some of the earliest street railway equipment operated on the West Coast. Beginning about 1888 the firm built some of the first cable cars operated in Seattle, Portland, and San Diego, and the first electric cars run in Salem, Oregon, and Oakland, Calif. During the early 1890's the company was one of the largest western carbuilders, and Stockton cars were to be found on almost every street railway system in the Far West. Carbuilding ceased around 1896 when the company turned its energies to agricultural equipment more in keeping with its title.

Southern Car Company, High Point, N. C. (1904-1917)

An outgrowth of the Briggs Car Company of Amesbury, Mass., Southern built a complete line of street and interurban railway cars for systems throughout the South and points as far distant as New York City and Puerto Rico. The car company went out of business in 1917.

Standard Steel Car Company, Pittsburgh, Pa. (1902-1930)

The celebrated railway equipment salesman "Diamond Jim" Brady and Chief Engineer John M. Hansen of Pressed Steel, dissatisfied with their opportunities at Pressed Steel Car Company, formed the Standard Steel Car Company in 1902 with a plant at Butler, Pa. Although Standard was mainly a steam railroad carbuilder, the company built a number of cars for street and interurban railways. Far more important than Standard's electric car production, however, was the extensive volume of electric car trucks of all types produced by the Standard Motor Truck Company, an outgrowth of the carbuilding firm organized in 1906. In 1930 the Standard Steel Car Company was absorbed by Pullman Car & Manufacturing Company.

Taylor Electric Truck Company, Troy, N. Y. (1895-   )

Successor to the Gilbert Car Manufacturing Company, the Taylor firm produced a wide range of trucks for both single- and double-truck street railway equipment. Taylor trucks were well designed and enjoyed a high degree of popularity among traction systems.

Perley A. Thomas Car Works, High Point, N. C. (1917-)

The Thomas works, although it was not a direct successor to the Southern Car Company, was organized by a former Southern employee who within a month after Southern went out of business took over its carbuilding plant at High Point. Thomas produced a line of extremely well-built cars which were ordered by street railway systems in almost every part of the U. S. and points as far removed as Cuba, Puerto Rico, and Central and South America. After electric car production ceased in 1930 the company turned to the fabrication of steel bus bodies and continues to produce these today.

Twin City Rapid Transit Company, Minneapolis-St. Paul, Minn.

Dissatisfied with the standard products of commercial carbuilding firms, the Twin City system designed and built its own distinctive rolling stock from just after the turn of the century until the advent of PCC car operation after World War II. Many larger systems built substantial numbers of cars for their own use, but none depended so completely on its own shops for car manufacture, and none manufactured cars for other systems as extensively as did Twin City's shops. In addition to manufacturing hundreds of cars for its own lines, the Twin City Rapid Transit's Snelling Shops produced a majority of the cars operated on the Duluth-Superior street railway system, and Twin City cars were found in Winnipeg and Seattle as well. For a brief period during the 1920's the Light Weight Noiseless Electric Street Car Company (q.v.) employed the facilities of the Snelling Shops to produce several orders of cars for other street railway systems.

Wason Manufacturing Company, Springfield, Mass. (1845-1931)

Wason, another of the New England wagon and coach builders that turned to carbuilding, constructed a substantial volume of cars for street and interurban railways as well as trucks of its own design. Although the company's production went largely to New England systems, Wason cars could be found almost everywhere in the U. S. After acquisition of the Springfield plant by J. G. Brill in 1906, production continued under the Wason name until 1931, when the name was changed to J. C. Brill of Massachusetts. Less than a year later, the new company was out of the carbuilding business.

Westinghouse Electric & Manufacturing Company, Pittsburgh, Pa.

Westinghouse, together with General Electric, dominated the electrical manufacturing field throughout the era of electric traction. Westinghouse produced a complete line of motors, controls, and other electrical equipment in activities that paralleled those of the rival General Electric organization.

Westinghouse Traction Brake Company, Pittsburgh, Pa.

Founded by air-brake pioneer George Westinghouse, the Westinghouse Traction Brake Company was the leading supplier of air-braking equipment throughout the history of the street railway organization. Still a leader in the field, the firm is currently active in the development of automatic braking and control systems for automation of rapid transit systems.

Woeber Brothers Carriage Company, Denver, Colo. (1880-1920)

Despite its misleading name, the Woeber works was an important builder of street railway equipment. With the exception of a single group of company-built cars, virtually every car ever operated by the Denver Tramways was constructed by Woeber Brothers, and the company also produced equipment for a number of other cities in the western states.

Where the cars still run

A DIRECTORY of the surviving electric street railways, rapid transit lines, and interurbans of North America, together with a listing of all museum projects at which electric railway equipment is operated, compiled with the assistance of James W. Walker Jr. Further details of all operating, as well as nonoperating, electric railway museums are contained in the annual museum survey of the Association of Railway Museums, 11307 Long Beach Boulevard, Lynwood, Calif. 90262, which is edited by Mr. Walker.

NEW ENGLAND STATES

MAINE

SEASHORE TROLLEY MUSEUM, Kennebunkport, operated by the New England Electric Railway Historical Society, represents the oldest and largest of all the electric railway museum projects. The museum's collection of some 85 pieces of equipment includes examples of virtually every important type of street railway equipment, as well as a number of items from rapid transit and interurban railways. Although most of the equipment is of U. S. origin, predominantly from the New England states, cars from such diverse areas as Canada, Australia, New Zealand, Japan, England, and Italy are included. Equipment runs over ½ mile of track on weekends during June and from Labor Day through October, and daily from June 30 to Labor Day.

MASSACHUSETTS

MASSACHUSETTS BAY TRANSPORTATION AUTHORITY, Boston, runs more than 300 PCC trolley cars on six routes consisting largely of reserved right of way and trolley subway, plus nearly 300 rapid transit cars on 23 miles of elevated, subway, and surface rapid transit line.

CONNECTICUT

BRANFORD ELECTRIC RAILWAY ASSOCIATION, Short Beach, conducts the second largest trolley museum project in the U. S. The Branford collection comprises some 75 items of equipment — examples of every major type of streetcar from a Toronto horsecar replica to the first production-model PCC streamliner built for Brooklyn in 1936, as well as representative specimens of interurban and rapid transit railway equipment. Cars run over a mile of former Connecticut Company line on Sunday afternoons from April through November, on Saturday and holiday afternoons from May 30 through Labor Day, and daily during July and August.

CONNECTICUT ELECTRIC RAILWAY ASSOCIATION, Warehouse Point, operates a collection of 25 electric cars, primarily from New England systems, over a mile of line constructed on the right of way of the former Hartford & Springfield Street Railway. Cars carry passengers on Sunday and holiday afternoons from May 30 until sometime in December.

MIDDLE AND SOUTH ATLANTIC STATES

NEW YORK

NEW YORK TRANSIT AUTHORITY, New York City, operates the largest electric railway system in North America. Some 6560 rapid transit cars serve over 37 routes comprising 237 miles of subway, elevated, and reserved right-of-way line.

STATEN ISLAND RAPID TRANSIT, New York City, a Baltimore & Ohio Railroad subsidiary, dispatches 48 rapid transit cars over 14 miles of suburban rapid transit line.

NEW JERSEY

PORT AUTHORITY TRANS-HUDSON TUBES, Newark, operated by the Port Authority of New York, sends 236 cars over four rapid transit routes totaling 14 miles of line between New York City and the New Jersey suburbs.

PUBLIC SERVICE COORDINATED TRANSPORT, Newark, operates 30 PCC trolleys on the 4-mile City Subway line.

PENNSYLVANIA

MAGEE TRANSPORTATION MUSEUM, Bloomsburg, has a ¼-mile trolley line and preserves seven city and interurban cars from the U. S.,

Canada, and Brazil. Operation is on weekends during summer and autumn.

PHILADELPHIA TRANSPORTATION COMPANY runs nearly 500 PCC trolley cars over 13 street railway routes, five of which reach downtown Philadelphia through a trolley subway; and nearly 500 rapid transit cars over three subway-elevated routes totaling 29 miles.

PHILADELPHIA SUBURBAN TRANSPORTATION COMPANY, Upper Darby, operates one of the two remaining interurban railway systems in North America. Lightweight trolley cars of several types are run over two broad-gauge suburban trolley lines, and "Liberty Liner" trains and "Bullet" interurbans serve on the 13-mile Norristown Division.

PORT AUTHORITY OF ALLEGHENY COUNTY, which acquired the transit properties of the Pittsburgh Railways Company early in 1964, operates a fleet of some 128 PCC cars over a trolley network of seven routes totaling 58 track-miles.

RAILWAYS TO YESTERDAY, Rockhill Furnace, runs a former Johnstown, Pa., trolley and a Chicago Aurora & Elgin interurban car on ⅓ mile of track. Operation is on Saturday and Sunday afternoons in conjunction with steam train trips on the East Broad Top line.

ARDEN ELECTRIC RAILWAY, near Washington, a project of the Pennsylvania Railway Museum Association, maintains a collection of 10 broad-gauge electric cars originally operated on several different Pennsylvania systems and at New Orleans. Cars make trips on an irregular Saturday and Sunday afternoon schedule on ½ mile of track.

NORTH CENTRAL STATES

OHIO

CLEVELAND TRANSIT SYSTEM schedules a fleet of 108 cars over more than 20 miles of reserved right-of-way rapid transit line.

SHAKER HEIGHTS RAPID TRANSIT, Cleveland, operates 55 PCC trolley cars over two semi-rapid-transit routes totaling 13 miles.

COLUMBIA PARK & SOUTHWESTERN RAILROAD, Olmsted Falls, num-

bers in its collection more than 20 street railway and interurban cars which are run over 1¼ miles of track. In addition to a variety of cars from Ohio cities and Chicago area lines, the collection includes two former Veracruz (Mexico) single-truck open cars. Operation is scheduled on weekends from 1 p.m. to 6 p.m.

OHIO RAILWAY MUSEUM, Worthington, operates over more than a mile of track with 10 items of electric railway equipment, including both street and interurban railway cars, from systems in Ohio, Michigan, and Missouri. Service is scheduled on Sunday afternoons from May through October, and on Saturday afternoons during July and August.

INDIANA

CHICAGO SOUTH SHORE & SOUTH BEND RAILROAD, Michigan City, operates a 57-mile heavy-duty interurban railway extending from Chicago to South Bend. Passenger service is handled with heavy steel multiple-unit cars and freight service with locomotives acquired from electrified steam railroads.

ILLINOIS

CHICAGO TRANSIT AUTHORITY runs in excess of 1200 rapid transit cars over five subway and elevated routes totaling some 80 miles. Additional routes totaling 15 miles will soon be under construction.

ILLINOIS RAILWAY MUSEUM, Union, operates on a mile of track and displays over 35 various units from midwest traction systems on weekend afternoons during summer and fall.

RELIC preserves seven interurban cars from Chicago area systems at South Elgin and runs over ¾ mile of track of the Aurora, Elgin & Fox River Railroad during summer and autumn weekends.

SOUTH CENTRAL STATES

LOUISIANA

NEW ORLEANS PUBLIC SERVICE maintains the only remaining non-streamlined streetcar system in the U. S. Standard two-man trolleys roll on a single 6-mile route on St. Charles Avenue.

TEXAS

LEONARDS M&O SUBWAY, Fort Worth, owned by Leonards department store, sponsors a small fleet of modified Washington (D. C.) PCC cars on a 1½-mile subway-surface route in downtown Fort Worth.

EL PASO CITY LINES runs 20 PCC cars on an international route extending across the Rio Grande from El Paso to Ciudad Juarez, Mexico.

MOUNTAIN AND PACIFIC STATES

CALIFORNIA

BAY AREA ELECTRIC RAILROAD ASSOCIATION displays a collection of over 25 pieces of rolling stock, mainly from San Francisco systems at Rio Vista Junction near Fairfield. Cars run over ¼ mile of track on weekend afternoons.

MUNICIPAL RAILWAY OF SAN FRANCISCO operates a fleet of 105 PCC cars on a network of five street railway routes, as well as the world's only three remaining cable railway lines.

ORANGE EMPIRE TROLLEY MUSEUM, Perris, maintains a collection of more than 65 items of electric railway equipment acquired since its founding in 1956. Although the greater part of the collection is devoted to a variety of Los Angeles equipment, cars from other parts of California and from Canada and Ireland are included. Operation is on weekend afternoons over ½ mile of track.

OREGON

OREGON ELECTRIC RAILWAY HISTORICAL SOCIETY, Glenwood, has a collection of five cars from the U. S., Canada, England, and Australia. It operates over a ¼-mile railway weekends during summer and autumn.

CANADA

ONTARIO

TORONTO TRANSIT COMMISSION owns one of the largest trolley car fleets in North America. A total of over 400 PCC cars run over 10 street railway routes. The Commission also operates some 340 rapid transit cars on a 14-mile subway system.

QUEBEC

MONTREAL MÉTRO opened an entirely new subway system late in 1966. A total of 369 unorthodox rubber-tired cars run on the 16-mile network.

EXPO EXPRESS at Montreal, a 3.7-mile automated rapid transit line, serves the six-month Expo 67 World's Fair.

MEXICO

SERVICIO DE TRANSPORTES ELECTRICOS DEL D.F., Mexico City, sends 274 PCC trolley cars over a network of 13 different street railway routes, portions of which are located on semi-rapid-transit reserved right of way.

COOPERATIVO DE TRANSPORTES URBANOS Y SUBURBANOS, Veracruz, operates a variety of trolley cars over seven street railway routes.

SOCIEDAD COOPERATIVA DE TRANSPORTES ELECTRICOS DE PASAJE Y CARGO TAMPICO-MIRAMAR, S.C.L., Tampico, has 29 PCC cars and some older equipment serving a 7-mile suburban route to Miramar.

427

Index

431

435